CAMBRIDGE TEXTS IN THE
HISTORY
OF PHILOSOPHY

REI

Meditatio

D0117901

CAMBRIDGE TEXTS IN THE
HISTORY OF PHILOSOPHY

Series Editors

KARL AMERIKS

Professor of Philosophy, University of Notre Dame

DESMOND M. CLARKE

Emeritus Professor of Philosophy, University College Cork

The main objective of Cambridge Texts in the History of Philosophy is to expand the range, variety, and quality of texts in the history of philosophy which are available in English. The series includes texts by familiar names (such as Descartes and Kant) and also by less well-known authors. Wherever possible, texts are published in complete and unabridged form, and translations are specially commissioned for the series. Each volume contains a critical introduction together with a guide to further reading and any necessary glossaries and textual apparatus. The volumes are designed for student use at undergraduate and postgraduate level, and will be of interest not only to students of philosophy but also to a wider audience of readers in the history of science, the history of theology, and the history of ideas.

For a list of titles published in the series, please see end of book.

RENÉ DESCARTES

Meditations on First Philosophy

with Selections from the Objections and Replies

TRANSLATED AND EDITED BY

JOHN COTTINGHAM

University of Reading

Second Edition

with an introductory essay by

BERNARD WILLIAMS

and a general introduction by

JOHN COTTINGHAM

CAMBRIDGE
UNIVERSITY PRESS

CAMBRIDGE
UNIVERSITY PRESS

University Printing House, Cambridge CB2 8BS, United Kingdom

Cambridge University Press is part of the University of Cambridge.

It furthers the University's mission by disseminating knowledge in the pursuit of education, learning and research at the highest international levels of excellence.

www.cambridge.org
Information on this title: www.cambridge.org/9781107665736

© Cambridge University Press 2017

First published 1986
Reprinted 1987, 1988 (twice), 1989, 1990, 1991 (twice), 1993 (twice)
Revised edition with new editorial matter 1996
21st printing 2015
Second edition first published 2017
6th printing 2019

Printed in Singapore by Markono Print Media Pte Ltd

A catalogue record for this publication is available from the British Library

Library of Congress Cataloging-in-Publication data
Descartes, René, 1596–1650.
[Meditationes de prima philosophia. English] Meditations on first philosophy / René Descartes.
With selections from the Objections and replies / [both] translated and edited by John Cottingham;
with an introductory essay by Bernard Williams and a new introduction for this edition by John
Cottingham. – Rev. ed. p. cm. – (Cambridge texts in the history of philosophy) Includes
bibliographical references and index. ISBN 0 521 55252 4 (hardback) ISBN 0 521 55818 2 (paperback)
1. First philosophy – Early works to 1800. 2. Metaphysics – Early works to 1800. I. Cottingham,
John, 1943–. II. Williams, Bernard Arthur Owen. III. Adjunctae sunt variae objectiones – cum
responsionibus authoris. English. Selections. IV Title. V. Series. B1853.E5C6713 1996
194–dc20 95–10664

ISBN 978-1-107-05920-7 Hardback
ISBN 978-1-107-66573-6 Paperback

Contents

Introductory essay

BERNARD WILLIAMS

'I would not urge anyone to read this book except those who are able and willing to meditate seriously with me', Descartes says to his readers in the Preface (p. 9, below), and he makes it clear that he means the *Meditations* not to be a treatise, a mere exposition of philosophical reasons and conclusions, but rather an exercise in thinking, presented as an encouragement and a guide to readers who will think philosophically themselves. Its thoughts, correspondingly, are presented as they might be conducted by its author – or rather, as though they were being conducted at the very moment at which you read them. Indeed, the 'I' who is having these thoughts may be yourself. Although we are conscious, in reading the *Meditations*, that they were written by a particular person, René Descartes, and at a particular time, about 1640, the 'I' that appears throughout them from the first sentence on does not specifically represent that person: it represents anyone who will step into the position it marks, the position of the thinker who is prepared to reconsider and recast his or her beliefs, as Descartes supposed we might, from the ground up.

This 'I' is different, then, from the 'I' that occurs in the *Replies* to the *Objections*. (Extracts from both of these also appear in this volume; how they came to be written is explained by the translator in his Note on the text, p. xlix.) In the *Replies*, Descartes speaks straightforwardly for himself, and the 'I' represents the author of the *Meditations*. The 'I' in the *Meditations* themselves represents their narrator or protagonist, whom we may call 'the thinker'. Of course the author has to take responsibility for the thinker's reflections. He takes responsibility both for the conduct of them and for their outcome, where that includes the beliefs to which we shall have been led if we are persuaded by the arguments, and also the improved states of mind that the author expects us to reach by following his work. But the author is not answerable for every notion entertained by the thinker and for every turn that the reflection takes on the way. The series of thoughts has an upshot or culmination, reached in the Sixth Meditation, and some of the thinker's earlier thoughts have been overcome and left behind in the process of reaching that final point.

Some of those who submitted the *Objections* found it hard to follow the working out of this idea, and to see how far the thinker had got at various points in the process of reflection. It is still hard today, and commentators' discussions of the *Meditations* often take the form of asking how much at a given stage Descartes takes himself to have established. In such discussions, it is *Descartes* and his intentions that come into question; the modern objectors address themselves, if less directly than the objectors whose texts appear in this volume, to the author. It was, after all, Descartes who gave the thinker the directions he follows. There is a suggestion implicit in the beginning of the work that the thinker does not know how it will all turn out: but that is a fiction.

To say that it is a fiction is not necessarily to say that in terms of the work itself it is untrue. This might have been a work in which the thinker's fictional ignorance of how his reflections would turn out was convincingly sustained. To some extent it is so, and to that extent, one of the gifts offered to the reader by this extraordinary work is a freedom to write it differently, to set out with the thinker and end up in a different place. The rewriting of Descartes's story in that way has constituted a good deal of modern philosophy.

However, it would be wrong to suggest that the *Meditations* offers no more than an invitation to philosophical reflection, by asking some questions and showing one way in which they might be answered. We are expected, rather, to sense the author's guiding hand throughout. Modern readers may take this for granted too easily, because they underestimate Descartes's intention to engage the reader in the argument. They may think of the *Meditations* as just a device that Descartes chose to get across the opinions that we now find ascribed to him in histories of philosophy. It is, certainly, a device for convincing us, but it is more than that, because it aims to convince us by making us conduct the argument ourselves.

The first readers of the *Meditations* may have felt the author's guiding presence for a different reason, that they were conscious of a kind of writing that it resembled. It was, and remains, a very unusual work, and there had never been a work of philosophy presented in such a form before. But there did exist, familiarly, works of religious meditation, and Descartes's book self-consciously resembles them. Like many of them, it is ostensibly divided between days of contemplation and, again like them, it encourages and helps the reader to overcome and get rid of misleading and seductive states of the soul, so as to arrive at an understanding of his or her own nature and of a created being's relations with God.

Those who wrote religious meditations were acting as guides to a spiritual discipline. Descartes's work gives his readers guidance in an intellectual discipline, and helps them to discover in themselves pure intellectual conceptions – of matter, of mind and of God – from which they will be able to form a true and unclouded understanding of the world. The inquiry in which he leads them does indeed yield a conviction of the existence of God. There is no reason at all to suppose that Descartes was insincere in these religious affirmations (though theories that ascribe to him complex strategies of deceit have a strange capacity to survive.) What is true is that the thoughts that lead to these conclusions are not in the least religious in spirit, and God's existence is established as a purely metaphysical conclusion. Anything to do with a religious life or, indeed, with any distinctively religious aspects of life, will have to come in after Descartes's reflections are over. The *Meditations*, though they have an analogy to traditional meditations that belong to the religious life, assuredly do not belong to it themselves.

A still greater difference lies in the authority with which the two kinds of works were offered. The authors of religious meditations claimed authority from their own experience, but also, most often, from a religious office. Descartes does not suppose that his right to claim a reader's attention lies in any sacramental, traditional or professional position. His authority to show us how to think lies only in this, that he has himself, as he supposes, uncovered methods of simple, clear-headed and rational inquiry which all reasonable people can conduct if they clear their minds of prejudice and address themselves in a straightforward way to the questions. No special training, no religious discipline, no knowledge of texts or of history is needed in order to do this. He was disposed to think, in fact, that such things could be an actual obstacle.

His justification for believing that his readers had these powers, if only they could use them, is to be found in the *Meditations* themselves. If we follow Descartes to the end of them and accept his considerations, we shall have come to a conception of ourselves as rational, immaterial selves born with pure intellectual ideas and a capacity for reasoning which enable us to grasp in basic respects the nature of the world. Each of us does indeed exist in some kind of union with a particular physical body. '*My* body', one says, and Descartes took this phrase to register a profound truth, that what one truly is, is a mind 'really distinct' from the body. We need sensory information provided through the body not only to survive in the material world, but to find out particular scientific laws. But our own nature, the existence of God and indeed the most abstract structural features of the physical world itself can be discovered, Descartes supposed, by directed intelligence and rational insight.

Among these things we discover, when we direct our intelligence in the right way, is that we are beings who are capable of making just such discoveries, and we gain insight into the way in which we can make them. So we discover also how the *Meditations*, a work of pure reflection aiming to free us from error and to help us understand these basic matters, can succeed. Its end lies in its beginning, not just because its author knows how the thinker will come out, but in the philosophical sense that if we undertake to follow its method of inquiry, our doing so, Descartes supposed, is justified by our being the kind of creatures that it finally shows us to be.

The method deployed and invoked in the *Meditations* works, to an important degree, through argument, clear chains of reasoning. This tells us something of how to read the book. We are asked to argue, not merely through it, but with it. Because of this, it is specially appropriate that the book was associated, at its first publication, with *Objections* and *Replies*. Descartes had some political motives in having the *Objections* assembled, as he also did in dedicating the book to the Sorbonne. He wanted to have his work accepted by the religious authorities. For the same reason, he did not welcome all the *Objections* that were collected by his friend Mersenne, who organised the enterprise, being embarrassed in particular by those of the English sceptic and materialist Hobbes.

But whatever the strategy of the publication, it was true to the spirit of the work, as Descartes clearly believed, that it should appear together with arguments attempting to refute it or defend it.

If we are to read the *Meditations* properly, we must remember that the thinker is not simply the author. We must not forget that the work is a carefully designed whole, of great literary cunning, and that it rarely lays out arguments in a complete or formal way. But this does not mean that it is not sustained by argument, or that arguing with it is inappropriate. It means only that we must read it carefully to find out what its arguments are, and what Descartes is taking for granted. If we reflect on what he is taking for granted or asking us by implication to accept, we are doing part of what he invited us to do, when he asked us to meditate with him.

A question of what he is taking for granted presents itself right at the beginning. 'Reason now leads me to think', he writes in the First Meditation (p. 15, below)

> that I should hold back my assent from opinions which are not completely certain and indubitable just as carefully as I do from those which are patently false. So, for the purpose of rejecting all my opinions, it will be enough if I find in each of them at least some reason for doubt. And to do this I will not need to run through them all individually... Once the foundations of a building are undermined, anything built on them collapses of its own accord; so I will go straight for the basic principles on which all my former beliefs rested.

Why does reason now lead him to think this? Everyone is engaged in trying to get information about matters of concern to him; some, such as Descartes, are involved in the sciences and want to arrive at systematic and reasoned beliefs about nature. But no one ordinarily supposes that the rational way to start on these things is to throw away or lay aside all the information one thinks one already has. Descartes thinks not only that this is the right course for him, but that it is self-evidently the right course for him. Why should he think this? Why should doubt seem the path to knowledge, if there is a path to knowledge at all?

We must notice first that the approach is not supposed to be applied to the ordinary affairs of life. Descartes makes that point over and over again, saying for instance that we must distinguish between 'the actions of life' and 'the search for truth'; and in the *Synopsis* to the *Meditations*

(p. 13, below) he is prepared to use such a distinction even to define what counts as serious: 'no sane person has ever seriously doubted these things'. He does not mean that the results of his reflections will not affect ordinary practice or the conduct of the sciences. On the contrary, this is what he hopes they will do, setting the sciences, for instance, on the right path. Nor does he think that these reflections are a trivial way of passing the time. They cannot be that, if eventually they could have these practical and scientific effects. He may think that it is particularly his own, the author's, use of the Doubt that will have those effects, but he also believes that it is a worthwhile exercise for any of us, once in a lifetime, to take temporarily the position of the thinker of such reflections, and this will not be a trivial undertaking, either. Indeed, he himself said that the meditation to which he invited us in the Preface was itself, in its own way, 'serious'.

When Descartes says that the thoughts deploying the Doubt are to be separated from practical life, and in that sense (but only in that sense) are not 'serious', he is defining a special kind of intellectual project which by its nature can be conducted only if it is separated from all other activities. In ordinary life, when we want the truth on a subject, we pursue it, necessarily, in a context of other things that we are aiming to do, including other inquiries we need to make. The pattern of our inquiries is formed by many constraints on how we can spend our time and energies, and by considerations of what we risk by failing to look into one thing or spending too long looking into another. These constant and often implicit calculations of the economics of inquiry help to shape the body of our beliefs; and they have the consequence that our beliefs, while they aim at truth, will, inevitably, only partly achieve it. Descartes conceived of a project that would be *purely* the search for truth, and would be unconstrained by any other objectives at all. Because it temporarily lays aside the demands of practical rationality, it has to be detached from practice; and because it is concerned with truth and nothing else, it has to raise its requirements to the highest conceivable level, and demand nothing less than absolute certainty.

The search has to take place out of this world, so to speak, and its nature, its internal purpose, explains why this should be. But there is still a question about its external purpose. Why should Descartes or anyone else, once in a lifetime, take time out of the world to pursue this project? Descartes can commend it to us in more than one way, but his own principal reason is that he is looking for what he calls, at the start of the First Meditation and in many other places, 'foundations' of knowledge. To serve this purpose, the Doubt has to be methodical. A refusal to take things for granted that might be doubtful is part of Descartes's general intellectual method, which he had introduced in his earlier work *The Discourse on the Method*; the Doubt is an extreme application of that idea, conditioned by the circumstances of the special project, the radical search for certainty. The Doubt is deployed for defined purposes, and from the start it is under control.

It was not a new idea that scepticism might be used for its beneficial effects. Sceptics in the ancient world, Pyrrhonians and others, had advocated such techniques for their own purposes; their teachings had been revived since the Reformation, and sceptical views were in the air at the time that Descartes wrote. Some of his critics complained that material he deployed, for instance about the errors of the senses, was old stuff. But Descartes could rightly reply that while scepticism was no new thing, his use of it was indeed new. When the Pyrrhonians deployed sceptical considerations, it was in order to calm and eradicate an unsatisfiable urge for knowledge; and it was rather in this spirit, sixty years before the *Meditations*, that Montaigne had written. But Descartes's aim was precisely the opposite, to use scepticism to help in acquiring knowledge, and to bring out from a sceptical inquiry the result that knowledge was, after all, possible. The Doubt served that purpose by eliminating false conceptions; and the fact that it was possible to use it in this way and then overcome it gave the fundamental reassurance that a proper science would have nothing to fear from the doubts of the sceptics. Descartes's Doubt was to be both revelatory and pre-emptive.

'Foundations of knowledge' can mean more than one thing. Descartes has often been thought to be searching for foundations in the sense of axioms from which the whole of knowledge or, more particularly, the whole of science, might be deduced, as in a geometrical system. In fact, this is rarely his concern, and it does not represent his understanding of what a completed science would be like. Historians classify Descartes as a 'rationalist', but this should not be taken to mean that he supposed mere rational reflection to be enough to establish scientific conclusions. He was a rationalist, rather, in his views about the origins of scientific *concepts*. He thought that the terms in which physics should describe the world were given to rational reflection, and he supposed them to be, in fact, purely mathematical. It was only by empirical investigation and experiment, however, that we could discover which descriptions, expressed in those terms, were true of the actual world.

Basically, the Doubt provides foundations for knowledge because it helps to eliminate error. Descartes's aim was not so much to find truths from which all scientific knowledge could be deduced, but rather to identify false or doubtful propositions which were implied by our everyday beliefs and so made those beliefs themselves unreliable. One belief of this kind was that objects in the external world had just the qualities that they seem to have, such as colour. The Doubt helped in eliminating this very general error, which could then be replaced by the sound conviction that objects, in themselves, had only the properties ascribed to them by mathematical physics. Once this corrected view had been laid bare and found indubitable in the process of orderly reflection, it could from then on serve as a sound foundation of our understanding of the world.

Proceeding in this way, Descartes could indeed 'go straight for the basic principles on which all my former beliefs rested'. The workings of the Doubt are adjusted to these aims. In its most extreme, 'hyperbolical', form, the Doubt is embodied in the fiction (p. 19) that a malicious demon, 'of the utmost power and cunning has employed all his energies in order to deceive me'. This device provides Descartes with a thought-experiment that can be generally applied: if there were an indefinitely powerful agency who was misleading me to the greatest conceivable extent, would *this* kind of belief or experience be correct? Thinking in these terms, Descartes is led to identify whole tracts of his ordinary experience he may lay aside, so that he suspends belief in the whole of the material world, including his own body.

It is significant, however, and characteristic of the way in which the *Meditations* unfolds, that Descartes does not start his sceptical inquiry with this extreme device. We are invited to get used to sceptical thinking gradually, by considering first more familiar and realistic occasions of error. He starts with illusions of the senses, in which we mistake the shape of a distant tower, for instance, or suppose a straight stick, partly in water, to be bent. Such examples remind us that we can be mistaken, and that even by everyday canons the world need not really be as it presents itself to our perception. There is little in these cases, however, to encourage the more generally sceptical idea that on any given occasion when we take ourselves to be perceiving something, we may be mistaken. He thinks that we are led to that further and more radical idea by reflection on the 'errors of our dreams'. The phenomenon of dreaming creates a more general and more puzzling scepticism because, first, it is true (or at least the sceptic pretends that it is true) that anything we can perceive we can dream we perceive; and, second, there is no way of telling at the time of dreaming whether we are dreaming or not. So it seems that at any moment I can ask 'how do I know that I am not dreaming now?', and find it hard to give an answer. But what I can do, at any rate, if the question has occurred to me, is to 'bracket' these experiences, and not commit myself on the question of whether they are waking experiences which are reliable, or dreams which are delusive.

Once I am prepared to do this, I am well started on the sceptical journey. So far I have reached only the distributive doubt, *on any occasion I may be mistaken*, but reflecting on the possibility that I can have a set of experiences that do not correspond to anything real, I am nearly ready to take the step, with the help of the malicious demon, to the final and collective doubt, *I may be mistaken all the time*. In his description of what dreams are Descartes already lays the ground for what is to come. In the Sixth Meditation (p. 61) he says that he did not believe that what he seemed to perceive when he was dreaming came 'from things located outside me'. In an everyday sense, certainly, that description of a dream must be correct. But the description has acquired some large implications by the time I reach the last Meditation, and, having accepted the 'real distinction' between mind and body, understand that my body is itself something 'outside me'.

Every step in the sceptical progress should be questioned. It is at the beginning that all the seeds are sown of the philosophical system that has come to life by the end of the *Meditations*. To take just one example of questions that the thinker's reflections invite, do these facts about dreaming, even if we accept them, really lead to the conclusion that I can never know whether I am awake? Why, in particular, does the thinker take dreaming so seriously for his purposes, and not madness? He simply dismisses the deranged people who think that their heads are made of earthenware, or that they are pumpkins, or made of glass (p. 16). Perhaps Bourdin, the author of the Seventh Objections, makes a good point in suggesting that the two conditions should be treated together (p. 80). There is of course this difference, that the mad are assumed unable to conduct the meditation at all: the thinker turns away from them, treats them in the third person, because they cannot join him and the reader in thinking through these things, whereas we who are the readers have dreams, as the thinker has. But is this enough of a difference? Descartes and his thinker cannot speak to us *when we are dreaming*. Descartes seemingly thinks that if we are sane, we can be sure that we are, even though mad people cannot tell that they are mad. So why should the fact that when we are dreaming, we cannot tell that we are, imply that we cannot be sure we are awake when we are awake? There may be an answer to that question; but we should not let the argument from dreams go by until we have considered what it might be.

The *Meditations* use the Doubt to lead out of the Doubt into knowledge and a correct conception of things. In doing that, they do not merely provide a sounder conception: they show that we can reach such a conception, and demonstrate that knowledge is to be had. The foundations that Descartes believes himself at the end to have discovered are also foundations of the *possibility* of knowledge. That is why the scepticism of the *Meditations* is pre-emptive. Descartes claimed that he had taken the doubts of the sceptics farther than the sceptics had taken them, and had been able to come out the other side.

The rebuttal of scepticism depends on the existence of a God who has created us and who is 'no deceiver'. If we do our own part in clarifying our thoughts (as thinker does in the *Meditations*) and we seek the truth as seriously as we can, God will not allow us to be systematically mistaken. However hard we think about these matters, however much we clarify our understanding of what an 'external' world might be, we are left with a conviction that there is such a world – a conviction so powerful that it needed the extreme device of the malicious demon temporarily to displace it. It would be contrary to the benevolence and the trustworthiness of God that this conviction should be untrue.

It is essential that we should have done our own part. God cannot be expected to underwrite confused conceptions which have not been carefully examined. If we do not accept a sound intellectual discipline, we deceive ourselves and are responsible for our errors. (This is one way in which Descartes thinks that the will is involved in belief.) Equally, God's benevolence does not guarantee us against every error, but only against general and systematic error. We remain liable to occasional mistakes, such as those of defective perception and also those of dreams, which before these reassurances seemed to offer a sceptical threat. Particular errors are caused by our bodily constitution, and it is not surprising that we should be subject to them. The sceptics' threat was that our entire picture of things might be wrong: now we have an assurance, because God is no deceiver, that this cannot be so.

But have we? Those who offered *Objections* were only the first among many to doubt whether Descartes's argument succeeds, even in its own terms. In the course of the *Meditations*, the sceptic has been allowed to cast doubt, it seems, even on the convictions that ground the belief in God. This doubt must be resisted, but how, in resisting it, can we appeal to the existence and nature of God, without arguing in a circle? Descartes's answer to this objection emphasises that a doubt about the proofs of God, and their implications for the validation of our thoughts, can be entertained only when one is not actually considering them. At the time they are clearly considered, these proofs are supposed to be as compelling as any other basic certainty – that I cannot think without existing, for instance, or that twice two is four. So when the sceptic professes to doubt the proofs of God, or any other such certainty, it can be only because he is not actually considering them at that time. All one can do is to refer him back to them; if he does properly consider them, he will, then, be convinced.

All this Descartes clearly says, but it is a little less clear what he expects us, and the sceptic, to make of it. His idea may be this, that if the sceptic reverts to his doubts when he has stopped thinking clearly about the proofs, we have earned the right by then simply to forget about him. He is merely insisting that we go on giving the answer – an answer we indeed have – to one question, his question, instead of getting on with our scientific inquiries or other practical activities, rather as though we were required to spend all our time out of the world with the thinker. We have offered all the justifications we could in principle offer, and now have the right to see the dispute as one about how to spend our time. If the sceptic were still to offer some basis for his doubts, it seems that it could now lie only in the idea that intellectual concentration was itself the enemy of truth: that you are more likely to be right about these matters if you do not think carefully about them than if you do. This idea is denied by the procedures of the sceptic, as well as by those of Descartes's thinker; in starting on the *Meditations* themselves, or any other inquiry, we implicitly reject it.

Modern readers will want to consider how exactly Descartes answers the problem of the 'Cartesian Circle', and whether his answer, in his own terms, is a good one. Few of them, however, will accept those terms, or agree that the theological foundation he offers for science and everyday belief is convincing. Descartes was very insistent that science itself should be thoroughly mechanistic and should not offer explanations in terms of God's purposes or any kind of teleology. In this, he was one of the major prophets of the seventeenth-century scientific revolution. Yet his justification of the possibility of such a science itself lay in God, and in a kind of teleology, a conviction that the world cannot be such that our desire to know must be ultimately misguided or frustrated. Perhaps we still have some version of that conviction, but if so, it is not for those reasons, and it could not be used to provide foundations for science.

To Descartes's contemporaries, it seemed much more obvious that God existed and was no deceiver than that natural science was possible. Neither the successes nor the institutions of modern science yet existed. For us, science is manifestly possible, and because it is so, the demand is less pressing than it seemed to Descartes that it should be justified from the ground up. We may feel happier than he did to live without foundations of knowledge. But that must leave us open to questions of how that can be so. We need to know what the science that is so manifestly possible, is. Does it describe a world that is there anyway, independently of us? What does this question itself mean? How do we, with our thoughts and our bodies, fit into our picture of the natural world? We cannot do with Descartes's *Meditations* everything that he hoped to achieve with them himself, but there remain many good reasons to accept his invitation to them.

BERNARD WILLIAMS

General introduction

The Meditations *and Cartesian Philosophy*

JOHN COTTINGHAM

Descartes's *Meditations on First Philosophy* is, indisputably, one of the greatest philosophical classics of all time. The challenge it offers is in many ways definitive of the philosophical enterprise: to leave behind the comfortable world of inherited prejudice and preconceived opinion; to take nothing for granted in the determination to achieve secure and reliable knowledge. Descartes talks of 'demolishing] everything completely and starting] again right from the foundations', and for this purpose he famously uses doubt, stretched to its limits, as an instrument which self-destructs, impelling him forwards on the journey towards certainty and truth.[1] These central themes are today part of every introductory course in the philosophy of knowledge: Descartes's masterpiece has achieved canonical status in that part of the philosophy syllabus we now call 'epistemology'. Yet for Descartes himself these epistemic concerns were but one part of a much wider project: the construction of a grand, all-embracing system of philosophy which would encompass metaphysics, natural science, psychology and morals, connecting all the objects within the scope of human understanding. In the words of the famous metaphor which he deployed some six years after the publication of the *Meditations*, 'the whole of philosophy is like a

---

[1] See the opening paragraph of the *Meditations*. Descartes's use of doubt, and other key philosophical issues in the *Meditations*, are discussed in the Introductory essay to the present volume, by Bernard Williams, pp. viiff., above.

tree. The roots are metaphysics, the trunk is physics, and the branches ... all the other sciences.'[2]

Descartes spent much of his career occupied with what we would nowadays call theoretical physics: he devised a radical new theory of the nature of matter, defined simply as extension in three dimensions, and formulated a number of mathematical laws describing the results of collisions of moving particles of matter. He then proposed to apply these principles to a wide variety of subjects, from cosmology and astronomy to physiology and medicine; and towards the end of his life he planned to include a science of man, which would develop prescriptions for how to understand and control the workings of our bodies, and how to live fulfilled and worthwhile lives. Examining the course of Descartes's life, and the context in which the *Meditations* was written, helps us deepen our understanding of the metaphysical and epistemological themes of his most famous book by seeing how they fit into the broader philosophical system which he devoted his life to creating.

The shaping of a philosopher

René Descartes was born in France on 31 March 1596 in the small town of La Haye (now renamed 'Descartes'), some fifty kilometres south of Tours. Not a very great deal is known of his early life, but it seems likely that his childhood was not a particularly happy one. His health was poor, and he appears not to have got on very well with his father, Joachim, who was often away discharging his duties as Counsellor at the Parliament of Brittany. Relations between the two in later life were certainly strained, and when René sent his father a copy of his first published book the father's only reported reaction was that he was displeased to have a son 'idiotic enough to have himself bound in vellum'.[3] Descartes's mother

---

[2] *Principles of Philosophy*, Preface to the French Edition of 1647 (AT IXB 14; CSM I 186). Throughout the present volume, 'AT' refers to the standard Franco-Latin edition of Descartes by C. Adam and P. Tannery, *Œuvres de Descartes*, rev. edn. (12 vols., Paris, Vrin/CNRS, 1964–76); 'CSM' refers to the English translation by J. Cottingham, R. Stoothoff and D. Murdoch, *The Philosophical Writings of Descartes*, vols. I and II (Cambridge, Cambridge University Press, 1985) and 'CSMK' to vol. III, *The Correspondence*, by the same translators and A. Kenny (Cambridge, Cambridge University Press, 1991). For the text of the *Meditations*, see 'Note on the text and the translation', p. l, below.

[3] Cf. AT XII 7, 8, and 433–4.

died, in childbirth, a year after his own birth,[4] and he was looked after by his maternal grandmother until, at the age of ten, he was sent away as a boarding pupil to the recently founded Jesuit college of La Flèche in Anjou, where he remained for eight or nine years. During Descartes's time there the school was steadily building up a reputation for excellence (he later described it as 'one of the most famous schools in Europe'[5]); pupils followed a comprehensive curriculum which included classical literature and traditional classics-based subjects such as history and rhetoric, as well as, in the senior years, higher mathematics and philosophy. The approach to philosophy taken by Descartes's teachers belonged to what we now know as the 'scholastic' tradition; that is to say, it was based on broadly Aristotelian principles, adapted in an attempt to make them consistent with the demands of Christian orthodoxy, and elaborated over many centuries by a host of learned commentators. Descartes's teachers at La Flèche would have been well versed in such commentaries, and would also have made use of compendious textbooks like the *Summa Philosophiae Quadripartita*, a four-part treatise by a noted contemporary Scholastic, Eustachius a Sancto Paulo, which provided a complete philosophical system, including logic, metaphysics, moral philosophy and 'natural philosophy' or physics.[6] Descartes was not impressed with the philosophy he learned at school, and later wrote that the subject, despite being 'cultivated for many centuries by the most excellent minds', contained no point which was not 'disputed and hence doubtful'. The 'shaky foundations' of the traditional system meant, in his view, that all the specific sciences built on them were equally suspect.[7]

In 1610, about halfway through Descartes's time at La Flèche, the College marked the death of its founder, Henry IV, with a series of grand observances, including the reciting of poems, one of which hailed the recent discovery by Galileo of the moons of Jupiter (which 'brightened

---

[4] Despite what the philosopher himself told a correspondent (letter to Elizabeth of May or June 1645, AT IV 220–1; CSMK 250–1), it was not René's own birth that cost his mother her life, but that of a younger brother (who lived only three days); see G. Rodis-Lewis, 'Descartes' Life and the Development of his Philosophy', in J. Cottingham (ed.), *The Cambridge Companion to Descartes* (Cambridge, Cambridge University Press, 1992), p. 23.

[5] *Discourse on the Method*, Part One (AT VI 5; CSM I 113).

[6] The *Summa Philosophiae Quadripartita* was published in 1609. For more on Eustachius, and on some of the commentaries on Aristotle which Descartes may have read at La Flèche, see R. Ariew, 'Descartes and Scholasticism', in Cottingham, *Cambridge Companion to Descartes*, pp. 74ff.

[7] See *Discourse*, Part One (AT VI 8; CSM I 115).

the gloom of the King's death').[8] We do not know what part if any Descartes played in these ceremonies (though some have suggested that he was the author of the poem honouring Galileo); what is certain is that Galileo's discovery came in due course to be widely acknowledged as strong experimental support for the new Copernican cosmology, dethroning the earth from its privileged place at the centre of the universe – a shift which, more than any other, has subsequently come to be seen as central to the philosophical and scientific revolution of the early modern period. Descartes himself was to become a convinced if cautious adherent of the new heliocentric model, and his own scientific career was to intertwine, at a crucial point, with that of Galileo. By his late thirties Descartes had produced a comprehensive treatise on cosmology and physics, *Le Monde* (*The World* or *The Universe*), which applied reductive mechanical principles to the explanation of a wide variety of celestial and terrestrial phenomena; in the course of the work (though carefully insisting that it was an account of how things *might* have evolved in an imaginary universe) he places the sun at the centre of the planetary system.[9] But on hearing of the condemnation of Galileo by the Inquisition for advocating the heliocentric hypothesis, Descartes decided to withdraw his own treatise from publication. 'I desire to live in peace', he wrote to his friend and chief correspondent, Marin Mersenne.[10]

The cautious and reclusive attitude which became typical of Descartes's middle years was in some respects at odds with the rather more active and outgoing life he pursued in his twenties. After taking a law degree at Poitiers, at the age of twenty-two Descartes went to Holland and enrolled in the army of Prince Maurice of Nassau; this was the prelude for a series of travels in Europe, inspired by the resolve, as Descartes later put it, 'to seek no knowledge other than that which could be found in myself or else in the great book of the world'.[11] The comment suggests that his motive for choosing the soldier's life was the prospect for travel it offered, though in later life he commented acidly that the chief attraction of a military career for the young was the opportunity it provided for 'idleness and debauchery'.[12] At all events,

8 See Rodis-Lewis, 'Descartes' Life', p. 26, and AT XII 29.
9 See *Le Monde*, ch. 10 (AT XI 69–70).   10 Letter of April 1634 (AT I 285–6; CSMK 43).
11 *Discourse*, Part One (AT VI 9; CSM I 115).
12 Letter to Pollot of 1648 (AT V 557; CSMK 359).

the most significant result of his initial journey to Holland was the friendship Descartes formed with the Dutch mathematician Isaac Beeckman, whom he met accidentally in 1618. Beeckman made Descartes party to a number of projects on which he was working in pure and applied mathematics, and was described by Descartes in terms reminiscent of those later used by Immanuel Kant when he acknowledged Hume as the one who had roused him from his 'dogmatic slumbers'. 'You alone', Descartes wrote to Beeckman in 1619, 'roused me from my state of indolence'; in another letter, he spoke of the 'gigantic task' which, inspired by Beeckman's ideas, he had set himself: that of devising a method which would provide 'a general solution of all possible equations involving any sort of quantity'.[13] Descartes continued to work on arithmetic, algebra and geometry (and the relationship between them) for much of the following decade, and it was to become a central theme of his later philosophy that mathematics possessed the kind of precision and certainty which the traditional philosophy he had learnt at school conspicuously lacked. Mathematics was a paradigm of what Descartes came to call *scientia* – genuine and systematic knowledge based on reliable principles.

Descartes's earliest work, the *Compendium Musicae*, written in 1618 and dedicated to Beeckman, applied quantitative principles to the study of musical harmony and dissonance. But the wider significance which mathematical reasoning later came to have for Descartes consisted in its being a model for all human understanding: 'Those long chains composed of very simple and easy reasonings, which geometers customarily use to arrive at their most difficult demonstrations, had given me occasion to suppose that all the things which fall within the scope of human knowledge are interconnected in the same way.'[14] This ambitious vision of a new model for the sciences was probably shaped and nurtured over a number of years, but according to Descartes himself it took root in his mind after an extraordinary experience which occurred during his European travels.

On 10 November 1619 Descartes found himself closeted in a 'stove-heated room' (*poêle*) in a town in southern Germany, where after a day of intense meditation, he fell asleep and had a series of three strikingly vivid

---

[13] Letters of 23 April and 26 March 1619 (AT X 163, 157–8; CSMK IV, 2–3).
[14] *Discourse*, Part Two (AT VI 19; CSM I 120).

dreams. In the first, he was assailed by phantoms and a violent whirl-wind, took refuge in a college, where he tried to reach the chapel, and was greeted by a friend who gave him a present which he took to be a 'melon brought from a foreign country'. As he woke up he felt a sharp pain in his side which made him fear that an 'evil demon was trying to deceive him'; such was the sense of dread produced by the dream that he lay awake for several hours. In the second dream he heard a terrible noise like a thunderclap, and saw a shower of bright sparks, whereupon he awoke at once, still in a state of terror. The last and most complex dream involved the appearance and disappearance of various books on a table: first an encyclopaedia, which he thought might be 'very useful to him'; then an anthology of poetry containing the Pythagorean motto for truth and falsity, '*Est et non*', and an ode of Ausonius beginning *Quod vitae sectabor iter?* ('What road in life shall I follow?'); and finally (after a long dialogue with a stranger about the contents of the books) the encyclopaedia again, this time incomplete. As he began to wake up, he immediately started interpreting the dream, the most significant feature being the encyclopaedia, which he took for a symbol of 'how the sciences are linked together'. The upshot of this night of troubled visions was that Descartes became convinced that his own life's journey should be devoted to completing the 'encyclopaedia': his mission was to found a new and comprehensive philosophical and scientific system.[15]

The development of Descartes's methodology

Returning to Paris after his travels, Descartes began work on a treatise in Latin entitled *Regulae ad Directionem Ingenii*, the *Rules for the Direction of our Native Intelligence*. Though never completed (and never published during his lifetime), the *Regulae* inaugurates the project, glimpsed in Descartes's dream, of founding a universal scientific system. The inspiration, as with so much of his work (particularly so during this early period) is mathematical, and much of the book is concerned with devising of 'rules' or methods for the solution of problems in arithmetic and

---

[15] The dreams are described in some detail by A. Baillet (*La Vie de Monsieur Des-Cartes*, Paris, Horthemels, 1691; photographic reprint Hildesheim, Olms, 1972, vol. 1, pp. 81ff.), but some of his embellishments are almost certainly apocryphal; see Rodis-Lewis, 'Descartes' Life' (pp. 30–2). Fragments which have survived from Descartes's own early notebooks provide more reliable, if somewhat sparse, information. See CSM I 2ff.

geometry. But Descartes pointedly observes that he 'would not value these Rules so highly if they were good only for solving those pointless problems with which arithmeticians and geometers are inclined to while away their time'. He goes on to speak of a general discipline that contains the 'rudiments of human reason' and can 'extend to the discovery of truths in any field whatever': 'there must be a general science which explains all the points that can be raised concerning order and measure irrespective of the subject-matter'.[16] The tool for the discovery of such truths would not be a study of traditional methods and authorities, but, instead, the ordinary 'native intelligence' of each individual: the simple and clear perceptions of the intellect, uncluttered by considerations of 'what other people have thought or what we ourselves conjecture'.[17]

This vision of how to proceed in philosophy remained Descartes's guiding principle when he came to write the *Meditations*, over ten years later. In the *Regulae*, Descartes uses the term 'intuition' (in Latin *intuitus*) for the kind of reliable cognition he is seeking – a word which suggests looking directly at something, a kind of straightforward inspection or vision (though of a purely intellectual, not an ocular, kind):

> By 'intuition' I do not mean the fluctuating testimony of the senses or the deceptive judgement of the imagination as it botches things together, but the conception of a clear and attentive mind, which is so easy and distinct that there can be no room for doubt about what we are understanding. Alternatively, and this comes to the same thing, intuition is the indubitable conception of a clear and attentive mind which proceeds solely from the light of reason.[18]

The 'light of reason' (*lux rationis*) which is invoked in this passage (and which reappears in the *Meditations* and elsewhere as the 'natural light') has a long ancestry. Plato, in the *Republic* (*c.* 380 BC), had used the simile of the sun to describe the Form of the Good which makes manifest the objects of abstract intellectual cognition (just as the sun sheds light on ordinary visible objects). In St John's Gospel (*c.* AD 100), the *Logos*, the 'Word' or divine creative intelligence, is identified with 'the Light that lighteth every man coming into the world' (1:9). And Augustine, in the *De Trinitate* (*c.* 410), welding together Platonic and Christian ideas,

---

[16] *Regulae*, Rule Four (AT X 374, 378; CSM I 17, 19).
[17] Ibid., Rule Three (AT X 366; CSM I 13).   [18] Ibid. (AT X 368; CSM I 14).

asserts that 'the mind, when directed to intelligible things in the natural order, according to the disposition of the Creator, sees them in a certain incorporeal light which has a nature all of its own, just as the body's eye sees nearby objects in the ordinary light'.[19] Descartes certainly shares with Platonic and Augustinian 'rationalism' a distrust of the 'fluctuating testimony' of the senses, and a belief in the pure inner light of the intellect as a vastly more reliable source of knowledge than anything which is received from the external world via the sensory organs.[20] This rationalist perspective remains strikingly present in the way the argument of the *Meditations* was later developed. And beyond this there is the deeper theological dimension (though this aspect tends to be played down by many modern commentators): Descartes's faith in the reliability of the intellectual light comes to be closely linked, in his later metaphysics, with the fact that it is bestowed on us by God, the source of all truth. Our own route to secure knowledge is, ultimately, illuminated by the 'immense light' proceeding from the perfect divine nature, and shining, albeit with diminished scope, in each individual mind.[21]

Back in the late 1620s, however, the relationship between the divine nature and the attainment of reliable human knowledge was an issue that Descartes had probably not examined in any detail. Despite the underlying theological implications of the notion of the 'light of reason', his early work in the *Rules for the Direction of our Native Intelligence* contains little if any metaphysical argument, and tends instead to proceed as if epistemology and methodology are relatively self-standing and self-contained disciplines capable of providing an autonomous route to 'certain and evident cognition'.[22] We know, however, that Descartes had at least begun to work on metaphysics around this time, since a letter to Marin Mersenne, mentions a 'little treatise' started in 1629, soon after he had decided to leave France to take up permanent residence in Holland. The 'little treatise' (now lost) aimed to prove 'the existence of God and of our souls when they are separate from the

---

[19] *De Trinitate*, XII xv 24. Cf. Plato, *Republic*, 514–18.

[20] Though he is very much *not* the caricature 'rationalist' who holds there is no role whatever for the senses in the development of science: see *Discourse*, Part Six (AT VI 65; CSM I 144).

[21] For the immensity of the divine light, see the resounding final paragraph of the Third Meditation, p. 41. For the limited scope of the natural light within the individual soul, see the Fourth Meditation, p. 47.

[22] AT X 362; CSM I 10.

body';[23] but the work was laid aside, and Descartes did not come back to a full treatment of these issues until the late 1630s.

The reasons for Descartes's self-imposed exile from his native land have been much disputed. He certainly complained of the 'innumerable distractions' of Paris,[24] but though many of his residences in Holland were in secluded country locations, he was not wholly averse to town life (soon after arriving he took lodgings in the bustling city of Amsterdam). It has been suggested that he hoped the Netherlands would provide a more tolerant and free-thinking atmosphere for the reception of his 'modern' views on physics and cosmology; but in the event his philosophical views provoked as much controversy and hostility from Protestant Dutch academics as any he might have expected from Catholic scholars in France. Most likely, Descartes experienced (at least at first) that sense of freedom and release which many expatriates discover on moving away from the culture in which they were born and brought up; the 'masked man', as Descartes had earlier called himself, spoke in his first (anonymously) published work of his pleasure at living amidst a mass of busy people 'more concerned with their own affairs than curious about those of others'.[25]

The main preoccupations of Descartes during the early and middle 1630s were scientific. His treatise on physics, *Le Monde* (already mentioned above), was completed by 1633. It contained a complete description of the origins and workings of the physical universe in accordance with the 'laws of mechanics', and a concluding section, known as the *Traité de l'homme* (*Treatise on Man*), supplied an account of human physiology employing the self-same mechanical principles. Descartes had a keen interest in physiology (which stayed with him all his life), and when he lived in Kalverstraat ('Calf Street') in Amsterdam he made a habit of collecting carcases from the butcher for dissection. His approach to the processes and functions of the living human body was strongly reductionistic: the body was essentially a 'machine', which, like 'clocks, artificial fountains and mills', has the power to operate purely in

---

[23] AT I 182; CSMK 29.   [24] Letter to Mersenne of 27 May 1638 (AT II 151–2).
[25] *Discourse*, Part Three (AT VI 31; CSM I 126). The image of the 'masked man' (*larvatus*) occurs in one of Descartes's early notebooks probably composed during his travels in Europe during the years 1619–22: 'Actors, taught not to let any embarrassment show on their faces, put on a mask. I will do the same. So far, I have been a spectator in this theatre which is the world, but I am now about to mount the stage, and I come forward masked' (AT X 213; CSM I 2).

accordance with its own internal principles, depending 'solely on the disposition of our organs'.[26] Cartesian physiology and biology entirely dispenses with the traditional Scholastic apparatus that had tried to explain such functions as movement, digestion and sensation by appeal to the operation of the so-called locomotive, nutritive and sensory 'souls'. In Descartes's programme for science, mechanism replaces psychism, and the workings of the animal, and indeed human, organism become no different, in principle, from the workings of any other material structure in the universe; all is to be explained purely in terms of size, shape and motion of the component parts. Only in the case of *thought* does Descartes find it necessary to have recourse to a 'rational soul' (*âme raisonable*), specially created by God and 'united' to the complex machinery of the human body.[27]

By 1637, Descartes was ready to publish three 'specimen essays' illustrating his new scientific method. The first was the *Optics* (*La Dioptrique*), which applied mathematical and mechanical principles to the explanation of 'refraction and the manufacture of lenses, ... of the eye, of light, of vision, and of everything belonging to catoptrics and optics'.[28] The achievement was a considerable one: in the course of the work, Descartes accurately sets out, in precise mathematical terms, a version of what is now known as Snell's law of refraction. The second essay, the *Meteorology* (*Les Météores*), applies the reductionistic mechanical approach to a wide variety of phenomena including 'vapours and exhalations, salt, winds, clouds, snow, rain and hail, storms and lightning, and the rainbow'.[29] The guiding principle here is one that remains dominant throughout Cartesian science: differences in the size, shape and motion of constituent particles are sufficient to explain all the phenomena we observe in the world around us and the sky above us, without the need to posit any of the traditional 'substantial forms', or indeed any qualitative differences between supposedly different 'kinds' of matter. 'I regard [these particles] as all being composed of one single kind of matter,' Descartes observes in the *Meteorology*, 'and believe that

[26] *Treatise on Man*, AT XI 120; CSM I 99.   [27] Ibid., AT XI 143; CSM I 102.
[28] Letter to Mersenne of March 1636 (AT I 339–40; CSMK 51). The scope of Descartes's essay was thus wider than its original French title *La Dioptrique* (literally 'Dioptrics') suggests. ('Dioptrics' was the traditional name given to the study of refracted light; 'catoptrics' to reflected light.)
[29] AT VI 231ff.; CSM I 175.

each of them could be divided repeatedly in infinitely many ways, and that there is no more difference between them than there is between stones of various different shapes cut from the same rock'.[30] Finally, in the published trio of specimen essays, comes the *Geometry* (*La Géométrie*), an accomplished work, reflecting Descartes's long-standing interest in pure mathematics, which laid down the foundations for what we now know as coordinate geometry.

The core of Descartes's philosophy

Prefaced to the three essays just mentioned was an extended introduction in six parts, the *Discourse on the Method of rightly conducting one's reason and seeking the truth in the sciences* (*Discours de la Méthode pour bien conduire sa raison, et chercher la vérité dans les sciences*). The whole volume consisting of the *Discourse and Essays* was published anonymously in Leiden in June 1637; in an earlier letter to Mersenne, Descartes had compared himself to the painter who wished to 'hide behind the picture in order to hear what people will say about it'.[31] The *Discourse*, which next to the *Meditations* is nowadays Descartes's best-known and most widely-read work, provides a remarkably clear and accessible overview of his philosophical and scientific ideas, though it is very different both in tone and content from the *Meditations*, published four years later. The latter work was composed in Latin, the international language of scholarship in the seventeenth century, whereas Descartes chose to write the *Discourse* in French, precisely in order to present his views more informally, and to a wider audience. Though the author's name did not appear on the title page, the *Discourse* is an intensely personal work, a kind of intellectual autobiography which describes (in Part One) the influences on Descartes's early development and his dissatisfaction with the traditional philosophical curriculum, and (in Part Two) his determination to establish a new, clear and orderly method, modelled on the reasoning found in mathematics: 'provided we refrain from accepting anything as true which is not, and always keep to the order required for deducing one thing from another, there can be nothing too remote to be reached in the end or too well hidden to be discovered'.[32] The project is

---

[30] AT VI 239; CSM II 173, n. 2.   [31] Letter of 8 October 1629 (AT I 23; CSMK 6).
[32] AT VI 19; CSM I 120.

nothing less than the construction of a new system of knowledge, starting from scratch – a complete 'rebuilding of the house' as Descartes puts it.[33]

Part Three of the *Discourse* then goes on to set out a 'provisional moral code',[34] which will provide a reliable practical shelter while the edifice of knowledge is being reconstructed; and Part Four (to be discussed below) gives a compelling account of how the metaphysical foundations of the new edifice are to be laid down. Part Five provides a discussion of some of Descartes's scientific work, and is by way of being a summary of the cosmology, physics and physiology covered in the earlier suppressed treatise on the universe and man (*Le Monde* and the *Traité de l'homme*). It includes a detailed account of the circulation of the blood,[35] as well as a series of arguments designed to show that the mechanistic schema which suffices to explain all observed functions in animals totally breaks down when it comes to explaining the capacity for thought and language in human beings. 'It is not conceivable', Descartes argues, that 'a machine should produce different arrangements of words so as to give an appropriately meaningful answer to whatever is said in its presence, as the dullest of men can do'. This leads to the idea of a radical difference between animals and men. The former are simply mechanical automata – natural machines (albeit highly complex ones) made, 'by the hand of God', out of the same material ingredients which compose the rest of the physical universe. But human beings, whose conceptual and linguistic abilities cannot be explained in this way, must possess a rational soul which 'cannot be derived in any way from the potentiality of matter, but must be specially created'.[36] Finally, in Part Six of the *Discourse*, Descartes says something of his plans for future research, and underlines the need for empirical observation to establish which hypotheses, of the several alternatives consistent with the general principles of his science, are in fact correct:

---

[33] *Discourse*, Part Three (AT VI 22; CSM I 122).　　[34] Ibid.

[35] In supporting the idea of the circulation of the blood, Descartes praises the 'English physician, who ... [broke] the ice on this subject', referring to William Harvey, whose *De Motu Cordis* was published in 1628. But Descartes takes the cause of circulation to be expansion caused by the 'heat of the heart', a view which led him to insist that the blood gushes from heart to arteries during the diastole phase, not (as Harvey had correctly maintained) during the systole (contraction) phase (AT VI 50, 52; CSM I 136, 137).

[36] AT VI 55–9; CSM I 139–41.

the power of nature is so ample and so vast, and these principles so simple and so general, that I notice hardly any particular effect of which I do not know at once that it can be deduced from the principles in many different ways; and my greatest difficulty is usually to discover in which of these ways it depends on them. I know no other means to discover this than by seeking further observations whose outcomes vary according to which of these ways provides the correct explanation.[37]

Interesting though these scientific and methodological issues are, it is Part Four of the *Discourse*, the metaphysical core of the work, which has called forth the greatest discussion and commentary. For students of the *Meditations* it is of particular interest, since, in the space of eight paragraphs, it anticipates, if only in outline, many of the more complex and extended arguments of the later work. Descartes begins Part Four of the *Discourse* by stressing the need to make sure the foundations of his new science are sufficiently firm and secure. The way to achieve this is to 'reject as if absolutely false everything in which I could imagine the least doubt, in order to see if I was left believing anything that was entirely indubitable'. He continues:

Thus, because our senses sometimes deceive us, I decided to suppose that nothing was such as they led us to imagine. And since there are people who make mistakes in reasoning, committing logical fallacies concerning the simplest questions in geometry, and because I judged that I was as prone to error as anyone else, I rejected as unsound all the arguments I had previously taken as demonstrative proofs. Lastly, considering that the very thoughts we have while awake may also occur while we sleep without any of them being at that time true, I resolved to pretend that all the things that had ever entered my mind were no more true than the illusions of my dreams. But immediately I noticed that even while I was endeavouring in this way to think that everything was false, it was necessary that I, who was thinking this, was something. And observing that this truth '*I am thinking, therefore I exist*' was so firm and sure that all the most extravagant suppositions of the sceptics were incapable of shaking it, I decided that I could accept it without scruple as the first principle of the philosophy I was seeking.[38]

[37] AT VI 64–5; CSM I 144.   [38] AT VI 32; CSM I 127.

Here we have the same technique for systematically 'leading the mind away from the senses' which is later found in the First Meditation (see Synopsis, p. 10). The unreliability of the senses is underscored by appeal to the fact that they 'sometimes deceive us'; the celebrated dreaming argument is deployed, first to cast doubt on our ability to distinguish between waking and sleeping experience, and then to raise more radical doubts about the existence of anything external to the mind. The possibility of error even with regard to the simple propositions of geometry is also raised, though without the appeal, found in the *Meditations*, to the possible existence of an all-powerful God who might bring it about that 'I . . . go wrong every time I . . . count the sides of a square' (p. 18).[39] And finally, the successive waves of doubt collapse on an immovable rock of certainty, as the doubter arrives at the indubitable awareness of his own existence: 'I am thinking, therefore I exist'. The original French phrase in the *Discourse* is *je pense donc je suis*, but the argument has come to be known as 'the Cogito' (from the Latin version *Cogito ergo sum* found in Descartes's later work, the *Principles of Philosophy*, as well as in the subsequent Latin edition of the *Discourse*). It is notable that the celebrated phrase does not appear in the *Meditations*, although there is a closely similar argument: despite the most extravagant doubts that can be raised, '*I am, I exist*, is necessarily true whenever it is put forward by me or conceived in my mind' (p. 21).

The argument of the *Discourse* now proceeds to a new phase. The narrator, having achieved certainty of his own existence, turns next to examining what *kind* of being he is. And here the methodical doubts just canvassed are taken to yield a remarkable result:

> I saw that while I could pretend that I had no body and that there was no world and no place for me to be in, I could not for all that pretend that I did not exist . . . From this I knew I was a substance whose whole essence or nature is only to think, and which does not require any place, or depend on any material thing, in order to exist. Accordingly this 'I' – that is, the soul by which I am what

---

39 The 'deceiving God' argument in the First Meditation takes the form of a dilemma: either God exists, in which case he has the power to make me go astray in the manner suggested, or there is no God, in which case I owe my origins to some less perfect cause, with the result that I have even less reason to suppose myself free of error in these matters. Neither this argument, nor the later scenario of a 'malicious demon of the utmost power and cunning' who 'employ[s] all his energies in order to deceive me' (p. 19) makes any appearance in the *Discourse*.

I am – is entirely distinct from the body, and indeed is easier to know than the body, and would not fail to be whatever it is, even if the body did not exist.[40]

Descartes is thus led to propound one of his most controversial theses, that the thinking self is essentially incorporeal. What makes me *me* is, by nature, entirely independent of the body and could exist without it. Though consistent with Descartes's earlier arguments in the *Treatise on Man*, that humans consist of a mechanical body plus an immaterial 'rational soul', it is a thesis that is harshly out of tune with the dominant approach to the philosophy of mind in our own time; the majority of modern philosophers have entirely rejected what has scathingly been called the Cartesian doctrine of the 'ghost in the machine'.[41] But even among Descartes's contemporaries there was serious criticism of the argument he offered in the *Discourse*. From what looks like a purely epistemological point, that I can doubt my body's existence, or that I am less certain of it than I am of my own thinking, how is it supposed to follow that the essential 'me' is, in reality, distinct from and independent of the body? How can we move so swiftly from epistemology to ontology, from questions about what we are capable of knowing, doubting or imagining to answers about the real and essential truth of things? Readers of the *Discourse* were quick to fasten on this difficulty, and when Descartes came to write the *Meditations*, although he refused to abandon the reasoning (it reappears in more elaborate form in the Second Meditation, p. 22), he did undertake to clarify his position and to strengthen his arguments. The clarification is offered in the Preface to the *Meditations* (p. 8), and the strengthening is offered in the Sixth Meditation (pp. 61, 67). It is for the reader to judge the merits of what appears in these passages, together with Descartes's attempts to defend his view against the powerful criticisms offered by the author of the Fourth Objections, Antoine Arnauld (p. 136ff., below). What is unmistakably clear is that Descartes continues to insist on the independence of the mind, *qua* 'thinking thing', from anything bodily: 'if a foot or arm or any other part of the body is cut off, nothing has thereby been taken away from the mind' (p. 68). The claim is revealed in its full starkness, and

---

[40] Part Four (AT VI 32–3; CSM I 127).
[41] The phrase is Gilbert Ryle's (*The Concept of Mind*, London, Hutchinson, 1949).

(to most philosophers nowadays) its overwhelming implausibility, when we remember that the *brain*, being a purely bodily organ, must, for Descartes, be as inessential to the mind's continued functioning as foot or arm.

The remainder of Part Four of the *Discourse* is concerned with the celebrated Cartesian 'truth rule' ('Whatever is very clearly and distinctly conceived is true'),[42] and with the proofs of the existence of a perfect God, which enable us to be sure that 'our ideas or notions, being real things and coming from God, cannot be anything but true, in every respect in which they are clear and distinct'.[43] This opens the gateway to the construction of a reliable science, based not on the deliverances of the senses, but on the divinely implanted truths of mathematics which give us clear and distinct knowledge of the material world. Making the transition from metaphysics to science at the start of Part Five of the *Discourse*, Descartes resoundingly declares: 'I have noticed certain laws which God has so established in nature, and of which he has implanted such notions in our minds, that after adequate reflection we cannot doubt that they are exactly observed in everything which exists or occurs in the world'.[44]

When Descartes came to write the *Meditations*, which he began to compose not long after the publication of the *Discourse*, his aim was to provide a richer and more detailed elaboration of these metaphysical themes, and thus ensure a firm and unshakable base for his new philosophical system. We have already drawn attention to a number of themes in the *Meditations* which had been prefigured in his earlier writings. The 'rationalistic' move away from the senses towards the inner light of the intellect – a movement which is steadily developed from the barrage of doubt which opens the First Meditation, through to the articulation of the mind's innate ideas in the Third – had been anticipated in the *Discourse*, and, much earlier, if less explicitly, in the *Regulae*. The Cogito argument set out in the *Discourse* provides the bones for the fuller and

---

[42] Cf. AT VI 33; CSM I 127. The invoking of God as the guarantor of the reliability of our clear and distinct ideas, which is even more prominent in the *Meditations*, gives rise to the notorious problem of the 'Cartesian Circle': if we can be sure of the reliability of such ideas only after we have proved the existence of a perfect God who created us, how can we, without circularity, rely on the ideas which we need to prove his existence in the first place? For more on this, see the Introductory essay (p. xvii, above), and the detailed exchange between Descartes and his contemporary critics (pp. 130–5, below).

[43] AT VI 38; CSM I 130.   [44] AT VI 41; CSM I 131.

more sophisticated treatment in the Second Meditation. The notion of the thinking self as essentially incorporeal, tentatively explored in the Second Meditation, and defended at length in the Sixth, was also a development of earlier reflections in the *Discourse*. And the central role of God as guarantor of the possibility of knowledge, a thread that runs right through the *Meditations*, has its roots in the doctrine of the 'light of reason' appearing in the *Regulae*, and the more direct appeal, in the *Discourse*, to divine perfection as the source of all truth in our ideas.

The theocentric character of Descartes's thinking here is underlined by the language of the *Meditations*, which, especially in the original Latin, is often strongly reminiscent of the patristic and medieval world that shaped the intellectual culture Descartes inherited. We often read the *Meditations* nowadays as a work of epistemology, as if Descartes's sole aim was to refute scepticism. But Descartes observes in the Preface to the *Meditations* that his aim is not to prove 'that there really is a world, and that human beings have bodies and so on – *since no sane person has ever seriously doubted these things.*' (below, p. 13, emphasis added). The Cartesian quest did not spring into existence as a set of intellectual puzzles or diversions, but fits into a long tradition (going back to Augustine and beyond), which sees the philosopher as using doubt and self-discovery as the first step in the search for objective truth. The point of his arguments establishing the external world, says Descartes, is that 'in considering [them] we come to realize that they are not as solid or as transparent as the arguments which lead us to knowledge of our own minds and of God' (ibid.). For Descartes himself the primary significance of the self-awareness he achieves is that it is the first step on the road to awareness of God.

Descartes's conception of himself as a thinking being immediately leads him to reflect on his finitude and imperfection; and this in turn leads him directly forward to contemplate the 'immense light' of the Godhead, the infinite incorporeal being whose image is reflected, albeit dimly, in the finite created intellect of the meditator.[45] Like Bonaventure nearly four hundred years earlier, whose own *Itinerarium mentis in Deum* (*The Journey of the Mind towards God*) was profoundly conditioned by the contemplative and immaterialist tradition of Plato and Augustine,

---

[45] Third Meditation, AT VII 51; CSM II 35.

Descartes has a conception of ultimate truth that required an *aversio* – a turning of the mind away from the world of the senses – in order to prepare it for glimpsing the reality that lies beyond the phenomenal world. Both Bonaventure and Descartes, following Augustine's famous slogan *In interiore homine habitat veritas* ('The truth dwells within the inner man'),[46] undertake an interior journey. 'Go back into yourself', says Augustine; 'let us return to ourselves, into our mind', says Bonaventure, that we may search for the '*lux veritatis in facie nostrae mentis*' – the light of truth shining in our minds, as through a glass, in which the image of the Blessed Trinity shines forth.[47] 'I turn my mind's eye upon myself', says Descartes, and find the idea of God stamped there, like the 'mark the craftsman has set on his work'.[48]

There is a paradox here which lies at the heart of Descartes's philosophy. On the one hand, it is clearly motivated by the desire of the independent-mind researcher to shake off the shackles of preconceived opinion and stride forward in search of the truth: this is the image of Descartes as inaugurator of the modern scientific age, and the champion of human autonomy and independence. But on the other hand, the path to truth is conditioned, in Descartes's conception, by the traditional religious idea of our creatureliness – the idea that we are sustained at every moment of our existence by a creative power who is the source of all truth and goodness, and without whom we would remain adrift in the darkness, bereft of that 'light of reason' which, for Descartes, is the divine gift to each human soul. The tension between independence and creatureliness pervades the entire structure of the *Meditations*.

'I am here quite alone', the meditator announces in the opening paragraph of the *Meditations* (p. 15). There follows, in vividly dramatic detail, a compelling account of the journey of discovery taken by the isolated thinker as he[49] searches for secure foundations for knowledge.

---

[46] 'Noli foras ire, in teipsum redi; in interiore homine habitat veritas' ('Go not outside, but return within thyself; in the inward man dwelleth the truth'). Augustine, *De vera religione* [391] XXXIX, 72.

[47] 'Ad nos reintraremus, in mentem scilicet nostram, in qua divina relucet imago; hinc … conari debemus per speculum videre Deum, ubi ad modum candelabri relucet lux veritatis in facie nostrae mentis, in qua scilicet resplendet imago beatissimae Trinitatis.' Bonaventure, *Itinerarium mentis in Deum* [1259], III, 1. For more on the theocentric character of Descartes's philosophy, see J. Cottingham, *Cartesian Reflections* (Oxford: Oxford University Press, 2008), ch. 13 and 14.

[48] Third Meditation, AT VII 51; CSM II 35.

[49] A genderless pronoun would be more appropriate here, since the meditator is identified purely as a 'thinking thing'; the existence of the body is at this stage still in doubt, and the subject is

A series of progressively more radical and extreme doubts are employed to question all preconceived opinions (First Meditation), but (soon after the start of the Second) an 'Archimedean point' of unshakable certainty is reached with the meditator's indubitable awareness of his own existence (p. 21). The meditator then reflects on his essence or nature as a 'thinking thing', and reasons that the mind is better known than the body (p. 27). The Third Meditation begins by laying down the rule that 'whatever I perceive very clearly and distinctly is true' (p. 29); but there remain doubts about the reliability of the mind that can only be allayed by establishing 'whether there is a God, and, if there is, whether he can be a deceiver' (p. 30). The meditator proceeds to reflect on the innate ideas he finds within him, and reasons that the representational content (or 'objective reality')[50] of one of these ideas, that of a supremely perfect being, is so great that it cannot have been constructed from the resources of the meditator's own finite mind; the conclusion is that God must really exist, and that 'in creating me, [he] . . . placed this idea in me to be, as it were, the mark of the craftsman stamped on his work' (p. 41).

The Fourth Meditation tackles the problem of truth and falsity, and argues that the way for humans to avoid error is to restrain their (infinite) will, so as to make judgements only when the perceptions of the (finite) intellect are clear and distinct. The intellect, though limited, is created by a perfect God, and what it *does* clearly perceive can therefore be guaranteed to be true.[51] The effect of the argument is to provide a kind of Cartesian 'theodicy' or vindication of God, which parallels the traditional theological project of trying to vindicate the goodness of God notwithstanding the existence of evil in the world. In the particular case of the frequent mistakes and errors in judgement to which we humans are prone, Descartes aims to show that such error is not to be laid at God's door, but is the result of an improper use of the gift of free will, when we jump in and give our assent to what is not clearly perceived. The Fifth Meditation prepares the way for Cartesian science by establishing

considered entirely in abstraction from the bodily attributes that make one male or female. Modern writers often use the plural 'they' and 'their' when a neutral pronoun is required, but unfortunately this useful convention would be highly misleading in the present context, since it is a crucial part of Descartes's argument that the meditator is a *singular* isolated individual (at this stage I cannot know whether anyone else exists apart from myself).

[50] For the meaning of this technical term, see pp. 32, n. 8, and 105–8.

[51] The problem of the 'Cartesian Circle' is never far beneath the surface here and in many other crucial stages of the argument of the *Meditations*. See n. 42, above.

the nature of matter as something extended and divisible, which can be accurately and correctly described in mathematical language (pp. 50, 56). We are also offered a second proof for God's existence, namely that the concept of a supremely perfect being (one who is the sum of all perfections) implies that such a being cannot lack the perfection of existence, and hence that such a being must, by its very nature, exist (p. 52).[52] Lastly, in the Sixth Meditation, the actual existence of the external world (called into doubt in the First Meditation) is finally re-established (p. 63), and we are offered a series of arguments which purport to demonstrate the 'real' distinction between mind and body: they are mutually independent substances, each of which can exist without the other. But having used philosophical reason to establish the distinction, the Sixth Meditation closes by invoking our everyday experience of the sensations 'of hunger, thirst, pain and so on' as showing that mind and body, though distinct, are closely 'intermingled' or 'united' (p. 64). The final paragraphs return to the problem of truth and error, arguing that 'notwithstanding the immense goodness of God, the nature of man as a combination of mind and body is such that it is bound to mislead him from time to time' (p. 69).[53] Descartes himself provided a tolerably informative *Synopsis* of the argument which is not only worth consulting as a summary, but also contains some interesting additional reflections by the author on his work (pp. 10–13). For detailed discussion of some of the chief philosophical difficulties arising from the argument of the *Meditations*, an invaluable starting point is the published *Objections* of Descartes's distinguished contemporaries, and the author's own *Replies* (extracts from some of the most important of these exchanges are provided in the present volume, pp. 73–153).[54]

---

[52] This is Descartes's version of the so-called 'Ontological' argument, first invented by St Anselm of Canterbury. Descartes was at pains to distinguish it from the *causal* argument of the Third Meditation, which proceeds from effect (the idea of God found in the meditator's mind) to cause (the God who placed it there, like a trademark). The Fifth Meditation argument, by contrast, is purely a priori, and depends merely on reflecting on the defining *essence* of a supremely perfect being. For criticism of the argument, and Descartes's replies, see pp. 121ff.

[53] The naturally ordained patterns of psycho-physical response in human beings (for example, a sensation of dryness when the nerves in the tongue and throat are in a certain state) are such as to conduce in general to the health of the mind–body composite. But because nature's laws are constant, there are bound to be occasions when such correlations will produce a desire to drink even in those rare and exceptional morbid conditions where fluid intake is not beneficial; see p. 70.

[54] For publication details relating to the *Meditations* and *Objections and Replies*, and information about the authors of the *Objections*, see Note on the text and the translation, p. l, below.

Descartes hoped that the arguments of the *Meditations*, in particular those purporting to demonstrate the existence of God and the 'real distinction' between soul and body, would find favour with the theologians, and he prefixed to the work a dedicatory letter to the members of the Theology Faculty at the Sorbonne, asking for their approval in his battle for the cause of religion against the atheists (pp. 3–7). The approbation of the Sorbonne was not, however, forthcoming, and the years following the publication of the *Meditations* saw Descartes embroiled in a series of bitter debates with a variety of theological and philosophical critics.[55] One may see some of these debates prefigured in some of the extracts from the *Objections and Replies* included in the present volume, which give an idea of the sensitivity of the questions about God and the soul tackled by Descartes in the *Meditations*, lying as they do at the very interface between philosophy and theology.

The Cartesian system and the human being

Notwithstanding the controversies and disputes that plagued him, Descartes's reputation continued to grow, particularly after the publication, in 1644, of the *Principia Philosophiae*, a grand exposition of the Cartesian system in four parts. Unlike Descartes's earlier writings, the *Principles of Philosophy* was explicitly planned as a university textbook, and like the traditional handbooks it was divided up into a series of small sections or 'articles' (there are 504 in all). Part One ('The Principles of Human Knowledge') covers much the same metaphysical ground as the *Meditations*, though the exposition is much more formal and impersonal; Part Two ('The Principles of Material Things') presents a complete account of Cartesian physics and the laws of matter in motion; Part Three ('The Visible Universe') describes the structure and workings of the solar system; and Part Four ('The Earth') offers explanations of a wide variety of terrestrial phenomena, as well as giving a brief account, in the closing articles, of Descartes's plans for future work on animals and man, with special reference to the explanation of sense perception and sensory awareness. A French version of the original Latin text was issued three

---

[55] Particularly savage were the attacks of the Dutch theologian Gisbertus Voetius, which led to the publication by Descartes of a lengthy defence of his views, the *Epistola ad Voetium* (1643). (Cf. AT VIIIB 25; CSMK 220.)

years later, in 1647, by which time the Cartesian philosophy, despite strong opposition from many parts of the academic establishment, was beginning to gain widespread support.

Descartes's programme for establishing a fully comprehensive philosophical system was, however, still incomplete in at least one important respect: he had as yet provided little indication of how his philosophy would deal with the psychological and ethical realms. In the preface to the 1647 French edition of the *Principles of Philosophy* he referred to the project of constructing a 'perfect morality' – *la plus parfaite morale* – which was to be the crowning achievement of his philosophical endeavours. The traditional goal of moral philosophy was to articulate 'the good for human kind';[56] but the concept of a *human beings*, an embodied creature of flesh and blood, had been left rather in limbo by the results of the *Meditations*. His metaphysical arguments, as we have seen, had led Descartes to the conclusion that the thinking subject was an essentially incorporeal entity whose nature was utterly distinct and alien from the body. And the implication of this was that a human being was an amalgam of seemingly incompatible elements, an immaterial spirit and a mechanical assemblage of bodily organs. Taking his cue from this, Descartes's zealous disciple Regius had insistently proclaimed that the Cartesian doctrine was that man was nothing more than an 'accidental entity' – in the jargon, an *ens per accidens*, as opposed to an *ens per se* (a genuine entity in its own right). Descartes, in correspondence, had angrily dissociated himself from this interpretation, insisting that his view was that 'the mind is united in a real and substantial manner to the body'.[57] But although the Sixth Meditation had called attention to how mind and body were 'very closely joined and, as it were, intermingled' (p. 64), it must have left most readers puzzled as to how such intermingling of incommensurable elements could come about.

One of those who was puzzled was the young Princess Elizabeth of Bohemia, only twenty-four years of age when, in 1643, she began a long and fruitful correspondence with Descartes, largely devoted to the topic of the mind–body union. Her initial question to the philosopher was about the possibility of interaction between 'thinking' and 'extended' substances: how can the soul, or thinking substance, causally influence

---

[56] The phrase is Aristotle's (*Nicomachean Ethics*, Book 1 ch. 7).
[57] Letter to Regius of January 1642 (AT III 493; CSMK 206).

the behaviour of the body to bring about voluntary actions? In his reply, Descartes acknowledged that this question was 'the one which can most properly be put to me in view of my published writings'. He went on to introduce a distinction between three 'primitive notions', which are 'the patterns on the basis of which we form all our other conceptions':

> ... as regards body we have only the notion of extension, which entails the notions of shape and motion. As regards the soul on its own, we have only the notion of thought, which includes the perceptions of the intellect and the inclinations of the will. Lastly, as regards the soul and body together, we have only the notion of their union, on which depends our notions of the soul's power to move the body, and the body's power to act on the soul and cause its sensations and passions.[58]

This third 'primitive notion' comprises, in effect, whatever is attributable to an embodied human being. The *Meditations* had mentioned 'hunger, thirst, pain' in this connection, while the *Principles of Philosophy* had provided a rather fuller list: 'first, appetites like hunger and thirst; secondly, the emotions or passions of the mind which do not consist of thought alone, such as the emotions of anger, joy, sadness and love; and finally, all the sensations, such as those of pain, pleasure, light, colours, sounds, smells, tastes, heat, hardness and the other tactile qualities'.[59]

Our life on this earth, as Descartes came increasingly to underline, involves far more than the intellectual and volitional activities that belong to our essence as immaterial 'thinking things'. If we were like angels (pure thinking beings), Descartes once observed, our existence would be entirely devoid of sensation;[60] we would lack the manifold and varied sensory awareness that is an inescapable part of our everyday human experience. And it is this sensory and affective dimension, with all the vivid phenomenal quality of the various feelings involved, that gives colour and richness to our lives as human beings. Of particular importance here is the category of the passions, which in his last work, *Les Passions de l'âme* (*The Passions of the Soul*, 1649), Descartes grouped under six basic kinds: wonder, love, hatred, desire, joy and sadness. Dissociating himself from earlier intellectualist approaches to ethics

---

[58] Letter of 21 May 1643 (AT III 664, 665; CSMK 217, 218); cf. AT III 660.
[59] Part One, art. 48 (AT VIIIA 23; CSM I 209).
[60] Letter to Regius of January 1642 (AT III 493; CSMK 206).

which had often attempted to suppress the passions as inimical to the good life, Descartes declared: 'The philosophy I cultivate is not so savage or grim as to outlaw the operation of the passions; on the contrary, it is here, in my view, that the entire sweetness and joy of life is to be found'.[61] Descartes's final project was to ground his ethics, his recipe for how humans could achieve fulfilling and worthwhile lives, in a systematic understanding of the operation of the passions, both on a physiological and on a psychological level. Here he hoped that his new method for science would yield a rich harvest. A detailed grasp of the bodily mechanisms which give rise to our emotional responses would, he envisaged, enable us to modify those responses where appropriate, and thus channel our feelings and emotions in such a way as to generate a harmonious human life, lived in accordance with our best perceptions of the good for mankind. Cartesian science, pressed into the service of ethics, would allow us to fulfill the dream first announced in the *Discourse on the Method* and reiterated in the *Principles of Philosophy*: instead of the abstract speculative philosophy of the past, we would have at our disposal a new and genuinely practical philosophy, one that would make us the 'lords and masters of nature', and bring us closer to achieving 'perfection and felicity of life'.[62]

The Cartesian legacy

Descartes's ambitious programme was cut short by his own untimely death, in Stockholm, where, after much hesitation, he had taken up residence at the invitation of Queen Christina of Sweden in 1649. His vitality sapped by the rigours of the Swedish winter, and the need to rise early in the morning to give philosophy tutorials to the Queen, he succumbed to pneumonia and died on 11 February 1650, just under two months short of his fifty-fourth birthday. But although he died leaving his philosophical system not fully complete, the remarkably wide range of what he had achieved, and the clarity and precision of its execution, meant that Cartesian ideas dominated the scientific and philosophical thinking of

---

[61] Letter to Silhon, March or April 1648 (AT V 135).
[62] *Discourse*, Part Six (AT VI 62; CSM I 142–3); Preface to the French edition of the *Principles of Philosophy* (AT IXB 20; CSM I 190).

Europe for a long time to come.[63] The writings of the philosophical giants of the early modern period, Spinoza, Malebranche and Leibniz, on the Continent, and Locke, Berkeley and Hume, in the British Isles, all, in different ways, bear the unmistakable imprint of Descartes's thought concerning the structure of human knowledge, the nature of the mind and the relationship between mind and matter. It is impossible to examine the arguments and conceptual apparatus of any of the canonical philosophers of the late seventeenth and early eighteenth century without seeing the irresistible aptness of the traditional accolade which is so often bestowed on Descartes: he is, indubitably, the true 'father of modern philosophy'.

The story in our own era has been very different. Much twentieth-century philosophy has developed along tracks that diverge sharply from those which Descartes laid down. In the theory of knowledge, what has come to be known as 'foundationalism' – the Cartesian project of trying to build a reliable belief system from scratch, starting from a supposedly self-standing and indubitably certain base – has come to be seen as radically misguided. In the philosophy of mind, Descartes's notion of an immaterial thinking substance has been derided as an explanatory dead-end, powerless to account in any illuminating way for the phenomenon of consciousness and its relationship to the physical world. And, perhaps most devastating of all, the very starting point of Cartesian metaphysics, with its focus on the private reflections of the isolated thinker, has been attacked as incoherent: in the aftermath of Wittgenstein, it has become a ruling orthodoxy that thought and language are inescapably public, socially mediated phenomena, and hence that there is something deeply wrong with the very idea of 'Cartesian privacy' – of solitary, introspective access to the truth. But for all that, the enduring influence of Descartes's ideas remains. It is of the nature of philosophy that its advances are always achieved by means of a continuing dialogue with the great thinkers of the past. The very fact that so much contemporary philosophy defines its goals and methods in stark opposition to Cartesian paradigms itself bears witness to the powerful pressures which Descartes's approach to philosophy still continues to exert. What is

---

[63] Cartesian physics, however, was by the end of the century to come under increasing pressure from the vastly more sophisticated (and accurate) Newtonian system.

called 'common sense' in any age frequently turns out to be the half-digested remains of earlier philosophical theories. Many people's supposedly 'pre-philosophical' intuitions about knowledge, the mind and the nature of certainty, the very intuitions which the philosophers of the twentieth century have struggled to dismantle, have been conditioned by the long-standing dominance of ways of thinking which Descartes helped create.

But there is a final point to be made. Though philosophers sometimes like to think of themselves as belonging to a quasi-scientific, progressive discipline, with steady 'advances' in research, the actual history of the subject shows that it does not, and cannot, proceed in this rectilinear way. Rather, it is a matter of currents and counter-currents, of theses conquered by antitheses which themselves then fall victim to newer and reinvigorated incarnations of earlier rejected ideas. For this reason alone, it is plausible to think that the anti-Cartesian thrust of contemporary philosophizing is destined, in some areas at least, to overreach itself. As far as Descartes's general conception of philosophy is concerned, philosophers nowadays live in a cautiously specialised world which is wary of grand systems; but just as the dominant Scholasticism prior to Descartes ran out of energy, so it is conceivable that today's compartmentalized approach to philosophy may lose its appeal, and give way to a faintly recognizable successor to the Cartesian vision of a comprehensive philosophy that strives to integrate the disparate areas of human cognition. Such speculations aside, one thing is certain, that over three and a half centuries after they were written, the *Meditations* have lost none of their power to fascinate. The vividly dramatic narrative in which Descartes presents the metaphysical core of his philosophy still exerts an extraordinary spell, whether as a specimen of a splendid but doomed enterprise, or as an inspiring exemplar of what the individual intellect can achieve when it casts off the bonds of authority and convention and sets out on the long search for security and truth. In his Preface to the first edition, Descartes observed that he did not expect his *Meditations* to attract 'any great crowd of readers' (p. 9).[64] History has proved him wrong, and will surely continue to do so for a very long time to come.

[64] *nuilam frequentiam lectorum* (AT VII 9, line 23).

Chronology of Descartes's life and works

1596	born at La Haye near Tours on 31 March
1606–14	attends Jesuit college of La Flèche in Anjou[1]
1616	takes *Baccalauréat* and *Licence* in law at University of Poitiers
1618	goes to Holland; joins army of Prince Maurice of Nassau; meets Isaac Beeckman; composes a short treatise on music, the *Compendium Musicae*
1619	travels in Germany; 10 November: has vision of new mathematical and scientific system
1622	returns to France; during next few years spends time in Paris, but also travels in Europe
1628	composes *Rules for the Direction of the Mind*; leaves for Holland, which is to be his home until 1649, though with frequent changes of address
1629	begins working on *The World*
1633	condemnation of Galileo; Descartes abandons plans to publish *The World*
1635	birth of Descartes's natural daughter Francine, baptized 7 August (died 1640)
1637	publishes *Discourse on the Method*, with *Optics*, *Meteorology* and *Geometry*
1641	*Meditations on First Philosophy* published, together with *Objections and Replies* (first six sets)

---

[1] Descartes is known to have stayed at La Flèche for eight or nine years, but the exact dates of his arrival and departure are uncertain. Baillet places Descartes's admission in 1604, the year of the College's foundation (A. Baillet, *La vie de M. Des-Cartes* (1691), vol. I, p. 18).

1642	second edition of *Meditations* published, with all seven sets of *Objections and Replies* and *Letter to Dinet*
1643	Cartesian philosophy condemned at the University of Utrecht; Descartes's long correspondence with Princess Elizabeth of Bohemia begins
1644	visits France; *Principles of Philosophy* published
1647	awarded a pension by King of France; begins work on *Description of the Human Body*
1648	publishes *Comments on a Certain Broadsheet*; interviewed by Frans Burman at Egmond-Binnen (*Conversation with Burman*)
1649	goes to Sweden on invitation of Queen Christina; *The Passions of the Soul* published
1650	dies at Stockholm on 11 February

Further reading

The standard complete edition of Descartes's writings in the original French and Latin is:

Adam, C. and P. Tannery (eds.), *Œuvres de Descartes*, rev. edn, 12 vols, (Paris: Vrin/CNRS, 1964–76). (referred to as 'AT')

The standard three-volume English Edition is:

Cottingham, J., R. Stoothoff and D. Murdoch (eds.), *The Philosophical Writings of Descartes*, Vols. I and II (Cambridge: Cambridge University Press, 1985) (referred to as 'CSM'); Vol. III, *The Correspondence*, by the same translators and A. Kenny (Cambridge: Cambridge University Press, 1991). (referred to as 'CSMK')

The following long-established and accessible introductions to Descartes's philosophy cover many of the topics in the *Meditations:*

Cottingham, J., *Descartes* (Oxford: Blackwell, 1986).

Kenny, A., *Descartes: A Study of His Philosophy* (New York: Random House, 1968).

Williams, B., *Descartes: The Project of Pure Inquiry* (London: Penguin, 1978).

Wilson, M., *Descartes* (London: Routledge & Kegan Paul, 1978).

Two helpful introductions to the arguments of the *Meditations* are

Hatfield, G., *Descartes and the Meditations* (London: Routledge, 2003), and

Wilson, C., *Descartes's Meditations: An Introduction* (Cambridge: Cambridge University Press, 2003).

Two valuable collections of essays devoted to the most important topics in the *Meditations* are

Cunning, D. (ed.), *The Cambridge Companion to Descartes' Meditations* (Cambridge: Cambridge University Press, 2014), and

Gaukroger, S., (ed.), *The Blackwell Guide to Descartes' Meditations* (Oxford: Blackwell, 2006).

The following is a wide-ranging collection of articles covering the full context and impact of Descartes's philosophy

Broughton, J. and John Carriero (ed.), *A Companion to Descartes* (Malden, MA: Wiley Blackwell, 2008).

See also the following collections of critical essays covering central aspects of Descartes's thought:

Cottingham, J. (ed.), *The Cambridge Companion to Descartes* (Cambridge, Cambridge University Press, 1992).

Moyal, J. D. (ed.), *René Descartes, Critical Assessments*, 4 vols., (London and New York, Routledge, 1991).

For illuminating accounts of important influences on Descartes's thought, see

Menn, S., *Descartes and Augustine* (Cambridge: Cambridge University Press, 1998), and

Carriero, J., *Between Two Worlds: A Reading of Descartes's Meditations* (Princeton, NJ.: Princeton University Press, 2009), which compares Descartes's arguments with those of Aquinas.

A useful collection of lesser known background sources is

Ariew, R., J. Cottingham, and T. Sorell (eds.), *Descartes' Meditations: Background Source Materials* (Cambridge: Cambridge University Press, 1998).

Other useful books on Descartes and his philosophy include:

Beyssade, J.-M., *La philosophie première de Descartes* (Paris: Flammarion, 1979).

Broughton, J., *Descartes's Method of Doubt* (Princeton, NJ: Princeton University Press, 2002).

Cottingham, J., *A Descartes Dictionary* (Oxford: Blackwell, 1993).

Frankfurt, H., *Demons, Dreamers and Madmen: The Defense of Reason in Descartes's Meditations* (New York: Bobbs-Merrill, 1970).

Garber, D., *Descartes' Metaphysical Physics* (Chicago, University of Chicago Press, 1992).

Gaukroger, S., *Descartes: An Intellectual Biography* (Oxford: Clarendon Press, 1995).

Rozemond, M., *Descartes's Dualism* (Cambridge, MA: Harvard University Press, 1998).

Note on the text and the translation

Descartes's most celebrated philosophical work was written in Latin during the period 1638–40, when the philosopher was living, for the most part, at Santpoort. This 'corner of north Holland', he wrote to Mersenne on 27 May 1638, was much more suitable for his work than the 'air of Paris' with its 'vast number of inevitable distractions'.[1] The work was completed by April 1640, and was first published in Paris in 1641 by Michel Soly under the title *Meditationes de Prima Philosophia* (*Meditations on First Philosophy*); the subtitle adds 'in which are demonstrated the existence of God and the immortality of the soul'. In earlier correspondence Descartes had referred to his work as the *Metaphysics*, but he eventually decided that 'the most suitable title is *Meditations on First Philosophy*, because the discussion is not confined to God and the soul but treats in general of all the first things to be discovered by philosophizing'.[2]

Descartes was not entirely satisfied with Soly as a publisher, and he arranged for a second edition of the *Meditations* to be brought out in Holland, by the house of Elzevir of Amsterdam. This second edition appeared in 1642, with a new and more appropriate subtitle, *viz.* 'in which are demonstrated the existence of God and the distinction between the human soul and the body'. The second edition contains a number of minor corrections to the text (though in practice the sense is seldom affected), and except where indicated it is this edition that is followed in the present translation.[3]

[1] AT II 152.   [2] Letter to Mersenne of 11 November 1640 (AT III 239; CSMK 157).
[3] A dual language edition which presents Descartes's Latin text in a facing-page format, alongside my English translation of the *Meditations with Selections from the Objections and Replies*, is published by Cambridge University Press, trans. and ed. J. Cottingham (hb 2013; pb 2015).

A French translation of the *Meditations* by Louis-Charles d'Albert, Duc de Luynes (1620–90) appeared in 1647. This is a tolerably accurate version which was published with Descartes's approval; Adrien Baillet, in his biography of Descartes, goes so far as to claim that the philosopher took advantage of the French edition to 'retouch his original work'.[4] In fact, however, the French version generally stays fairly close to the Latin. There are a number of places where phrases in the original are paraphrased or expanded somewhat, but it is impossible to say which of these modifications, if any, were directly initiated by Descartes (some are certainly too clumsy to be his work). There is thus no good case for giving the French version greater authority than the original Latin text, which we know that Descartes himself composed; and the present translation therefore always provides, in the first instance, a direct rendering of the original Latin. But where expansions or modifications to be found in the French version offer useful glosses on, or additions to, the original, these are also translated, but always in diamond brackets, or in footnotes, to avoid confusion.

As soon as he had completed the *Meditations*, Descartes began to circulate them among his friends, asking for comments and criticisms. He also sent the manuscript to Friar Marin Mersenne (1588–1648), his friend and principal correspondent, asking him to obtain further criticisms. He wrote to Mersenne in a letter of 28 January 1641: 'I will be very glad if people put to me many objections, the strongest they can find, for I hope that the truth will stand out all the better.'[5] The resulting six sets of Objections (the first set collected by Descartes himself, the remainder by Mersenne) were published in Latin, together with Descartes's Replies, in the same volume as the first (1641) edition of the *Meditations*. The second edition of the *Meditations* (1642) contained in addition the Seventh Set of Objections together with Descartes's Replies, and also the Letter to Dinet (all in Latin). The terms 'Objections' and 'Replies' were suggested by Descartes himself, who asked that his own comments should be called 'Replies' rather than 'Solutions' in order to leave the reader to judge whether his replies contained solutions to the difficulties offered.[6]

---

[4] *La Vie de Monsieur Des-Cartes* (Paris, Horthemels, 1691; photographic reprint Hildesheim, Olms, 1972), vol. II, p. 172.

[5] AT III 297; CSMK 172.

[6] Letters to Mersenne of 30 September 1640 and 18 March 1641 (AT III 184, 340; CSMK 153, 177).

The volume containing the French translation of the *Meditations* (by de Luynes), which appeared in 1647, also contained a French version of the first six sets of *Objections and Replies* by Descartes's disciple Claude Clerselier (1614–84). Although it is frequently said that Descartes saw and approved of this translation, there is, as with the *Meditations* proper, no good case for preferring the French version to the original Latin which Descartes himself composed. It should also be remembered that all the objectors wrote in Latin, and had before them only the Latin text of the *Meditations* when they wrote. The present extracts from the *Objections and Replies* are therefore based entirely on the original Latin.

The First Set of Objections is by a Catholic theologian from Holland, Johannes Caterus (Johan de Kater), who was priest in charge of the church of St Laurens at Alkmaar from 1632–56. Caterus had been asked to comment on the *Meditations* by two fellow priests who were friends of Descartes, Bannius and Bloemaert; and it is to these two intermediaries that both Caterus' Objections and Descartes's Replies are addressed. Descartes wrote to Mersenne on 24 December 1640 that Caterus himself wished to remain anonymous.[7]

The Second Set of Objections is simply attributed to 'theologians and philosophers' in the index to the first edition, but the French version of 1647 announces that they were 'collected by the Reverend Father Mersenne'. In fact they are largely the work of Mersenne himself.

The Third Set of Objections ('by a celebrated English philosopher', says the 1647 edition) is by Thomas Hobbes (1588–1679) who had fled to France, for political reasons, in 1640. Although many of Hobbes' points are of considerable philosophical interest, Descartes's comments are mostly curt and dismissive in the extreme.

The Fourth Set of Objections is by the French theologian and logician Antoine Arnauld (1612–94), who became Doctor of Theology at the Sorbonne in 1641. Both the Objections and Replies are addressed to Mersenne as intermediary, and the tone of both authors is courteous and respectful throughout.

The Fifth Set of Objections is by the philosopher Pierre Gassendi (1592–1655). His comments are very lengthy and come near to being a paragraph by paragraph commentary on the *Meditations*. Gassendi's tone

---

7 AT III 265; CSMK 163.

is often acerbic, and Descartes frequently reacts with bristly defensiveness. (Gassendi went on to publish a further set of criticisms, in 1644, to which Descartes published a further reply, which was included in the French translation of the *Objections and Replies*, published in 1647.)

The Sixth Set of Objections was printed with no indication of the author in the first and second editions, and is described in the 1647 French edition as being 'by various theologians and philosophers'. The compiler, as in the case of the Second Objections, is Mersenne.

The Seventh Set of Objections is by the Jesuit, Pierre Bourdin (1595–1653). Descartes had been eager to obtain the support of the Jesuits for his philosophy, but he was very disappointed with what he called 'the quibbles of Father Bourdin'; he wrote to Mersenne 'I have treated him as courteously as possible, but I have never seen a paper so full of faults.'[8]

The English translation in the present volume is based on the version which I originally prepared for the two (later three) volume Cambridge edition of *The Philosophical Writings of Descartes*.[9] It was subsequently published with minor changes in my one-volume edition of the *Meditations with Selections from the Objections and Replies*, and later reissued, with revisions, in the *Cambridge Texts in the History of Philosophy* series.[10] I have taken the opportunity of the present revised edition to include several additional extracts from the *Objections and Replies*, and to make some further corrections to the text.

The selecting of extracts from the *Objections and Replies* has been done specially for this edition, and the reader should note that the extracts do not necessarily come in the order in which they appear in the original. Instead, I have arranged the material thematically, so as to indicate the main points of criticism that occurred to Descartes's contemporaries as

[8] Letter of March 1642 (AT III 543; CSMK 211).
[9] J. Cottingham, R. Stoothoff and D. Murdoch, *The Philosophical Writings of Descartes*, vols. I and II (Cambridge, Cambridge University Press, 1985), known as 'CSM', and vol. III, *The Correspondence*, by the same translators and A. Kenny (Cambridge, Cambridge University Press, 1991), known as 'CSMK'. In the division of labour adopted for the first two volumes, it fell to me to translate the *Meditations* and the *Objections and Replies*. I should like, however, to underline once again the debt I owe to my friends and colleagues Bob Stoothoff and Dugald Murdoch, who during the original project scrutinized my work at every stage, and made numerous corrections and suggestions for improvement
[10] René Descartes, *Meditations on First Philosophy with Selections from the Objections and Replies*, trans. and ed. J. Cottingham (Cambridge: Cambridge University Press, 1986). Revised edition with new Introduction, 1996.

they read through the *Meditations*, and to show how Descartes clarified and developed his arguments in response to those criticisms. In condensing some 320 pages of text down to some 50 pages of extracts for the present volume, I have of course had to be ruthlessly selective. My aim has been to assist the student in coming to terms with the complex and subtle reasoning of the *Meditations* by focusing attention on some of the principal philosophical difficulties which arise out of Descartes's deceptively lucid masterpiece. Before each extract, or group of extracts, I have supplied a title indicating the topic dealt with, and at the end of each extract the reader will find a note of the set of Objections or Replies to which it belongs, together with a page reference to Volume II of CSM, where the unabridged English text may be found. The translations, both of the *Meditations* and of the selections from the *Objections and Replies*, are based on the Latin text in Volume VII of the standard edition of Descartes, *Œuvres de Descartes*, ed. C. Adam and P. Tannery (known as 'AT'). Running references to the relevant page numbers of AT vol. VII are supplied in the margins.[11]

J.C.

---

[11] Where a marginal reference appears in parentheses ( ), this indicates that the extract in question begins part way down an AT page, rather than at the start of the page.

Meditations on First Philosophy

[Dedicatory letter to the Sorbonne]

To those most learned and distinguished men, the Dean and
Doctors of the sacred Faculty of Theology at Paris,
from René Descartes.

I have a very good reason for offering this book to you, and I am
confident that you will have an equally good reason for giving it your
protection once you understand the principle behind my undertaking; so
much so, that my best way of commending it to you will be to tell you
briefly of the goal which I shall be aiming at in the book.

I have always thought that two topics – namely God and the soul – are
prime examples of subjects where demonstrative proofs ought to be
given with the aid of philosophy rather than theology. For us who are
believers, it is enough to accept on faith that the human soul does not
die with the body, and that God exists; but in the case of unbelievers, it
seems that there is no religion, and practically no moral virtue, that they
can be persuaded to adopt until these two truths are proved to them by
natural reason. And since in this life the rewards offered to vice are often
greater than the rewards of virtue, few people would prefer what is right
to what is expedient if they did not fear God or have the expectation of
an after-life. It is of course quite true that we must believe in the
existence of God because it is a doctrine of Holy Scripture, and conversely, that we must believe Holy Scripture because it comes from God;
for since faith is the gift of God, he who gives us grace to believe other
things can also give us grace to believe that he exists. But this argument

3

cannot be put to unbelievers because they would judge it to be circular. Moreover, I have noticed both that you and all other theologians assert that the existence of God is capable of proof by natural reason, and also that the inference from Holy Scripture is that the knowledge of God is easier to acquire than the knowledge we have of many created things – so easy, indeed, that those who do not acquire it are at fault. This is clear from a passage in the Book of Wisdom, Chapter 13: 'Howbeit they are not to be excused; for if their knowledge was so great that they could value this world, why did they not rather find out the Lord thereof?' And in Romans, Chapter 1 it is said that they are 'without excuse'. And in the same place, in the passage 'that which is known of God is manifest in them', we seem to be told that everything that may be known of God can be demonstrated by reasoning which has no other source but our own mind. Hence I thought it was quite proper for me to inquire how this may be, and how God may be more easily and more certainly known than the things of this world.

3   As regards the soul, many people have considered that it is not easy to discover its nature, and some have even had the audacity to assert that, as far as human reasoning goes, there are persuasive grounds for holding that the soul dies along with the body and that the opposite view is based on faith alone. But in its eighth session the Lateran Council held under Leo X condemned those who take this position,[1] and expressly enjoined Christian philosophers to refute their arguments and use all their powers to establish the truth; so I have not hesitated to attempt this task as well.

In addition, I know that the only reason why many irreligious people are unwilling to believe that God exists and that the human mind is distinct from the body is the alleged fact that no one has hitherto been able to demonstrate these points. Now I completely disagree with this: I think that when properly understood almost all the arguments that have been put forward on these issues by the great men have the force of demonstrations, and I am convinced that it is scarcely possible to provide any arguments which have not already been produced by someone else. Nevertheless, I think there can be no more useful service to be rendered in philosophy than to conduct a careful search, once and for all, for the best of these arguments, and to set them out so precisely and clearly as to

---

[1] The Lateran Council of 1513 condemned the Averroist heresy which denied personal immortality.

produce for the future a general agreement that they amount to demonstrative proofs. And finally, I was strongly pressed to undertake this task
by several people who knew that I had developed a method for resolving
certain difficulties in the sciences – not a new method (for nothing is
older than the truth), but one which they had seen me use with some
success in other areas; and I therefore thought it my duty to make some
attempt to apply it to the matter in hand.

The present treatise contains everything that I have been able to   4
accomplish in this area. Not that I have attempted to collect here all
the different arguments that could be put forward to establish the same
results, for this does not seem worthwhile except in cases where no
single argument is regarded as sufficiently reliable. What I have done is
to take merely the principal and most important arguments and develop
them in such a way that I would now venture to put them forward as
very certain and evident demonstrations. I will add that these proofs are
of such a kind that I reckon they leave no room for the possibility that
the human mind will ever discover better ones. The vital importance of
the cause and the glory of God, to which the entire undertaking is
directed, here compel me to speak somewhat more freely about my
own achievements than is my custom. But although I regard the proofs
as quite certain and evident, I cannot therefore persuade myself that they
are suitable to be grasped by everyone. In geometry there are many
writings left by Archimedes, Apollonius, Pappus and others which are
accepted by everyone as evident and certain because they contain absolutely nothing that is not very easy to understand when considered on its
own, and each step fits in precisely with what has gone before; yet
because they are somewhat long, and demand a very attentive reader,
it is only comparatively few people who understand them. In the same
way, although the proofs I employ here are in my view as certain and
evident as the proofs of geometry, if not more so, it will, I fear, be
impossible for many people to achieve an adequate perception of them,
both because they are rather long and some depend on others, and also,
above all, because they require a mind which is completely free from
preconceived opinions and which can easily detach itself from involve-
ment with the senses. Moreover, people who have an aptitude for
metaphysical studies are certainly not to be found in the world in any
greater numbers than those who have an aptitude for geometry. What is
more, there is the difference that in geometry everyone has been taught   5

to accept that as a rule no proposition is put forward in a book without there being a conclusive demonstration available; so inexperienced students make the mistake of accepting what is false, in their desire to appear to understand it, more often than they make the mistake of rejecting what is true. In philosophy, by contrast, the belief is that everything can be argued either way; so few people pursue the truth, while the great majority build up their reputation for ingenuity by boldly attacking whatever is most sound.

Hence, whatever the quality of my arguments may be, because they have to do with philosophy I do not expect they will enable me to achieve any very worthwhile results unless you come to my aid by granting me your patronage.[2] The reputation of your Faculty is so firmly fixed in the minds of all, and the name of the Sorbonne has such authority that, with the exception of the Sacred Councils, no institution carries more weight than yours in matters of faith; while as regards human philosophy, you are thought of as second to none, both for insight and soundness and also for the integrity and wisdom of your pronouncements. Because of this, the results of your careful attention to this book, if you deigned to give it, would be threefold. First, the errors in it would be corrected – for when I remember not only that I am a human being, but above all that I am an ignorant one, I cannot claim it is free of mistakes. Secondly, any passages which are defective, or insufficiently developed or requiring further explanation, would be supplemented, completed and clarified, either by yourselves or by me after you have given me your advice. And lastly, once the arguments in the book proving that God exists and that the mind is distinct from the body have been brought, as I am sure they can be, to such a pitch of clarity that they are fit to be regarded as very exact demonstrations, you may be willing to declare as much, and make a public statement to that effect. If all this were to happen, I do not doubt that all the errors which have ever existed on these subjects would soon be eradicated from the minds of men. In the case of all those who share your intelligence and learning, the truth itself will readily ensure that they subscribe to your opinion. As for the atheists, who are generally posers rather than people of real intelligence or learning, your authority

---

[2] Although the title page of the first edition of the *Meditations* carries the words 'with the approval of the learned doctors', Descartes never in fact obtained the endorsement from the Sorbonne which he sought.

will induce them to lay aside the spirit of contradiction; and, since they know that the arguments are regarded as demonstrations by all who are intellectually gifted, they may even go so far as to defend them, rather than appear not to understand them. And finally, everyone else will confidently go along with so many declarations of assent, and there will be no one left in the world who will dare to call into doubt either the existence of God or the real distinction between the human soul and body. The great advantage that this would bring is something which you, in your singular wisdom, are in a better position to evaluate than anyone;[3] and it would ill become me to spend any more time commending the cause of God and religion to you, who have always been the greatest tower of strength to the Catholic Church.

Preface to the reader[4]

I briefly touched on the topics of God and the human mind in my *Discourse on the method of rightly conducting reason and seeking the truth in the sciences*, which was published in French in 1637. My purpose there was not to provide a full treatment, but merely to offer a sample, and learn from the views of my readers how I should handle these topics at a later date. The issues seemed to me of such great importance that I considered they ought to be dealt with more than once; and the route which I follow in explaining them is so untrodden and so remote from the normal way, that I thought it would not be helpful to give a full account of it in a book written in French and designed to be read by all and sundry, in case weaker intellects might believe that they ought to set out on the same path.

In the *Discourse* I asked anyone who found anything worth criticizing in what I had written to be kind enough to point it out to me.[5] In the case of my remarks concerning God and the soul, only two objections worth mentioning were put to me, which I shall now briefly answer before embarking on a more precise elucidation of these topics.

---

[3] 'It is for you to judge the advantage that would come from establishing these beliefs firmly, since you see all the disorders which come from their being doubted' (French version).
[4] The French version of 1647 does not translate this preface, but substitutes a brief foreword, *Le Libraire au Lecteur* ('The Publisher to the Reader'), which is probably not by Descartes.
[5] See *Discourse*, Part Six; AT VI 75; CSM I 149.

The first objection is this. From the fact that the human mind, when directed towards itself, does not perceive itself to be anything other than a thinking thing, it does not follow that its nature or essence consists only in its being a thinking thing, where the word 'only' excludes everything else that could be said to belong to the nature of the soul. My answer to this objection is that in that passage it was not my intention to make those exclusions in an order corresponding to the actual truth of the matter (which I was not dealing with at that stage) but merely in an order corresponding to my own perception. So the sense of the passage was that I was aware of nothing at all that I knew belonged to my essence, except that I was a thinking thing, or a thing possessing within itself the faculty of thinking.[6] I shall, however, show below how it follows from the fact that I am aware of nothing else belonging to my essence, that nothing else does in fact belong to it.

The second objection is this. From the fact that I have within me an idea of a thing more perfect than myself, it does not follow that the idea itself is more perfect than me, still less that what is represented by the idea exists. My reply is that there is an ambiguity here in the word 'idea'. 'Idea' can be taken materially, as an operation of the intellect, in which case it cannot be said to be more perfect than me. Alternatively, it can be taken objectively, as the thing represented by that operation; and this thing, even if it is not regarded as existing outside the intellect, can still, in virtue of its essence, be more perfect than myself. As to how, from the mere fact that there is within me an idea of something more perfect than me, it follows that this thing really exists, this is something which will be fully explained below.

Apart from these objections, there are two fairly lengthy essays which I have looked at,[7] but these did not attack my reasoning on these matters so much as my conclusions, and employed arguments lifted from the standard sources of the atheists. But arguments of this sort can carry no weight with those who understand my reasoning. Moreover, the judgement of many people is so silly and weak that, once they have accepted a view, they continue to believe it, however false and irrational it may be, in preference to a true and well-grounded refutation which they hear

---

[6] See *Discourse*, Part Four: AT VI 32; CSM I 127.
[7] One of the critics referred to here is Petit: see letter to Mersenne of 27 May 1638 (AT XI 144; CSMK 104). The other is unknown.

subsequently. So I do not wish to reply to such arguments here, if only to avoid having to state them. I will only make the general point that all the objections commonly tossed around by atheists to attack the existence of God invariably depend either on attributing human feelings to God or on arrogantly supposing our own minds to be so powerful and wise that we can attempt to grasp and set limits to what God can or should perform. So, provided only that we remember that our minds must be regarded as finite, while God is infinite and beyond our comprehension, such objections will not cause us any difficulty.

But now that I have, after a fashion, taken an initial sample of people's opinions, I am again tackling the same questions concerning God and the human mind; and this time I am also going to deal with the foundations of First Philosophy in its entirety. But I do not expect any popular approval, or indeed any great crowd of readers. On the contrary I would not urge anyone to read this book except those who are able and willing to meditate seriously with me, and to withdraw their minds from the senses and from all preconceived opinions. Such readers, as I well know, are few and far between. Those who do not bother to grasp the proper order of my arguments and the connection between them, but merely try to carp at individual sentences, as is the fashion, will not get much benefit   10 from reading this book. They may well find an opportunity to quibble in many places, but it will not be easy for them to produce objections which are telling or worth replying to.

But I certainly do not promise to satisfy my other readers straightaway on all points, and I am not so presumptuous as to be sure that I am capable of foreseeing all the difficulties which anyone may find. So first of all, in the *Meditations*, I will set out the very thoughts which have enabled me, in my view, to arrive at a certain and evident knowledge of the truth, so that I can find out whether the same arguments which have convinced me will enable me to convince others. Next, I will reply to the objections of various men of outstanding intellect and scholarship who had these Meditations sent to them for scrutiny before they went to press. For the objections they raised were so many and so varied that I would venture to hope that it will be hard for anyone else to think of any point – at least of any importance – which these critics have not touched on. I therefore ask my readers not to pass judgement on the *Meditations* until they have been kind enough to read through all these objections and my replies to them.

Synopsis of the following Six Meditations

In the First Meditation reasons are provided which give us possible grounds for doubt about all things, especially material things, so long as we have no foundations for the sciences other than those which we have had up till now. Although the usefulness of such extensive doubt is not apparent at first sight, its greatest benefit lies in freeing us from all our preconceived opinions, and providing the easiest route by which the mind may be led away from the senses. The eventual result of this doubt is to make it impossible for us to have any further doubts about what we subsequently discover to be true.

In the Second Meditation, the mind uses its own freedom and supposes the non-existence of all the things about whose existence it can have even the slightest doubt; and in so doing the mind notices that it is impossible that it should not itself exist during this time. This exercise is also of the greatest benefit, since it enables the mind to distinguish without difficulty what belongs to itself, i.e. to an intellectual nature, from what belongs to the body. But since some people may perhaps expect arguments for the immortality of the soul in this section, I think they should be warned here and now that I have tried not to put down anything which I could not precisely demonstrate. Hence the only order which I could follow was that normally employed by geometers, namely to set out all the premises on which a desired proposition depends, before drawing any conclusions about it. Now the first and most important prerequisite for knowledge of the immortality of the soul is for us to form a concept of the soul which is as clear as possible and is also quite distinct from every concept of body; and that is just what has been done in this section. A further requirement is that we should know that everything that we clearly and distinctly understand is true in a way which corresponds exactly to our understanding of it; but it was not possible to prove this before the Fourth Meditation. In addition we need to have a distinct concept of corporeal nature, and this is developed partly in the Second Meditation itself, and partly in the Fifth and Sixth Meditations. The inference to be drawn from these results is that all the things that we clearly and distinctly conceive of as different substances (as we do in the case of mind and body) are in fact substances which are really distinct one from the other; and this conclusion is drawn in the Sixth Meditation. The conclusion is confirmed in the same Meditation by the fact that we cannot understand a body except as being divisible, while by contrast we cannot understand a mind except as being indivisible. For we cannot conceive of half of a mind, while we can always conceive of half of a body, however small; and this leads us to recognize that the natures of mind and body are not only different, but in some way opposite. But I have not pursued this topic any further in this book, first because these arguments are enough to show that the decay of the body does not imply the destruction of the mind, and are hence enough to give mortals the hope of an after-life, and secondly because the premises which lead to the conclusion that the soul is immortal depend on an account of the whole of physics. This is required for two reasons. First, we need to know that absolutely all substances, or things which must be created by God in order to exist, are by their nature incorruptible and cannot ever cease to exist unless they are reduced to nothingness by God's denying his concurrence[8] to them. Secondly, we need to recognize that body, taken in the general sense, is a substance, so that it too never perishes. But the human body, in so far as it differs from other bodies, is simply made up of a certain configuration of limbs and other accidents[9] of this sort; whereas the human mind is not made up of any accidents in this way, but is a pure substance. For even if all the accidents of the mind change, so that it has different objects of the understanding and different desires and sensations, it does not on that account become a different mind; whereas a human body loses its identity merely as a result of a change in the shape of some of its parts. And it follows from this that while the body can very easily perish, the mind[10] is immortal by its very nature.

In the Third Meditation I have explained quite fully enough, I think, my principal argument for proving the existence of God. But in order to draw my readers' minds away from the senses as far as possible, I was not willing to use any comparison taken from bodily things. So it may be that many obscurities remain; but I hope they will be completely removed later, in my Replies to the Objections. One such problem, among others, is how the idea of a supremely perfect being, which is in us, possesses so

14

---

[8] The continuous divine action necessary to maintain things in existence.
[9] Descartes here uses this scholastic term to refer to those features of a thing which may alter, e.g. the particular size, shape etc. of a body, or the particular thoughts, desires etc. of a mind.
[10] '... or the soul of man, for I make no distinction between them' (added in French version).

much objective[11] reality that it can come only from a cause which is supremely perfect. In the Replies this is illustrated by the comparison of a very perfect machine, the idea of which is in the mind of some engineer. Just as the objective intricacy belonging to the idea must have some cause, namely the scientific knowledge of the engineer, or of someone else who passed the idea on to him, so the idea of God which is in us must have God himself as its cause.

In the Fourth Meditation it is proved that everything that we clearly and distinctly perceive is true, and I also explain what the nature of falsity consists in. These results need to be known both in order to confirm what has gone before and also to make intelligible what is to come later. (But it should be noted in passing that I do not here deal at all with sin, i.e. the error which is committed in pursuing good and evil, but only with the error that occurs in distinguishing truth from falsehood. And there is no discussion of matters pertaining to faith or the conduct of life, but simply of speculative truths which are known solely by means of the natural light.)[12]

In the Fifth Meditation, besides an account of corporeal nature taken in general, there is a new argument demonstrating the existence of God. Again, several difficulties may arise here, but these are resolved later in the Replies to the Objections. Finally I explain the sense in which it is true that the certainty even of geometrical demonstrations depends on the knowledge of God.

Lastly, in the Sixth Meditation, the intellect is distinguished from the imagination; the criteria for this distinction are explained; the mind is proved to be really distinct from the body, but is shown, notwithstanding, to be so closely joined to it that the mind and the body make up a kind of unit; there is a survey of all the errors which commonly come from the senses, and an explanation of how they may be avoided; and, lastly, there is a presentation of all the arguments which enable the existence of material things to be inferred. The great benefit of these arguments is not, in my view, that they prove what they establish – namely that there really is a world, and that human beings have bodies

---

[11] For Descartes's use of this term, see Med. III, below, p. 32.

[12] Descartes added this passage on the advice of Arnauld (cf. AT VII 215; CSM II 151). He told Mersenne 'Put the words between brackets so that it can be seen that they have been added' (letter of 18 March 1641: AT III 335; CSMK 175).

and so on – since no sane person has ever seriously doubted these things. The point is that in considering these arguments we come to realize that they are not as solid or as transparent as the arguments which lead us to knowledge of our own minds and of God, so that the latter are the most certain and evident of all possible objects of knowledge for the human intellect. Indeed, this is the one thing that I set myself to prove in these Meditations. And for that reason I will not now go over the various other issues in the book which are dealt with as they come up.

Meditations on First Philosophy

*in which are demonstrated the existence of God and the
distinction between the human soul and the body*[1]

First Meditation

What can be called into doubt

Some years ago I was struck by the large number of falsehoods that I had
accepted as true in my childhood, and by the highly doubtful nature of the
whole edifice that I had subsequently based on them. I realized that it was
necessary, once in the course of my life, to demolish everything completely and start again right from the foundations if I wanted to establish
anything at all in the sciences that was stable and likely to last. But the task
looked an enormous one, and I began to wait until I should reach a mature
enough age to ensure that no subsequent time of life would be more
suitable for tackling such inquiries. This led me to put the project off for
so long that I would now be to blame if by pondering over it any further
I wasted the time still left for carrying it out. So today I have expressly rid
my mind of all worries and arranged for myself a clear stretch of free time.
I am here quite alone, and at last I will devote myself sincerely and without
reservation to the general demolition of my opinions.

But to accomplish this, it will not be necessary for me to show that all
my opinions are false, which is something I could perhaps never manage.
Reason now leads me to think that I should hold back my assent from
opinions which are not completely certain and indubitable just as carefully as I do from those which are patently false. So, for the purpose of
rejecting all my opinions, it will be enough if I find in each of them at
least some reason for doubt. And to do this I will not need to run

---

[1] This subtitle is from the 1642 title page. The 1641 title page has 'In which is demonstrated the
existence of God and the immortality of the soul.'

through them all individually, which would be an endless task. Once the foundations of a building are undermined, anything built on them collapses of its own accord; so I will go straight for the basic principles on which all my former beliefs rested.

Whatever I have up till now accepted as most true I have acquired either from the senses or through the senses. But from time to time I have found that the senses deceive, and it is prudent never to trust completely those who have deceived us even once.

Yet although the senses occasionally deceive us with respect to objects which are very small or in the distance, there are many other beliefs about which doubt is quite impossible, even though they are derived from the senses – for example, that I am here, sitting by the fire, wearing a winter dressing-gown, holding this piece of paper in my hands, and so on. Again, how could it be denied that these hands or this whole body are mine? Unless perhaps I were to liken myself to madmen, whose brains are so damaged by the persistent vapours of melancholia that they firmly maintain they are kings when they are paupers, or say they are dressed in purple when they are naked, or that their heads are made of earthenware, or that they are pumpkins, or made of glass. But such people are insane, and I would be thought equally mad if I took anything from them as a model for myself.

A brilliant piece of reasoning! As if I were not a man who sleeps at night, and regularly has all the same experiences[2] while asleep as madmen do when awake – indeed sometimes even more improbable ones. How often, asleep at night, am I convinced of just such familiar events – that I am here in my dressing-gown, sitting by the fire – when in fact I am lying undressed in bed! Yet at the moment my eyes are certainly wide awake when I look at this piece of paper; I shake my head and it is not asleep; as I stretch out and feel my hand I do so deliberately, and I know what I am doing. All this would not happen with such distinctness to someone asleep. Indeed! As if I did not remember other occasions when I have been tricked by exactly similar thoughts while asleep! As I think about this more carefully, I see plainly that there are never any sure signs by means of which being awake can be distinguished from being asleep. The result is that I begin to feel dazed, and this very feeling only reinforces the notion that I may be asleep.

19

---

[2] '... and in my dreams regularly represent to myself the same things' (French version).

Suppose then that I am dreaming, and that these particulars – that my eyes are open, that I am moving my head and stretching out my hands – are not true. Perhaps, indeed, I do not even have such hands or such a body at all. Nonetheless, it must surely be admitted that the visions which come in sleep are like paintings, which must have been fashioned in the likeness of things that are real, and hence that at least these general kinds of things – eyes, head, hands and the body as a whole – are things which are not imaginary but are real and exist. For even when painters try to create sirens and satyrs with the most extraordinary bodies, they cannot give them natures which are new in all respects; they simply jumble up the limbs of different animals. Or if perhaps they manage to think up something so new that nothing remotely similar has ever been seen before – something which is therefore completely fictitious and unreal – at least the colours used in the composition must be real. By similar reasoning, although these general kinds of things – eyes, head, hands and so on – could be imaginary, it must at least be admitted that certain other even simpler and more universal things are real. These are as it were the real colours from which we form all the images of things, whether true or false, that occur in our thought. 20

This class appears to include corporeal nature in general, and its extension; the shape of extended things; the quantity, or size and number of these things; the place in which they may exist, the time through which they may endure,[3] and so on.

So a reasonable conclusion from this might be that physics, astronomy, medicine, and all other disciplines which depend on the study of composite things, are doubtful; while arithmetic, geometry and other subjects of this kind, which deal only with the simplest and most general things, regardless of whether they really exist in nature or not, contain something certain and indubitable. For whether I am awake or asleep, two and three added together are five, and a square has no more than four sides. It seems impossible that such transparent truths should incur any suspicion of being false.

And yet firmly rooted in my mind is the long-standing opinion that 21 there is an omnipotent God who made me the kind of creature that I am. How do I know that he has not brought it about that there is no earth,

---

[3] '. . . the place where they are, the time which measures their duration' (French version).

no sky, no extended thing, no shape, no size, no place, while at the same time ensuring that all these things appear to me to exist just as they do now? What is more, just as I consider that others sometimes go astray in cases where they think they have the most perfect knowledge, how do I know that God has not brought it about that I too go wrong every time I add two and three or count the sides of a square, or in some even simpler matter, if that is imaginable? But perhaps God would not have allowed me to be deceived in this way, since he is said to be supremely good. But if it were inconsistent with his goodness to have created me such that I am deceived all the time, it would seem equally foreign to his goodness to allow me to be deceived even occasionally; yet this last assertion cannot be made.[4]

Perhaps there may be some who would prefer to deny the existence of so powerful a God rather than believe that everything else is uncertain. Let us not argue with them, but grant them that everything said about God is a fiction. According to their supposition, then, I have arrived at my present state by fate or chance or a continuous chain of events, or by some other means; yet since deception and error seem to be imperfections, the less powerful they make my original cause, the more likely it is that I am so imperfect as to be deceived all the time. I have no answer to these arguments, but am finally compelled to admit that there is not one of my former beliefs about which a doubt may not properly be raised; and this is not a flippant or ill-considered conclusion, but is based on powerful and well thought-out reasons. So in future I must withhold my assent from these former beliefs just as carefully as I would from obvious falsehoods, if I want to discover any certainty.[5]

But it is not enough merely to have noticed this; I must make an effort to remember it. My habitual opinions keep coming back, and, despite my wishes, they capture my belief, which is as it were bound over to them as a result of long occupation and the law of custom. I shall never get out of the habit of confidently assenting to these opinions, so long as I suppose them to be what in fact they are, namely highly probable opinions – opinions which, despite the fact that they are in a sense doubtful, as has just been shown, it is still much more reasonable to believe than to deny. In view of this, I think it will be a good plan to turn my will in completely

[4] '... yet I cannot doubt that he does allow this' (French version).
[5] '... in the sciences' (added in French version).

the opposite direction and deceive myself, by pretending for a time that these former opinions are utterly false and imaginary. I shall do this until the weight of preconceived opinion is counter-balanced and the distorting influence of habit no longer prevents my judgement from perceiving things correctly. In the meantime, I know that no danger or error will result from my plan, and that I cannot possibly go too far in my distrustful attitude. This is because the task now in hand does not involve action but merely the acquisition of knowledge.

I will suppose therefore that not God, who is supremely good and the source of truth, but rather some malicious demon of the utmost power and cunning has employed all his energies in order to deceive me. I shall think that the sky, the air, the earth, colours, shapes, sounds and all external things are merely the delusions of dreams which he has devised to ensnare my judgement. I shall consider myself as not having hands or eyes, or flesh, or blood or senses, but as falsely believing that I have all these things. I shall stubbornly and firmly persist in this meditation; and, even if it is not in my power to know any truth, I shall at least do what is in my power,[6] that is, resolutely guard against assenting to any falsehoods, so that the deceiver, however powerful and cunning he may be, will be unable to impose on me in the slightest degree. But this is an arduous undertaking, and a kind of laziness brings me back to normal life. I am like a prisoner who is enjoying an imaginary freedom while asleep; as he begins to suspect that he is asleep, he dreads being woken up, and goes along with the pleasant illusion as long as he can. In the same way, I happily slide back into my old opinions and dread being shaken out of them, for fear that my peaceful sleep may be followed by hard labour when I wake, and that I shall have to toil not in the light, but amid the inextricable darkness of the problems I have now raised.

[6] '... nevertheless it is in my power to suspend my judgement' (French version).

Second Meditation

The nature of the human mind, and how it is better known than the body

So serious are the doubts into which I have been thrown as a result of yesterday's meditation that I can neither put them out of my mind nor see any way of resolving them. It feels as if I have fallen unexpectedly into a deep whirlpool which tumbles me around so that I can neither stand on the bottom nor swim up to the top. Nevertheless I will make an effort and once more attempt the same path which I started on yesterday. Anything which admits of the slightest doubt I will set aside just as if I had found it to be wholly false; and I will proceed in this way until I recognize something certain, or, if nothing else, until I at least recognize for certain that there is no certainty. Archimedes used to demand just one firm and immovable point in order to shift the entire earth; so I too can hope for great things if I manage to find just one thing, however slight, that is certain and unshakeable.

I will suppose then, that everything I see is spurious. I will believe that my memory tells me lies, and that none of the things that it reports ever happened. I have no senses. Body, shape, extension, movement and place are chimeras. So what remains true? Perhaps just the one fact that nothing is certain.

Yet apart from everything I have just listed, how do I know that there is not something else which does not allow even the slightest occasion for doubt? Is there not a God, or whatever I may call him, who puts into me[1] the thoughts I am now having? But why do I think this, since I myself may perhaps be the author of these thoughts? In that case am not I, at least, something? But I have just said that I have no senses and no body. This is the sticking point: what follows from this? Am I not so bound up with a body and with senses that I cannot exist without them? But I have convinced myself that there is absolutely nothing in the world, no sky, no earth, no minds, no bodies. Does it now follow that I too do not exist? No: if I convinced myself of something[2] then I certainly existed. But there is a deceiver of supreme power and cunning who is deliberately and constantly deceiving me. In that case I too undoubtedly exist, if he is deceiving me; and let him deceive me as much as he can, he will never bring it about that I am nothing so long as I think that I am something. So after considering everything very thoroughly, I must finally conclude that this proposition, *I am, I exist*, is necessarily true whenever it is put forward by me or conceived in my mind.

But I do not yet have a sufficient understanding of what this 'I' is, that now necessarily exists. So I must be on my guard against carelessly taking something else to be this 'I', and so making a mistake in the very item of knowledge that I maintain is the most certain and evident of all. I will therefore go back and meditate on what I originally believed myself to be, before I embarked on this present train of thought. I will then subtract anything capable of being weakened, even minimally, by the arguments now introduced, so that what is left at the end may be exactly and only what is certain and unshakeable.

What then did I formerly think I was? A man. But what is a man? Shall I say 'a rational animal'? No; for then I should have to inquire what an animal is, what rationality is, and in this way one question would lead me down the slope to other harder ones, and I do not now have the time to waste on subtleties of this kind. Instead I propose to concentrate on what came into my thoughts spontaneously and quite naturally whenever I used to consider what I was. Well, the first thought to come to mind was that I had a face, hands, arms and the whole mechanical structure of limbs which can be seen in a corpse, and which I called the body. The next thought was that I was nourished, that I moved about, and

25

26

---

[1] '... puts into my mind' (French version).   [2] '... or thought anything at all' (French version).

that I engaged in sense-perception and thinking; and these actions I attributed to the soul. But as to the nature of this soul, either I did not think about this or else I imagined it to be something tenuous, like a wind or fire or ether, which permeated my more solid parts. As to the body, however, I had no doubts about it, but thought I knew its nature distinctly. If I had tried to describe the mental conception I had of it, I would have expressed it as follows: by a body I understand whatever has a determinable shape and a definable location and can occupy a space in such a way as to exclude any other body; it can be perceived by touch, sight, hearing, taste or smell, and can be moved in various ways, not by itself but by whatever else comes into contact with it. For, according to my judgement, the power of self-movement, like the power of sensation or of thought, was quite foreign to the nature of a body; indeed, it was a source of wonder to me that certain bodies were found to contain faculties of this kind.

But what shall I now say that I am, when I am supposing that there is some supremely powerful and, if it is permissible to say so, malicious deceiver, who is deliberately trying to trick me in every way he can? Can I now assert that I possess even the most insignificant of all the attributes which I have just said belong to the nature of a body? I scrutinize them, think about them, go over them again, but nothing suggests itself; it is tiresome and pointless to go through the list once more. But what about the attributes I assigned to the soul? Nutrition or movement? Since now I do not have a body, these are mere fabrications. Sense-perception? This surely does not occur without a body, and besides, when asleep I have appeared to perceive through the senses many things which I afterwards realized I did not perceive through the senses at all. Thinking? At last I have discovered it – thought; this alone is inseparable from me. I am, I exist – that is certain. But for how long? For as long as I am thinking. For it could be that were I totally to cease from thinking, I should totally cease to exist. At present I am not admitting anything except what is necessarily true. I am, then, in the strict sense only a thing that thinks;[3] that is, I am a mind, or intelligence,

---

[3] The word 'only' is most naturally taken as going with 'a thing that thinks', and this interpretation is followed in the French version. When discussing this passage with Gassendi, however, Descartes suggests that he meant the 'only' to govern 'in the strict sense'; cf AT IXA 215; CSM II 276.

or intellect, or reason – words whose meaning I have been ignorant of until now. But for all that I am a thing which is real and which truly exists. But what kind of a thing? As I have just said – a thinking thing.

What else am I? I will use my imagination.[4] I am not that structure of limbs which is called a human body. I am not even some thin vapour which permeates the limbs – a wind, fire, air, breath, or whatever I depict in my imagination; for these are things which I have supposed to be nothing. Let this supposition stand;[5] for all that I am still something. And yet may it not perhaps be the case that these very things which I am supposing to be nothing, because they are unknown to me, are in reality identical with the 'I' of which I am aware? I do not know, and for the moment I shall not argue the point, since I can make judgements only about things which are known to me. I know that I exist; the question is, what is this 'I' that I know? If the 'I' is understood strictly as we have been taking it, then it is quite certain that knowledge of it does not depend on things of whose existence I am as yet unaware; so it cannot depend on any of the things which I invent in my imagination. And this very word 'invent' shows me my mistake. It would indeed be a case of fictitious invention if I used my imagination to establish that I was something or other; for imagining is simply contemplating the shape or image of a corporeal thing. Yet now I know for certain both that I exist and at the same time that all such images and, in general, everything relating to the nature of body, could be mere dreams <and chimeras>. Once this point has been grasped, to say 'I will use my imagination to get to know more distinctly what I am' would seem to be as silly as saying 'I am now awake, and see some truth; but since my vision is not yet clear enough, I will deliberately fall asleep so that my dreams may provide a truer and clearer representation.' I thus realize that none of the things that the imagination enables me to grasp is at all relevant to this knowledge of myself which I possess, and that the mind must therefore be most carefully diverted from such things[6] if it is to perceive its own nature as distinctly as possible.

28

---

[4] '. . . to see if I am not something more' (added in French version).

[5] Lat. *maneat* ('let it stand'), first edition. The second edition has the indicative *manet*: 'The proposition still stands, *viz.* that I am nonetheless something.' The French version reads: 'without changing this supposition, I find that I am still certain that I am something'.

[6] '. . . from this manner of conceiving things' (French version).

But what then am I? A thing that thinks. What is that? A thing that doubts, understands, affirms, denies, is willing, is unwilling, and also imagines and has sensory perceptions.

This is a considerable list, if everything on it belongs to me. But does it? Is it not one and the same 'I' who is now doubting almost everything, who nonetheless understands some things, who affirms that this one thing is true, denies everything else, desires to know more, is unwilling to be deceived, imagines many things even involuntarily, and is aware of many things which apparently come from the senses? Are not all these things just as true as the fact that I exist, even if I am asleep all the time, and even if he who created me is doing all he can to deceive me? Which of all these activities is distinct from my thinking? Which of them can be said to be separate from myself? The fact that it is I who am doubting and understanding and willing is so evident that I see no way of making it any clearer. But it is also the case that the 'I' who imagines is the same 'I'. For even if, as I have supposed, none of the objects of imagination are real, the power of imagination is something which really exists and is part of my thinking. Lastly, it is also the same 'I' who has sensory perceptions, or is aware of bodily things as it were through the senses. For example, I am now seeing light, hearing a noise, feeling heat. But I am asleep, so all this is false. Yet I certainly *seem* to see, to hear, and to be warmed. This cannot be false; what is called 'having a sensory perception' is strictly just this, and in this restricted sense of the term it is simply thinking.

From all this I am beginning to have a rather better understanding of what I am. But it still appears – and I cannot stop thinking this – that the corporeal things of which images are formed in my thought, and which the senses investigate, are known with much more distinctness than this puzzling 'I' which cannot be pictured in the imagination. And yet it is surely surprising that I should have a more distinct grasp of things which I realize are doubtful, unknown and foreign to me, than I have of that which is true and known – my own self. But I see what it is: my mind enjoys wandering off and will not yet submit to being restrained within the bounds of truth. Very well then; just this once let us give it a completely free rein, so that after a while, when it is time to tighten the reins, it may more readily submit to being curbed.

Let us consider the things which people commonly think they understand most distinctly of all; that is, the bodies which we touch and see. I do not mean bodies in general – for general perceptions are apt to be somewhat

29

30

24

more confused – but one particular body. Let us take, for example, this piece of wax. It has just been taken from the honeycomb; it has not yet quite lost the taste of the honey; it retains some of the scent of the flowers from which it was gathered; its colour, shape and size are plain to see; it is hard, cold and can be handled without difficulty; if you rap it with your knuckle it makes a sound. In short, it has everything which appears necessary to enable a body to be known as distinctly as possible. But even as I speak, I put the wax by the fire, and look: the residual taste is eliminated, the smell goes away, the colour changes, the shape is lost, the size increases; it becomes liquid and hot; you can hardly touch it, and if you strike it, it no longer makes a sound. But does the same wax remain? It must be admitted that it does; no one denies it, no one thinks otherwise. So what was it in the wax that I understood with such distinctness? Evidently none of the features which I arrived at by means of the senses; for whatever came under taste, smell, sight, touch or hearing has now altered – yet the wax remains.

Perhaps the answer lies in the thought which now comes to my mind; namely, the wax was not after all the sweetness of the honey, or the fragrance of the flowers, or the whiteness, or the shape, or the sound, but was rather a body which presented itself to me in these various forms a little while ago, but which now exhibits different ones. But what exactly ³¹ is it that I am now imagining? Let us concentrate, take away everything which does not belong to the wax, and see what is left: merely something extended, flexible and changeable. But what is meant here by 'flexible' and 'changeable'? Is it what I picture in my imagination: that this piece of wax is capable of changing from a round shape to a square shape, or from a square shape to a triangular shape? Not at all; for I can grasp that the wax is capable of countless changes of this kind, yet I am unable to run through this immeasurable number of changes in my imagination, from which it follows that it is not the faculty of imagination that gives me my grasp of the wax as flexible and changeable. And what is meant by 'extended'? Is the extension of the wax also unknown? For it increases if the wax melts, increases again if it boils, and is greater still if the heat is increased. I would not be making a correct judgement about the nature of wax unless I believed it capable of being extended in many more different ways than I will ever encompass in my imagination. I must therefore admit that the nature of this piece of wax is in no way revealed by my imagination, but is perceived by the mind alone. (I am speaking of this particular piece of wax; the point is even clearer with regard to wax in general.) But what is this wax which is perceived by the mind alone?[7] It is of course the same wax which I see, which I touch, which I picture in my imagination, in short the same wax which I thought it to be from the start. And yet, and here is the point, the perception I have of it[8] is a case not of vision or touch or imagination – nor has it ever been, despite previous appearances – but of purely mental scrutiny; and this can be imperfect and confused, as it was before, or clear and distinct as it is now, depending on how carefully I concentrate on what the wax consists in.

But as I reach this conclusion I am amazed at how <weak and> prone to error my mind is. For although I am thinking about these matters within myself, silently and without speaking, nonetheless the actual words bring me up short, and I am almost tricked by ordinary ways of talking. We say that we see the wax itself, if it is there before us, not that we judge it to be there from its colour or shape; and this might lead me to conclude without more ado that knowledge of the wax comes from what the eye sees, and not from the scrutiny of the mind alone. But then if I look out of the window and see men crossing the square, as I just happen to have done, I normally say that I see the men themselves, just as I say that I see the wax. Yet do I see any more than hats and coats which could conceal automatons? I *judge* that they are men. And so something which I thought I was seeing with my eyes is in fact grasped solely by the faculty of judgement which is in my mind.

However, one who wants to achieve knowledge above the ordinary level should feel ashamed at having taken ordinary ways of talking as a basis for doubt. So let us proceed, and consider on which occasion my perception of the nature of the wax was more perfect and evident. Was it when I first looked at it, and believed I knew it by my external senses, or at least by what they call the 'common' sense[9] – that is, the power of imagination? Or is my knowledge more perfect now, after a more careful investigation of the nature of the wax and of the means by which it is known? Any doubt on this issue would clearly be foolish; for what distinctness was there in my earlier perception? Was there anything in it which an animal could not possess? But when I distinguish the wax from its outward forms – take the clothes off, as it were, and consider it

[7] '. . . which can be conceived only by the understanding or the mind' (French version).
[8] '. . . or rather the act whereby it is perceived' (added in French version).
[9] See note 15, p. 68, below.

naked – then although my judgement may still contain errors, at least my perception now requires a human mind.

But what am I to say about this mind, or about myself? (So far, remember, I am not admitting that there is anything else in me except a mind.) What, I ask, is this 'I' which seems to perceive the wax so distinctly? Surely my awareness of my own self is not merely much truer and more certain than my awareness of the wax, but also much more distinct and evident. For if I judge that the wax exists from the fact that I see it, clearly this same fact entails much more evidently that I myself also exist. It is possible that what I see is not really the wax; it is possible that I do not even have eyes with which to see anything. But when I see, or think I see (I am not here distinguishing the two), it is simply not possible that I who am now thinking am not something. By the same token, if I judge that the wax exists from the fact that I touch it, the same result follows, namely that I exist. If I judge that it exists from the fact that I imagine it, or for any other reason, exactly the same thing follows. And the result that I have grasped in the case of the wax may be applied to everything else located outside me. Moreover, if my perception of the wax seemed more distinct[10] after it was established not just by sight or touch but by many other considerations, it must be admitted that I now know my self even more distinctly. This is because every consideration whatsoever which contributes to my perception of the wax, or of any other body, cannot but establish even more effectively the nature of my own mind. But besides this, there is so much else in the mind itself which can serve to make my knowledge of it more distinct, that it scarcely seems worth going through the contributions made by considering bodily things.

I see that without any effort I have now finally got back to where I wanted. I now know that even bodies are not strictly perceived by the senses or the faculty of imagination but by the intellect alone, and that this perception derives not from their being touched or seen but from their being understood; and in view of this I know plainly that I can achieve an easier and more evident perception of my own mind than of anything else. But since the habit of holding on to old opinions cannot be set aside so quickly, I should like to stop here and meditate for some time on this new knowledge I have gained, so as to fix it more deeply in my memory.

10 The French version has 'more clear and distinct' and, at the end of this sentence, 'more evidently, distinctly and clearly'.

Third Meditation

The existence of God

I will now shut my eyes, stop my ears, and withdraw all my senses. I will eliminate from my thoughts all images of bodily things, or rather, since this is hardly possible, I will regard all such images as vacuous, false and worthless. I will converse with myself and scrutinize myself more deeply; and in this way I will attempt to achieve, little by little, a more intimate knowledge of myself. I am a thing that thinks: that is, a thing that doubts, affirms, denies, understands a few things, is ignorant of many things,[1] is willing, is unwilling, and also which imagines and has sensory perceptions; for as I have noted before, even though the objects of my sensory experience and imagination may have no existence outside me, nonetheless the modes of thinking which I refer to as cases of sensory perception and imagination, in so far as they are simply modes of thinking, do exist within me – of that I am certain.

In this brief list I have gone through everything I truly know, or at least everything I have so far discovered that I know. Now I will cast around more carefully to see whether there may be other things within me which I have not yet noticed. I am certain that I am a thinking thing. Do I not therefore also know what is required for my being certain about anything? In this first item of knowledge there is simply a clear and distinct perception of what I am asserting; this would not be enough to make me certain of the truth of the matter if it could ever turn out that

---

[1] The French version here inserts 'loves, hates'.

something which I perceived with such clarity and distinctness was false. So I now seem to be able to lay it down as a general rule that whatever I perceive very clearly and distinctly is true.[2]

Yet I previously accepted as wholly certain and evident many things which I afterwards realized were doubtful. What were these? The earth, sky, stars, and everything else that I apprehended with the senses. But what was it about them that I perceived clearly? Just that the ideas, or thoughts, of such things appeared before my mind. Yet even now I am not denying that these ideas occur within me. But there was something else which I used to assert, and which through habitual belief I thought I perceived clearly, although I did not in fact do so. This was that there were things outside me which were the sources of my ideas and which resembled them in all respects. Here was my mistake; or at any rate, if my judgement was true, it was not thanks to the strength of my perception.[3]

But what about when I was considering something very simple and straightforward in arithmetic or geometry, for example that two and three added together make five, and so on? Did I not see at least these things clearly enough to affirm their truth? Indeed, the only reason for my later judgement that they were open to doubt was that it occurred to me that perhaps some God could have given me a nature such that I was deceived even in matters which seemed most evident. But whenever my preconceived belief in the supreme power of God comes to mind, I cannot but admit that it would be easy for him, if he so desired, to bring it about that I go wrong even in those matters which I think I see utterly clearly with my mind's eye. Yet when I turn to the things themselves which I think I perceive very clearly, I am so convinced by them that I spontaneously declare: let whoever can do so deceive me, he will never bring it about that I am nothing, so long as I continue to think I am something; or make it true at some future time that I have never existed, since it is now true that I exist; or bring it about that two and three added together are more or less than five, or anything of this kind in which I see a manifest contradiction. And since I have no cause to think that there is a deceiving God, and I do not yet even know for sure whether there is a God at all, any reason for doubt which depends simply

36

[2] '... all the things which we conceive very clearly and very distinctly are true' (French version).
[3] '... it was not because of any knowledge I possessed' (French version).

on this supposition is a very slight and, so to speak, metaphysical one. But in order to remove even this slight reason for doubt, as soon as the opportunity arises I must examine whether there is a God, and, if there is, whether he can be a deceiver. For if I do not know this, it seems that I can never be quite certain about anything else.

First, however, considerations of order appear to dictate that I now classify my thoughts into definite kinds,[4] and ask which of them can properly be said to be the bearers of truth and falsity. Some of my thoughts are as it were the images of things, and it is only in these cases that the term 'idea' is strictly appropriate – for example, when I think of a man, or a chimera, or the sky, or an angel, or God. Other thoughts have various additional forms: thus when I will, or am afraid, or affirm, or deny, there is always a particular thing which I take as the object of my thought, but my thought includes something more than the likeness of that thing. Some thoughts in this category are called volitions or emotions, while others are called judgements.

Now as far as ideas are concerned, provided they are considered solely in themselves and I do not refer them to anything else, they cannot strictly speaking be false; for whether it is a goat or a chimera that I am imagining, it is just as true that I imagine the former as the latter. As for the will and the emotions, here too one need not worry about falsity; for even if the things which I may desire are wicked or even non-existent, that does not make it any less true that I desire them. Thus the only remaining thoughts where I must be on my guard against making a mistake are judgements. And the chief and most common mistake which is to be found here consists in my judging that the ideas which are in me resemble, or conform to, things located outside me. Of course, if I considered just the ideas themselves simply as modes of my thought, without referring them to anything else, they could scarcely give me any material for error.

Among my ideas, some appear to be innate, some to be adventitious,[5] and others to have been invented by me. My understanding of what a thing is, what truth is, and what thought is, seems to derive simply from

---

4 The opening of this sentence is greatly expanded in the French version: 'In order that I may have the opportunity of examining this without interrupting the order of meditating which I have decided upon, which is to start only from those notions which I find first of all in my mind and pass gradually to those which I may find later on, I must here divide my thoughts . . .'
5 '. . . foreign to me and coming from outside' (French version).

my own nature. But my hearing a noise, as I do now, or seeing the sun, or feeling the fire, comes from things which are located outside me, or so I have hitherto judged. Lastly, sirens, hippogriffs and the like are my own invention. But perhaps all my ideas may be thought of as adventitious, or they may all be innate, or all made up; for as yet I have not clearly perceived their true origin.

But the chief question at this point concerns the ideas which I take to be derived from things existing outside me: what is my reason for thinking that they resemble these things? Nature has apparently taught me to think this. But in addition I know by experience that these ideas do not depend on my will, and hence that they do not depend simply on me. Frequently I notice them even when I do not want to: now, for example, I feel the heat whether I want to or not, and this is why I think that this sensation or idea of heat comes to me from something other than myself, namely the heat of the fire by which I am sitting. And the most obvious judgement for me to make is that the thing in question transmits to me its own likeness rather than something else.

I will now see if these arguments are strong enough. When I say 'Nature taught me to think this', all I mean is that a spontaneous impulse leads me to believe it, not that its truth has been revealed to me by some natural light. There is a big difference here. Whatever is revealed to me by the natural light – for example that from the fact that I am doubting it follows that I exist, and so on – cannot in any way be open to doubt. This is because there cannot be another faculty[6] both as trustworthy as the natural light and also capable of showing me that such things are not true. But as for my natural impulses, I have often judged in the past that they were pushing me in the wrong direction when it was a question of choosing the good, and I do not see why I should place any greater confidence in them in other matters.[7]

Then again, although these ideas do not depend on my will, it does not follow that they must come from things located outside me. Just as the impulses which I was speaking of a moment ago seem opposed to my will even though they are within me, so there may be some other faculty not yet fully known to me, which produces these ideas without

39

---

[6] '... or power for distinguishing truth from falsehood' (French version).
[7] '... concerning truth and falsehood' (French version).

any assistance from external things; this is, after all, just how I have always thought ideas are produced in me when I am dreaming.

And finally, even if these ideas did come from things other than myself, it would not follow that they must resemble those things. Indeed, I think I have often discovered a great disparity <between an object and its idea> in many cases. For example, there are two different ideas of the sun which I find within me. One of them, which is acquired as it were from the senses and which is a prime example of an idea which I reckon to come from an external source, makes the sun appear very small. The other idea is based on astronomical reasoning, that is, it is derived from certain notions which are innate in me (or else it is constructed by me in some other way), and this idea shows the sun to be several times larger than the earth. Obviously both these ideas cannot resemble the sun which exists outside me; and reason persuades me that the idea which seems to have emanated most directly from the sun itself has in fact no resemblance to it at all.

40   All these considerations are enough to establish that it is not reliable judgement but merely some blind impulse that has made me believe up till now that there exist things distinct from myself which transmit to me ideas or images of themselves through the sense organs or in some other way.

But it now occurs to me that there is another way of investigating whether some of the things of which I possess ideas exist outside me. In so far as the ideas are <considered> simply <as> modes of thought, there is no recognizable inequality among them: they all appear to come from within me in the same fashion. But in so far as different ideas <are considered as images which> represent different things, it is clear that they differ widely. Undoubtedly, the ideas which represent substances to me amount to something more and, so to speak, contain within themselves more objective[8] reality than the ideas which merely represent modes or accidents. Again, the idea that gives me my understanding of a supreme God, eternal, infinite, <immutable,> omniscient, omnipotent

---

[8] '... i.e. participate by representation in a higher degree of being or perfection' (added in French version). According to the scholastic distinction invoked in the paragraphs that follow, the 'formal' reality of anything is its own intrinsic reality, while the 'objective' reality of an idea is a function of its representational content. Thus if an idea A represents some object X which is F, then F-ness will be contained 'formally' in X but 'objectively' in A. See below, pp. 105ff.

and the creator of all things that exist apart from him, certainly has in it more objective reality than the ideas that represent finite substances.

Now it is manifest by the natural light that there must be at least as much <reality> in the efficient and total cause as in the effect of that cause. For where, I ask, could the effect get its reality from, if not from the cause? And how could the cause give it to the effect unless it possessed it? It follows from this both that something cannot arise from nothing, and also that what is more perfect – that is, contains in itself more reality – cannot arise from what is less perfect. And this is transparently true not only in the case of effects which possess <what the philosophers call> actual or formal reality, but also in the case of ideas, where one. is considering only <what they call> objective reality. A stone, for example, which previously did not exist, cannot begin to exist unless it is produced by something which contains, either formally or eminently everything to be found in the stone;[9] similarly, heat cannot be produced in an object which was not previously hot, except by something of at least the same order <degree or kind> of perfection as heat, and so on. But it is also true that the *idea* of heat, or of a stone, cannot exist in me unless it is put there by some cause which contains at least as much reality as I conceive to be in the heat or in the stone. For although this cause does not transfer any of its actual or formal reality to my idea, it should not on that account be supposed that it must be less, real.[10] The nature of an idea is such that of itself it requires no formal reality except what it derives from my thought, of which it is a mode.[11] But in order for a given idea to contain such and such objective reality, it must surely derive it from some cause which contains at least as much formal reality as there is objective reality in the idea. For if we suppose that an idea contains something which was not in its cause, it must have got this from nothing; yet the mode of being by which a thing exists objectively <or representatively> in the intellect by way of an idea, imperfect though it may be, is certainly not nothing, and so it cannot come from nothing.

41

[9] '... i.e. it will contain in itself the same things as are in the stone or other more excellent things' (added in French version). In scholastic terminology, to possess a property 'formally' is to possess it literally, in accordance with its definition; to possess it 'eminently' is to possess it in some higher form.
[10] '... that this cause must be less real' (French version).
[11] '... i.e. a manner or way of thinking' (added in French version).

And although the reality which I am considering in my ideas is merely objective reality, I must not on that account suppose that the same reality need not exist formally in the causes of my ideas, but that it is enough for it to be present in them objectively. For just as the objective mode of being belongs to ideas by their very nature, so the formal mode of being belongs to the causes of ideas – or at least the first and most important ones – by *their* very nature. And although one idea may perhaps originate from another, there cannot be an infinite regress here; eventually one must reach a primary idea, the cause of which will be like an archetype which contains formally <and in fact> all the reality <or perfection> which is present only objectively <or representatively> in the idea. So it is clear to me, by the natural light, that the ideas in me are like <pictures, or> images which can easily fall short of the perfection of the things from which they are taken, but which cannot contain anything greater or more perfect.

The longer and more carefully I examine all these points, the more clearly and distinctly I recognize their truth. But what is my conclusion to be? If the objective reality of any of my ideas turns out to be so great that I am sure the same reality does not reside in me, either formally or eminently, and hence that I myself cannot be its cause, it will necessarily follow that I am not alone in the world, but that some other thing which is the cause of this idea also exists. But if no such idea is to be found in me, I shall have no argument to convince me of the existence of anything apart from myself. For despite a most careful and comprehensive survey, this is the only argument I have so far been able to find.

Among my ideas, apart from the idea which gives me a representation of myself, which cannot present any difficulty in this context, there are ideas which variously represent God, corporeal and inanimate things, angels, animals and finally other men like myself.

As far as concerns the ideas which represent other men, or animals, or angels, I have no difficulty in understanding that they could be put together from the ideas I have of myself, of corporeal things and of God, even if the world contained no men besides me, no animals and no angels.

As to my ideas of corporeal things, I can see nothing in them which is so great <or excellent> as to make it seem impossible that it originated in myself. For if I scrutinize them thoroughly and examine them one by one, in the way in which I examined the idea of the wax yesterday,

I notice that the things which I perceive clearly and distinctly in them are very few in number. The list comprises size, or extension in length, breadth and depth; shape, which is a function of the boundaries of this extension; position, which is a relation between various items possessing shape; and motion, or change in position; to these may be added substance, duration and number. But as for all the rest, including light and colours, sounds, smells, tastes, heat and cold and the other tactile qualities, I think of these only in a very confused and obscure way, to the extent that I do not even know whether they are true or false, that is, whether the ideas I have of them are ideas of real things or of non-things.[12] For although, as I have noted before, falsity in the strict sense, or formal falsity, can occur only in judgements, there is another kind of falsity, material falsity, which occurs in ideas, when they represent non-things as things. For example, the ideas which I have of heat and cold contain so little clarity and distinctness that they do not enable me to tell whether cold is merely the absence of heat or vice versa, or whether both of them are real qualities, or neither is. And since there can be no ideas which are not as it were of things,[13] if it is true that cold is nothing but the absence of heat, the idea which represents it to me as something real and positive deserves to be called false; and the same goes for other ideas of this kind. 44

Such ideas obviously do not require me to posit a source distinct from myself. For on the one hand, if they are false, that is, represent non-things, I know by the natural light that they arise from nothing – that is, they are in me only because of a deficiency and lack of perfection in my nature. If on the other hand they are true, then since the reality which they represent is so extremely slight that I cannot even distinguish it from a non-thing, I do not see why they cannot originate from myself.

With regard to the clear and distinct elements in my ideas of corporeal things, it appears that I could have borrowed some of these from my idea of myself, namely substance, duration, number and anything else of this kind. For example, I think that a stone is a substance, or is a thing capable of existing independently, and I also think that I am a substance. Admittedly I conceive of myself as a thing that thinks and is not extended,

---

[12] '... chimerical things which cannot exist' (French version).
[13] 'And since ideas, being like images, must in each case appear to us to represent something' (French version).

whereas I conceive of the stone as a thing that is extended and does not think, so that the two conceptions differ enormously; but they seem to agree with respect to the classification 'substance'.[14] Again, I perceive that I now exist, and remember that I have existed for some time; moreover, I have various thoughts which I can count; it is in these ways that I acquire the ideas of duration and number which I can then transfer to other things. As for all the other elements which make up the ideas of corporeal things, namely extension, shape, position and movement, these are not formally contained in me, since I am nothing but a thinking thing; but since they are merely modes of a substance,[15] and I am a substance, it seems possible that they are contained in me eminently.

So there remains only the idea of God; and I must consider whether there is anything in the idea which could not have originated in myself. By the word 'God' I understand a substance that is infinite, <eternal, immutable,> independent, supremely intelligent, supremely powerful, and which created both myself and everything else (if anything else there be) that exists. All these attributes are such that, the more carefully I concentrate on them, the less possible it seems that they[16] could have originated from me alone. So from what has been said it must be concluded that God necessarily exists.

It is true that I have the idea of substance in me in virtue of the fact that I am a substance; but this would not account for my having the idea of an infinite substance, when I am finite, unless this idea proceeded from some substance which really was infinite.

And I must not think that, just as my conceptions of rest and darkness are arrived at by negating movement and light, so my perception of the infinite is arrived at not by means of a true idea but merely by negating the finite. On the contrary, I clearly understand that there is more reality in an infinite substance than in a finite one, and hence that my perception of the infinite, that is God, is in some way prior to my perception of the finite, that is myself. For how could I understand that I doubted or desired – that is, lacked something – and that I was not wholly perfect, unless there were in me some idea of a more perfect being which enabled me to recognize my own defects by comparison?

---

[14] '... in so far as they represent substances' (French version).
[15] '... and as it were the garments under which corporeal substance appears to us' (French version).
[16] '... that the idea I have of them' (French version).

Nor can it be said that this idea of God is perhaps materially false and so could have come from nothing,[17] which is what I observed just a moment ago in the case of the ideas of heat and cold, and so on. On the contrary, it is utterly clear and distinct, and contains in itself more objective reality than any other idea; hence there is no idea which is in itself truer or less liable to be suspected of falsehood. This idea of a supremely perfect and infinite being is, I say, true in the highest degree; for although perhaps one may imagine that such a being does not exist, it cannot be supposed that the idea of such a being represents something unreal, as I said with regard to the idea of cold. The idea is, moreover, utterly clear and distinct; for whatever I clearly and distinctly perceive as being real and true, and implying any perfection, is wholly contained in it. It does not matter that I do not grasp the infinite, or that there are countless additional attributes of God which I cannot in any way grasp, and perhaps cannot even reach in my thought; for it is in the nature of the infinite not to be grasped by a finite being like myself. It is enough that I understand[18] the infinite, and that I judge that all the attributes which I clearly perceive and know to imply some perfection – and perhaps countless others of which I am ignorant – are present in God either formally or eminently. This is enough to make the idea that I have of God the truest and most clear and distinct of all my ideas.

But perhaps I am something greater than I myself understand, and all the perfections which I attribute to God are somehow in me potentially, though not yet emerging or actualized. For I am now experiencing a gradual increase in my knowledge, and I see nothing to prevent its increasing more and more to infinity. Further, I see no reason why I should not be able to use this increased knowledge to acquire all the other perfections of God. And finally, if the potentiality for these perfections is already within me, why should not this be enough to generate the idea of such perfections? 47

But all this is impossible. First, though it is true that there is a gradual increase in my knowledge, and that I have many potentialities which are not yet actual, this is all quite irrelevant to the idea of God, which

---

[17] '. . . i.e. could be in me in virtue of my imperfection' (added in French version).
[18] According to Descartes one can know or understand something without fully grasping it: 'In the same way we can touch a mountain with our hands but we cannot put our arms around it . . . To grasp something is to embrace it in one's thought; to know something, it is sufficient to touch it with one's thought' (letter to Mersenne, 27 May 1630: AT I 152; CSMK 25).

contains absolutely nothing that is potential;[19] indeed, this gradual increase in knowledge is itself the surest sign of imperfection. What is more, even if my knowledge always increases more and more, I recognize that it will never actually be infinite, since it will never reach the point where it is not capable of a further increase; God, on the other hand, I take to be actually infinite, so that nothing can be added to his perfection. And finally, I perceive that the objective being of an idea cannot be produced merely by potential being, which strictly speaking is nothing, but only by actual or formal being.

If one concentrates carefully, all this is quite evident by the natural light. But when I relax my concentration, and my mental vision is blinded by the images of things perceived by the senses, it is not so easy for me to remember why the idea of a being more perfect than myself must necessarily proceed from some being which is in reality more perfect. I should therefore like to go further and inquire whether I myself, who have this idea, could exist if no such being existed.

From whom, in that case, would I derive my existence? From myself presumably, or from my parents, or from some other beings less perfect than God; for nothing more perfect than God, or even as perfect, can be thought of or imagined.

Yet if I derived my existence from myself,[20] then I should neither doubt nor want, nor lack anything at all; for I should have given myself all the perfections of which I have any idea, and thus I should myself be God. I must not suppose that the items I lack would be more difficult to acquire than those I now have. On the contrary, it is clear that, since I am a thinking thing or substance, it would have been far more difficult for me to emerge out of nothing than merely to acquire knowledge of the many things of which I am ignorant – such knowledge being merely an accident of that substance. And if I had derived my existence from myself, which is a greater achievement, I should certainly not have denied myself the knowledge in question, which is something much easier to acquire, or indeed any of the attributes which I perceive to be contained in the idea of God; for none of them seem any harder to achieve. And if any of them were harder to achieve, they would certainly

---

[19] '... but only what is actual and real' (added in French version).
[20] '... and were independent of every other being' (added in French version).

appear so to me, if I had indeed got all my other attributes from myself, since I should experience a limitation of my power in this respect.

I do not escape the force of these arguments by supposing that I have always existed as I do now, as if it followed from this that there was no need to look for any author of my existence. For a lifespan can be divided into countless parts, each completely independent of the others, so that it does not follow from the fact that I existed a little while ago that I must exist now, unless there is some cause which as it were creates me afresh at this moment – that is, which preserves me. For it is quite clear to anyone who attentively considers the nature of time that the same power and action are needed to preserve anything at each individual moment of its duration as would be required to create that thing anew if it were not yet in existence. Hence the distinction between preservation and creation is only a conceptual one,[21] and this is one of the things that are evident by the natural light.

I must therefore now ask myself whether I possess some power enabling me to bring it about that I who now exist will still exist a little while from now. For since I am nothing but a thinking thing – or at least since I am now concerned only and precisely with that part of me which is a thinking thing – if there were such a power in me, I should undoubtedly be aware of it. But I experience no such power, and this very fact makes me recognize most clearly that I depend on some being distinct from myself.

But perhaps this being is not God, and perhaps I was produced either by my parents or by other causes less perfect than God. No; for as I have said before, it is quite clear that there must be at least as much in the cause as in the effect.[22] And therefore whatever kind of cause is eventually proposed, since I am a thinking thing and have within me some idea of God, it must be admitted that what caused me is itself a thinking thing and possesses the idea of all the perfections which I attribute to God. In respect of this cause one may again inquire whether it derives its existence from itself or from another cause. If from itself, then it is clear from what has been said that it is itself God, since if it has the power of existing through its own might,[23] then undoubtedly it also has the power

49

50

---

[21] Cf. *Principles*, Part 1, art. 62: AT VII 30; CSM I 214.
[22] '. . . at least as much reality in the cause as in its effect' (French version).
[23] Lat. *per se*; literally 'through itself'.

of actually possessing all the perfections of which it has an idea – that is, all the perfections which I conceive to be in God. If, on the other hand, it derives its existence from another cause, then the same question may be repeated concerning this further cause, namely whether it derives its existence from itself or from another cause, until eventually the ultimate cause is reached, and this will be God.

It is clear enough that an infinite regress is impossible here, especially since I am dealing not just with the cause that produced me in the past, but also and most importantly with the cause that preserves me at the present moment.

Nor can it be supposed that several partial causes contributed to my creation, or that I received the idea of one of the perfections which I attribute to God from one cause and the idea of another from another – the supposition here being that all the perfections are to be found somewhere in the universe but not joined together in a single being, God. On the contrary, the unity, the simplicity, or the inseparability of all the attributes of God is one of the most important of the perfections which I understand him to have. And surely the idea of the unity of all his perfections could not have been placed in me by any cause which did not also provide me with the ideas of the other perfections; for no cause could have made me understand the interconnection and inseparability of the perfections without at the same time making me recognize what they were.

Lastly, as regards my parents, even if everything I have ever believed about them is true, it is certainly not they who preserve me; and in so far as I am a thinking thing, they did not even make me; they merely placed certain dispositions in the matter which I have always regarded as containing me, or rather my mind, for that is all I now take myself to be. So there can be no difficulty regarding my parents in this context. Altogether then, it must be concluded that the mere fact that I exist and have within me an idea of a most perfect being, that is, God, provides a very clear proof that God indeed exists.

It only remains for me to examine how I received this idea from God. For I did not acquire it from the senses; it has never come to me unexpectedly, as usually happens with the ideas of things that are perceivable by the senses, when these things present themselves to the external sense organs – or seem to do so. And it was not invented by me either; for I am plainly unable either to take away anything from it or to add anything to it. The only remaining alternative is that it is innate in me, just as the idea of myself is innate in me.

And indeed it is no surprise that God, in creating me, should have placed this idea in me to be, as it were, the mark of the craftsman stamped on his work – not that the mark need be anything distinct from the work itself. But the mere fact that God created me is a very strong basis for believing that I am somehow made in his image and likeness, and that I perceive that likeness, which includes the idea of God, by the same faculty which enables me to perceive myself. That is, when I turn my mind's eye upon myself, I understand that I am a thing which is incomplete and dependent on another and which aspires without limit to ever greater and better things; but I also understand at the same time that he on whom I depend has within him all those greater things, not just indefinitely and potentially but actually and infinitely, and hence that he is God. The whole force of the argument lies in this: I recognize that it would be impossible for me to exist with the kind of nature I have – that is, having within me the idea of God – were it not the case that God really existed. By 'God' I mean the very being the idea of whom is within me, that is, the possessor of all the perfections which I cannot grasp, but can somehow reach in my thought, who is subject to no defects whatsoever.[24] It is clear enough from this that he cannot be a deceiver, since it is manifest by the natural light that all fraud and deception depend on some defect. 52

But before examining this point more carefully and investigating other truths which may be derived from it, I should like to pause here and spend some time in the contemplation of God; to reflect on his attributes, and to gaze with wonder and adoration on the beauty of this immense light, so far as the eye of my darkened intellect can bear it. For just as we believe through faith that the supreme happiness of the next life consists solely in the contemplation of the divine majesty, so experience tells us that this same contemplation, albeit much less perfect, enables us to know the greatest joy of which we are capable in this life.

[24] '... and has not one of the things which indicate some imperfection' (added in French version).

Fourth Meditation
Truth and falsity

During these past few days I have accustomed myself to leading my mind away from the senses; and I have taken careful note of the fact that there is very little about corporeal things that is truly perceived, whereas much more is known about the human mind, and still more about God. The result is that I now have no difficulty in turning my mind away from imaginable things[1] and towards things which are objects of the intellect alone and are totally separate from matter. And indeed the idea I have of the human mind, in so far as it is a thinking thing, which is not extended in length, breadth or height and has no other bodily characteristics, is much more distinct than the idea of any corporeal thing. And when I consider the fact that I have doubts, or that I am a thing that is incomplete and dependent, then there arises in me a clear and distinct idea of a being who is independent and complete, that is, an idea of God. And from the mere fact that there is such an idea within me, or that I who possess this idea exist, I clearly infer that God also exists, and that every single moment of my entire existence depends on him. So clear is this conclusion that I am confident that the human intellect cannot know anything that is more evident or more certain. And now, from this contemplation of the true God, in whom all the treasures of wisdom and the sciences lie hidden, I think I can see a way forward to the knowledge of other things.[2]

[1] '. . . from things which can be perceived by the senses or imagined' (French version).
[2] '. . . of the other things in the universe' (French version).

To begin with, I recognize that it is impossible that God should ever deceive me. For in every case of trickery or deception some imperfection is to be found; and although the ability to deceive appears to be an indication of cleverness or power, the will to deceive is undoubtedly evidence of malice or weakness, and so cannot apply to God.

Next, I know by experience that there is in me a faculty of judgement which, like everything else which is in me, I certainly received from God. And since God does not wish to deceive me, he surely did not give me the kind of faculty which would ever enable me to go wrong while using it correctly. 54

There would be no further doubt on this issue were it not that what I have just said appears to imply that I am incapable of ever going wrong. For if everything that is in me comes from God, and he did not endow me with a faculty for making mistakes, it appears that I can never go wrong. And certainly, so long as I think only of God, and turn my whole attention to him, I can find no cause of error or falsity. But when I turn back to myself, I know by experience that I am prone to countless errors. On looking for the cause of these errors, I find that I possess not only a real and positive idea of God, or a being who is supremely perfect, but also what may be described as a negative idea of nothingness, or of that which is farthest removed from all perfection. I realize that I am, as it were, something intermediate between God and nothingness, or between supreme being and non-being: my nature is such that in so far as I was created by the supreme being, there is nothing in me to enable me to go wrong or lead me astray; but in so far as I participate in nothingness or non-being, that is, in so far as I am not myself the supreme being and am lacking in countless respects, it is no wonder that I make mistakes. I understand, then, that error as such is not something real which depends on God, but merely a defect. Hence my going wrong does not require me to have a faculty specially bestowed on me by God; it simply happens as a result of the fact that the faculty of true judgement which I have from God is in my case not infinite.

But this is still not entirely satisfactory. For error is not a pure negation,[3] but rather a privation or lack of some knowledge which 55

---

[3] '. . . i.e. not simply the defect or lack of some perfection to which I have no proper claim' (added in French version).

somehow should be in me. And when I concentrate on the nature of God, it seems impossible that he should have placed in me a faculty which is not perfect of its kind, or which lacks some perfection which it ought to have. The more skilled the craftsman the more perfect the work produced by him; if this is so, how can anything produced by the supreme creator of all things not be complete and perfect in all respects? There is, moreover, no doubt that God could have given me a nature such that I was never mistaken; again, there is no doubt that he always wills what is best. Is it then better that I should make mistakes than that I should not do so?

As I reflect on these matters more attentively, it occurs to me first of all that it is no cause for surprise if I do not understand the reasons for some of God's actions; and there is no call to doubt his existence if I happen to find that there are other instances where I do not grasp why or how certain things were made by him. For since I now know that my own nature is very weak and limited, whereas the nature of God is immense, incomprehensible and infinite, I also know without more ado that he is capable of countless things whose causes are beyond my knowledge. And for this reason alone I consider the customary search for final causes to be totally useless in physics; there is considerable rashness in thinking myself capable of investigating the <impenetrable> purposes of God.

It also occurs to me that whenever we are inquiring whether the works of God are perfect, we ought to look at the whole universe, not just at one created thing on its own. For what would perhaps rightly appear very imperfect if it existed on its own is quite perfect when its function as a part of the universe is considered. It is true that, since my decision to doubt everything, it is so far only myself and God whose existence I have been able to know with certainty; but after considering the immense power of God, I cannot deny that many other things have been made by him, or at least could have been made, and hence that I may have a place in the universal scheme of things.

Next, when I look more closely at myself and inquire into the nature of my errors (for these are the only evidence of some imperfection in me), I notice that they depend on two concurrent causes, namely on the faculty of knowledge which is in me, and on the faculty of choice or freedom of the will; that is, they depend on both the intellect and the will simultaneously. Now all that the intellect does is to enable me to perceive[4] the ideas which are subjects for possible judgements; and when regarded strictly in this light, it turns out to contain no error in the proper sense of that term. For although countless things may exist without there being any corresponding ideas in me, it should not, strictly speaking, be said that I am deprived of these ideas,[5] but merely that I lack them, in a negative sense. This is because I cannot produce any reason to prove that God ought to have given me a greater faculty of knowledge than he did; and no matter how skilled I understand a craftsman to be, this does not make me think he ought to have put into every one of his works all the perfections which he is able to put into some of them. Besides, I cannot complain that the will or freedom of choice which I received from God is not sufficiently extensive or perfect, since I know by experience that it is not restricted in any way. Indeed, I think it is very noteworthy that there is nothing else in me which is so perfect and so great that the possibility of a further increase in its perfection or greatness is beyond my understanding. If, for example, I consider the faculty of understanding, I immediately recognize that in my case it is extremely slight and very finite, and I at once form the idea of an understanding which is much greater – indeed supremely great and infinite; and from the very fact that I can form an idea of it, I perceive that it belongs to the nature of God. Similarly, if I examine the faculties of memory or imagination, or any others, I discover that in my case each one of these faculties is weak and limited, while in the case of God it is immeasurable. It is only the will, or freedom of choice, which I experience within me to be so great that the idea of any greater faculty is beyond my grasp; so much so that it is above all in virtue of the will that I understand myself to bear in some way the image and likeness of God. For although God's will is incomparably greater than mine, both in virtue of the knowledge and power that accompany it and make it more firm and efficacious, and also in virtue of its object, in that it ranges over a greater number of items, nevertheless it does not seem any greater than mine when considered as will in the essential and strict sense. This is because the will simply consists in our ability to do or not do something (that is, to affirm or deny, to pursue or avoid); or rather, it consists simply in the fact that when the intellect puts

---

[4] '. . . without affirming or denying anything' (added in French version).
[5] '. . . it cannot be said that my understanding is deprived of these ideas, as if they were something to which its nature entitles it' (French version).

something forward, we are moved to affirm or deny or to pursue or avoid it in such a way that we do not feel ourselves to be determined by any external force. For in order to be free, there is no need for me to be capable of going in each of two directions; on the contrary, the more I incline in one direction – either because I clearly understand that reasons of truth and goodness point that way, or because of a divinely produced disposition of my inmost thoughts – the freer is my choice. Neither divine grace nor natural knowledge ever diminishes freedom; on the contrary, they increase and strengthen it. But the indifference I feel when there is no reason pushing me in one direction rather than another is the lowest grade of freedom; it is evidence not of any perfection of freedom, but rather of a defect in knowledge or a kind of negation. For if I always saw clearly what was true and good, I should never have to deliberate about the right judgement or choice; in that case, although I should be wholly free, it would be impossible for me ever to be in a state of indifference.

From these considerations I perceive that the power of willing which I received from God is not, when considered in itself, the cause of my mistakes; for it is both extremely ample and also perfect of its kind. Nor is my power of understanding to blame; for since my understanding comes from God, everything that I understand I undoubtedly understand correctly, and any error here is impossible. So what then is the source of my mistakes? It must be simply this: the scope of the will is wider than that of the intellect; but instead of restricting it within the same limits, I extend its use to matters which I do not understand. Since the will is indifferent in such cases, it easily turns aside from what is true and good, and this is the source of my error and sin.

For example, during these past few days I have been asking whether anything in the world exists, and I have realized that from the very fact of my raising this question it follows quite evidently that I exist. I could not but judge that something which I understood so clearly was true; but this was not because I was compelled so to judge by any external force, but because from a great light in the intellect there followed a great inclination in the will, and thus the spontaneity and freedom of my belief was all the greater in proportion to my lack of indifference. But now, besides the knowledge that I exist, in so far as I am a thinking thing, an idea of corporeal nature comes into my mind; and I happen to be in doubt as to whether the thinking nature which is in me, or rather which I am, is distinct from this corporeal nature or identical with it. I am making the further supposition that my intellect has not yet come upon any persuasive reason in favour of one alternative rather than the other. This obviously implies that I am indifferent as to whether I should assert or deny either alternative, or indeed refrain from making any judgement on the matter.

What is more, this indifference does not merely apply to cases where the intellect is wholly ignorant, but extends in general to every case where the intellect does not have sufficiently clear knowledge at the time when the will deliberates. For although probable conjectures may pull me in one direction, the mere knowledge that they are simply conjectures, and not certain and indubitable reasons, is itself quite enough to push my assent the other way. My experience in the last few days confirms this: the mere fact that I found that all my previous beliefs were in some sense open to doubt was enough to turn my absolutely confident belief in their truth into the supposition that they were wholly false.

If, however, I simply refrain from making a judgement in cases where I do not perceive the truth with sufficient clarity and distinctness, then it is clear that I am behaving correctly and avoiding error. But if in such cases I either affirm or deny, then I am not using my free will correctly. If I go for the alternative which is false, then obviously I shall be in error; 60 if I take the other side, then it is by pure chance that I arrive at the truth, and I shall still be at fault since it is clear by the natural light that the perception of the intellect should always precede the determination of the will. In this incorrect use of free will may be found the privation which constitutes the essence of error. The privation, I say, lies in the operation of the will in so far as it proceeds from me, but not in the faculty of will which I received from God, nor even in its operation, in so far as it depends on him.

And I have no cause for complaint on the grounds that the power of understanding or the natural light which God gave me is no greater than it is; for it is in the nature of a finite intellect to lack understanding of many things, and it is in the nature of a created intellect to be finite. Indeed, I have reason to give thanks to him who has never owed me anything for the great bounty that he has shown me, rather than thinking myself deprived or robbed of any gifts he did not bestow.[6]

---

[6] '... rather than entertaining so unjust a thought as to imagine that he deprived me of, or unjustly withheld, the other perfections which he did not give me' (French version).

Nor do I have any cause for complaint on the grounds that God gave me a will which extends more widely than my intellect. For since the will consists simply of one thing which is, as it were, indivisible, it seems that its nature rules out the possibility of anything being taken away from it. And surely, the more widely my will extends, then the greater thanks I owe to him who gave it to me.

Finally, I must not complain that the forming of those acts of will or judgements in which I go wrong happens with God's concurrence. For in so far as these acts depend on God, they are wholly true and good; and my ability to perform them means that there is in a sense more perfection in me than would be the case if I lacked this ability. As for the privation involved – which is all that the essential definition of falsity and wrong consists in – this does not in any way require the concurrence of God, since it is not a thing; indeed, when it is referred to God as its cause, it should be called not a privation but simply a negation.[7] For it is surely no imperfection in God that he has given me the freedom to assent or not to assent in those cases where he did not endow my intellect with a clear and distinct perception; but it is undoubtedly an imperfection in me to misuse that freedom and make judgements about matters which I do not fully understand. I can see, however, that God could easily have brought it about that without losing my freedom, and despite the limitations in my knowledge, I should nonetheless never make a mistake. He could, for example, have endowed my intellect with a clear and distinct perception of everything about which I was ever likely to deliberate; or he could simply have impressed it unforgettably on my memory that I should never make a judgement about anything which I did not clearly and distinctly understand. Had God made me this way, then I can easily understand that, considered as a totality,[8] I would have been more perfect than I am now. But I cannot therefore deny that there may in some way be more perfection in the universe as a whole because some of its parts are not immune from error, while others are immune, than there would be if all the parts were exactly alike. And I have no right to complain that the role God wished me to undertake in the world is not the principal one or the most perfect of all.

61

---

[7] '... understanding these terms in accordance with scholastic usage' (added in French version).
[8] '... as if there were only myself in the world' (added in French version).

What is more, even if I have no power to avoid error in the first way just mentioned, which requires a clear perception of everything I have to deliberate on, I can avoid error in the second way, which depends merely on my remembering to withhold judgement on any occasion when the truth of the matter is not clear. Admittedly, I am aware of a certain weakness in me, in that I am unable to keep my attention fixed on one and the same item of knowledge at all times; but by attentive and repeated meditation I am nevertheless able to make myself remember it as often as the need arises, and thus get into the habit of avoiding error.

It is here that man's greatest and most important perfection is to be found, and I therefore think that today's meditation, involving an investigation into the cause of error and falsity, has been very profitable. The cause of error must surely be the one I have explained; for if, whenever I have to make a judgement, I restrain my will so that it extends to what the intellect clearly and distinctly reveals, and no further, then it is quite impossible for me to go wrong. This is because every clear and distinct perception is undoubtedly something,[9] and hence cannot come from nothing, but must necessarily have God for its author. Its author, I say, is God, who is supremely perfect, and who cannot be a deceiver on pain of contradiction; hence the perception is undoubtedly true. So today I have learned not only what precautions to take to avoid ever going wrong, but also what to do to arrive at the truth. For I shall unquestionably reach the truth, if only I give sufficient attention to all the things which I perfectly understand, and separate these from all the other cases where my apprehension is more confused and obscure. And this is just what I shall take good care to do from now on.

62

---

[9] '. . . something real and positive' (French version).

49

Fifth Meditation

*The essence of material things, and the existence of God
considered a second time*

There are many matters which remain to be investigated concerning the
attributes of God and the nature of myself, or my mind; and perhaps
I shall take these up at another time. But now that I have seen what to do
and what to avoid in order to reach the truth, the most pressing task
seems to be to try to escape from the doubts into which I fell a few days
ago, and see whether any certainty can be achieved regarding material
objects.

But before I inquire whether any such things exist outside me, I must
consider the ideas of these things, in so far as they exist in my thought,
and see which of them are distinct, and which confused.

Quantity, for example, or 'continuous' quantity as the philosophers
commonly call it, is something I distinctly imagine. That is, I distinctly
imagine the extension of the quantity (or rather of the thing which is
quantified) in length, breadth and depth. I also enumerate various parts
of the thing, and to these parts I assign various sizes, shapes, positions
and local motions; and to the motions I assign various durations.

Not only are all these things very well known and transparent to me
when regarded in this general way, but in addition there are countless
particular features regarding shapes, number, motion and so on, which
I perceive when I give them my attention. And the truth of these matters
is so open and so much in harmony with my nature, that on first
discovering them it seems that I am not so much learning something

50

new as remembering what I knew before; or it seems like noticing for the first time things which were long present within me although I had never turned my mental gaze on them before.

But I think the most important consideration at this point is that I find within me countless ideas of things which even though they may not exist anywhere outside me still cannot be called nothing; for although in a sense they can be thought of at will, they are not my invention but have their own true and immutable natures. When, for example, I imagine a triangle, even if perhaps no such figure exists, or has ever existed, anywhere outside my thought, there is still a determinate nature, or essence, or form of the triangle which is immutable and eternal, and not invented by me or dependent on my mind. This is clear from the fact that various properties can be demonstrated of the triangle, for example that its three angles equal two right angles, that its greatest side subtends its greatest angle, and the like; and since these properties are ones which I now clearly recognize whether I want to or not, even if I never thought of them at all when I previously imagined the triangle, it follows that they cannot have been invented by me.

It would be beside the point for me to say that since I have from time to time seen bodies of triangular shape, the idea of the triangle may have come to me from external things by means of the sense organs. For I can think up countless other shapes which there can be no suspicion of my ever having encountered through the senses, and yet I can demonstrate various properties of these shapes, just as I can with the triangle. All these properties are certainly true, since I am clearly aware of them, and therefore they are something, and not merely nothing; for it is obvious that whatever is true is something; and I have already amply demonstrated that everything of which I am clearly aware is true. And even if I had not demonstrated this, the nature of my mind is such that I cannot but assent to these things, at least so long as I clearly perceive them. I also remember that even before, when I was completely preoccupied with the objects of the senses, I always held that the most certain truths of all were the kind which I recognized clearly in connection with shapes, or numbers or other items relating to arithmetic or geometry, or in general to pure and abstract mathematics.

But if the mere fact that I can produce from my thought the idea of something entails that everything which I clearly and distinctly perceive to belong to that thing really does belong to it, is not this a possible basis

65

51

for another argument to prove the existence of God? Certainly, the idea of God, or a supremely perfect being, is one which I find within me just as surely as the idea of any shape or number. And my understanding that it belongs to his nature that he always exists[1] is no less clear and distinct than is the case when I prove of any shape or number that some property belongs to its nature. Hence, even if it turned out that not everything on which I have meditated in these past days is true, I ought still to regard the existence of God as having at least the same level of certainty as I have hitherto attributed to the truths of mathematics.[2]

66

At first sight, however, this is not transparently clear, but has some appearance of being a sophism. Since I have been accustomed to distinguish between existence and essence in everything else, I find it easy to persuade myself that existence can also be separated from the essence of God, and hence that God can be thought of as not existing. But when I concentrate more carefully, it is quite evident that existence can no more be separated from the essence of God than the fact that its three angles equal two right angles can be separated from the essence of a triangle, or than the idea of a mountain can be separated from the idea of a valley. Hence it is just as much of a contradiction to think of God (that is, a supremely perfect being) lacking existence (that is, lacking a perfection), as it is to think of a mountain without a valley.

However, even granted that I cannot think of God except as existing, just as I cannot think of a mountain without a valley, it certainly does not follow from the fact that I think of a mountain with a valley that there is any mountain in the world; and similarly, it does not seem to follow from the fact that I think of God as existing that he does exist. For my thought does not impose any necessity on things; and just as I may imagine a winged horse even though no horse has wings, so I may be able to attach existence to God even though no God exists.

But there is a sophism concealed here. From the fact that I cannot think of a mountain without a valley, it does not follow that a mountain and valley exist anywhere, but simply that a mountain and a valley, whether they exist or not, are mutually inseparable. But from the fact that I cannot think of God except as existing, it follows that existence is inseparable from God, and hence that he really exists. It is not that my

67

[1] '. . . that actual and eternal existence belongs to his nature' (French version).
[2] '. . . which concern only figures and numbers' (added in French version).

52

thought makes it so, or imposes any necessity on anything; on the contrary, it is the necessity of the thing itself, namely the existence of God, which determines my thinking in this respect. For I am not free to think of God without existence (that is, a supremely perfect being without a supreme perfection) as I am free to imagine a horse with or without wings.

And it must not be objected at this point that while it is indeed necessary for me to suppose God exists, once I have made the supposition that he has all perfections (since existence is one of the perfections), nevertheless the original supposition was not necessary. Similarly, the objection would run, it is not necessary for me to think that all quadrilaterals can be inscribed in a circle; but given this supposition, it will be necessary for me to admit that a rhombus can be inscribed in a circle – which is patently false. Now admittedly, it is not necessary that I ever light upon any thought of God; but whenever I do choose to think of the first and supreme being, and bring forth the idea of God from the treasure house of my mind as it were, it is necessary that I attribute all perfections to him, even if I do not at that time enumerate them or attend to them individually. And this necessity plainly guarantees that, when I later realize that existence is a perfection, I am correct in inferring that the first and supreme being exists. In the same way, it is not necessary for me ever to imagine a triangle; but whenever I do wish to consider a rectilinear figure having just three angles, it is necessary that I attribute to it the properties which license the inference that its three angles equal no more than two right angles, even if I do not notice this at the time. 68 By contrast, when I examine what figures can be inscribed in a circle, it is in no way necessary for me to think that this class includes all quadrilaterals. Indeed, I cannot even imagine this, so long as I am willing to admit only what I clearly and distinctly understand. So there is a great difference between this kind of false supposition and the true ideas which are innate in me, of which the first and most important is the idea of God. There are many ways in which I understand that this idea is not something fictitious which is dependent on my thought, but is an image of a true and immutable nature. First of all, there is the fact that, apart from God, there is nothing else of which I am capable of thinking such that existence belongs[3] to its essence. Second, I cannot understand

---

[3] '. . . necessarily belongs' (French version).

how there could be two or more Gods of this kind; and after supposing that one God exists, I plainly see that it is necessary that he has existed from eternity and will abide for eternity. And finally, I perceive many other attributes of God, none of which I can remove or alter.

But whatever method of proof I use, I am always brought back to the fact that it is only what I clearly and distinctly perceive that completely convinces me. Some of the things I clearly and distinctly perceive are obvious to everyone, while others are discovered only by those who look more closely and investigate more carefully; but once they have been discovered, the latter are judged to be just as certain as the former. In the case of a right-angled triangle, for example, the fact that the square on the hypotenuse is equal to the square on the other two sides is not so readily apparent as the fact that the hypotenuse subtends the largest angle; but once one has seen it, one believes it just as strongly. But as regards God, if I were not overwhelmed by preconceived opinions, and if the images of things perceived by the senses did not besiege my thought on every side, I would certainly acknowledge him sooner and more easily than anything else. For what is more self-evident than the fact that the supreme being exists, or that God, to whose essence alone existence belongs,[4] exists?

Although it needed close attention for me to perceive this, I am now just as certain of it as I am of everything else which appears most certain. And what is more, I see that the certainty of all other things depends on this, so that without it nothing can ever be perfectly known.

Admittedly my nature is such that so long as[5] I perceive something very clearly and distinctly I cannot but believe it to be true. But my nature is also such that I cannot fix my mental vision continually on the same thing, so as to keep perceiving it clearly; and often the memory of a previously made judgement may come back, when I am no longer attending to the arguments which led me to make it. And so other arguments can now occur to me which might easily undermine my opinion, if I were unaware of God; and I should thus never have true and certain knowledge about anything, but only shifting and changeable opinions. For example, when I consider the nature of a triangle, it appears most evident to me, steeped as I am in the principles of geometry, that its

69

---

[4] '... in the idea of whom alone necessary and eternal existence is comprised' (French version).
[5] '... as soon as' (French version).

three angles are equal to two right angles; and so long as I attend to the 70
proof, I cannot but believe this to be true. But as soon as I turn my mind's
eye away from the proof, then in spite of still remembering that
I perceived it very clearly, I can easily fall into doubt about its truth, if
I am unaware of God. For I can convince myself that I have a natural
disposition to go wrong from time to time in matters which I think
I perceive as evidently as can be. This will seem even more likely when
I remember that there have been frequent cases where I have regarded
things as true and certain, but have later been led by other arguments to
judge them to be false.

Now, however, I have perceived that God exists, and at the same time
I have understood that everything else depends on him, and that he is no
deceiver; and I have drawn the conclusion that everything which
I clearly and distinctly perceive is of necessity true. Accordingly, even
if I am no longer attending to the arguments which led me to judge that
this is true, as long as I remember that I clearly and distinctly perceived
it, there are no counter-arguments which can be adduced to make me
doubt it, but on the contrary I have true and certain knowledge of it. And
I have knowledge not just of this matter, but of all matters which
I remember ever having demonstrated, in geometry and so on. For what
objections can now be raised?[6] That the way I am made makes me prone
to frequent error? But I now know that I am incapable of error in those
cases where my understanding is transparently clear. Or can it be
objected that I have in the past regarded as true and certain many things
which I afterwards recognized to be false? But none of these were things
which I clearly and distinctly perceived: I was ignorant of this rule for
establishing the truth, and believed these things for other reasons which
I later discovered to be less reliable. So what is left to say? Can one raise
the objection I put to myself a while ago, that I may be dreaming, or that
everything which I am now thinking has as little truth as what comes to
the mind of one who is asleep? Yet even this does not change anything.
For even though I might be dreaming, if there is anything which is 71
evident to my intellect, then it is wholly true.

Thus I see plainly that the certainty and truth of all knowledge
depends uniquely on my awareness of the true God, to such an extent

---

[6] '. . . to oblige me to call these matters into doubt' (added in French version).

that I was incapable of perfect knowledge about anything else until I became aware of him. And now it is possible for me to achieve full and certain knowledge of countless matters, both concerning God himself and other things whose nature is intellectual, and also concerning the whole of that corporeal nature which is the subject-matter of pure mathematics.[7]

---

[7] '... and also concerning things which belong to corporeal nature in so far as it can serve as the object of geometrical demonstrations which have no concern with whether that object exists' (French version).

Sixth Meditation

The existence of material things, and the real distinction between mind and body[1]

It remains for me to examine whether material things exist. And at least I now know they are capable of existing, in so far as they are the subject-matter of pure mathematics, since I perceive them clearly and distinctly. For there is no doubt that God is capable of creating everything that I am capable of perceiving in this manner; and I have never judged that something could not be made by him except on the grounds that there would be a contradiction in my perceiving it distinctly. The conclusion that material things exist is also suggested by the faculty of imagination, which I am aware of using when I turn my mind to material things. For when I give more attentive consideration to what imagination is, it seems to be nothing else but an application of the cognitive faculty to a body which is intimately present to it, and which therefore exists.

To make this clear, I will first examine the difference between imagination and pure understanding. When I imagine a triangle, for example, I do not merely understand that it is a figure bounded by three lines, but at the same time I also see the three lines with my mind's eye as if they were present before me; and this is what I call imagining. But if I want to think of a chiliagon, although I understand that it is a figure consisting of a thousand sides just as well as I understand the triangle to be a three-sided figure, I do not in the same way imagine the thousand sides or see

72

---

[1] '... between the soul and body of a man' (French version).

57

them as if they were present before me. It is true that since I am in the habit of imagining something whenever I think of a corporeal thing, I may construct in my mind a confused representation of some figure; but it is clear that this is not a chiliagon. For it differs in no way from the representation I should form if I were thinking of a myriagon, or any figure with very many sides. Moreover, such a representation is useless for recognizing the properties which distinguish a chiliagon from other polygons. But suppose I am dealing with a pentagon: I can of course understand the figure of a pentagon, just as I can the figure of a chiliagon, without the help of the imagination; but I can also imagine a pentagon, by applying my mind's eye to its five sides and the area contained within them. And in doing this I notice quite clearly that imagination requires a peculiar effort of mind which is not required for understanding; this additional effort of mind clearly shows the difference between imagination and pure understanding.

73

Besides this, I consider that this power of imagining which is in me, differing as it does from the power of understanding, is not a necessary constituent of my own essence, that is, of the essence of my mind. For if I lacked it, I should undoubtedly remain the same individual as I now am; from which it seems to follow that it depends on something distinct from myself. And I can easily understand that, if there does exist some body to which the mind is so joined that it can apply itself to contemplate it, as it were, whenever it pleases, then it may possibly be this very body that enables me to imagine corporeal things. So the difference between this mode of thinking and pure understanding may simply be this: when the mind understands, it in some way turns towards itself and inspects one of the ideas which are within it; but when it imagines, it turns towards the body and looks at something in the body which conforms to an idea understood by the mind or perceived by the senses. I can, as I say, easily understand that this is how imagination comes about, if the body exists; and since there is no other equally suitable way of explaining imagination that comes to mind, I can make a probable conjecture that the body exists. But this is only a probability; and despite a careful and comprehensive investigation, I do not yet see how the distinct idea of corporeal nature which I find in my imagination can provide any basis for a necessary inference that some body exists.

74

But besides that corporeal nature which is the subject-matter of pure mathematics, there is much else that I habitually imagine, such as

58

colours, sounds, tastes, pain and so on – though not so distinctly. Now I perceive these things much better by means of the senses, which is how, with the assistance of memory, they appear to have reached the imagination. So in order to deal with them more fully, I must pay equal attention to the senses, and see whether the things which are perceived by means of that mode of thinking which I call 'sensory perception' provide me with any sure argument for the existence of corporeal things.

To begin with, I will go back over all the things which I previously took to be perceived by the senses, and reckoned to be true; and I will go over my reasons for thinking this. Next, I will set out my reasons for subsequently calling these things into doubt. And finally I will consider what I should now believe about them.

First of all then, I perceived by my senses that I had a head, hands, feet and other limbs making up the body which I regarded as part of myself, or perhaps even as my whole self. I also perceived by my senses that this body was situated among many other bodies which could affect it in various favourable or unfavourable ways; and I gauged the favourable effects by a sensation of pleasure, and the unfavourable ones by a sensation of pain. In addition to pain and pleasure, I also had sensations within me of hunger, thirst, and other such appetites, and also of physical propensities towards cheerfulness, sadness, anger and similar emotions. And outside me, besides the extension, shapes and movements of bodies, I also had sensations of their hardness and heat, and of the other tactile qualities. In addition, I had sensations of light, colours, smells, tastes and sounds, the variety of which enabled me to distinguish the sky, the earth, the seas, and all other bodies, one from another. Considering the ideas of all these qualities which presented themselves to my thought, although the ideas were, strictly speaking, the only immediate objects of my sensory awareness, it was not unreasonable for me to think that the items which I was perceiving through the senses were things quite distinct from my thought, namely bodies which produced the ideas. For my experience was that these ideas came to me quite without my consent, so that I could not have sensory awareness of any object, even if I wanted to, unless it was present to my sense organs; and I could not avoid having sensory awareness of it when it was present. And since the ideas perceived by the senses were much more lively and vivid and even, in their own way, more distinct than any of those which I deliberately formed through meditating or which I found

75

impressed on my memory, it seemed impossible that they should have come from within me; so the only alternative was that they came from other things. Since the sole source of my knowledge of these things was the ideas themselves, the supposition that the things resembled the ideas was bound to occur to me. In addition, I remembered that the use of my senses had come first, while the use of my reason came only later; and I saw that the ideas which I formed myself were less vivid than those which I perceived with the senses and were, for the most part, made up of elements of sensory ideas. In this way I easily convinced myself that I had nothing at all in the intellect which I had not previously had in

76 sensation. As for the body which by some special right I called 'mine', my belief that this body, more than any other, belonged to me had some justification. For I could never be separated from it, as I could from other bodies; and I felt all my appetites and emotions in, and on account of, this body; and finally, I was aware of pain and pleasurable ticklings in parts of this body, but not in other bodies external to it. But why should that curious sensation of pain give rise to a particular distress of mind; or why should a certain kind of delight follow on a tickling sensation? Again, why should that curious tugging in the stomach which I call hunger tell me that I should eat, or a dryness of the throat tell me to drink, and so on? I was not able to give any explanation of all this, except that nature taught me so. For there is absolutely no connection (at least that I can understand) between the tugging sensation and the decision to take food, or between the sensation of something causing pain and the mental apprehension of distress that arises from that sensation. These and other judgements that I made concerning sensory objects, I was apparently taught to make by nature; for I had already made up my mind that this was how things were, before working out any arguments to prove it.

Later on, however, I had many experiences which gradually undermined all the faith I had had in the senses. Sometimes towers which had looked round from a distance appeared square from close up; and enormous statues standing on their pediments did not seem large when observed from the ground. In these and countless other such cases, I found that the judgements of the external senses were mistaken. And this applied not just to the external senses but to the internal senses as

77 well. For what can be more internal than pain? And yet I had heard that those who had had a leg or an arm amputated sometimes still seemed to

feel pain intermittently in the missing part of the body. So even in my own case it was apparently not quite certain that a particular limb was hurting, even if I felt pain in it. To these reasons for doubting, I recently added two very general ones.[2] The first was that every sensory experience I have ever thought I was having while awake I can also think of myself as sometimes having while asleep; and since I do not believe that what I seem to perceive in sleep comes from things located outside me, I did not see why I should be any more inclined to believe this of what I think I perceive while awake. The second reason for doubt was that since I did not yet know the author of my being (or at least was pretending not to), I saw nothing to rule out the possibility that my natural constitution made me prone to error even in matters which seemed to me most true. As for the reasons for my previous confident belief in the truth of the things perceived by the senses, I had no trouble in refuting them. For since I apparently had natural impulses towards many things which reason told me to avoid, I reckoned that a great deal of confidence should not be placed in what I was taught by nature. And despite the fact that the perceptions of the senses were not dependent on my will, I did not think that I should on that account infer that they proceeded from things distinct from myself, since I might perhaps have a faculty not yet known to me which produced them.[3]

But now, when I am beginning to achieve a better knowledge of myself and the author of my being, although I do not think I should heedlessly accept everything I seem to have acquired from the senses, neither do I think that everything should be called into doubt.

First, I know that everything which I clearly and distinctly understand is capable of being created by God so as to correspond exactly with my understanding of it. Hence the fact that I can clearly and distinctly understand one thing apart from another is enough to make me certain that the two things are distinct, since they are capable of being separated, at least by God. The question of what kind of power is required to bring about such a separation does not affect the judgement that the two things are distinct. Thus, simply by knowing that I exist and seeing at the same time that absolutely nothing else belongs to my nature or essence except that I am a thinking thing, I can infer correctly that my essence consists

78

---

[2] Cf. Med. I, above, pp. 16–18.   [3] Cf. Med. III, above, pp. 31–2.

solely in the fact that I am a thinking thing. It is true that I may have
(or, to anticipate, that I certainly have) a body that is very closely joined
to me. But nevertheless, on the one hand I have a clear and distinct idea
of myself, in so far as I am simply a thinking, non-extended thing; and on
the other hand I have a distinct idea of body,[4] in so far as this is simply
an extended, non-thinking thing. And accordingly, it is certain that I[5] am
really distinct from my body, and can exist without it.

Besides this, I find in myself faculties for certain special modes of
thinking,[6] namely imagination and sensory perception. Now I can clearly
and distinctly understand myself as a whole without these faculties; but
I cannot, conversely, understand these faculties without me, that is,
without an intellectual substance to inhere in. This is because there is
an intellectual act included in their essential definition; and hence
I perceive that the distinction between them and myself corresponds to
the distinction between the modes of a thing and the thing itself.[7] Of
course I also recognize that there are other faculties (like those of
changing position, of taking on various shapes, and so on) which, like
sensory perception and imagination, cannot be understood apart from
some substance for them to inhere in, and hence cannot exist without it.
But it is clear that these other faculties, if they exist, must be in a
corporeal or extended substance and not an intellectual one; for the clear
and distinct conception of them includes extension, but does not include
any intellectual act whatsoever. Now there is in me a passive faculty of
sensory perception, that is, a faculty for receiving and recognizing the
ideas of sensible objects; but I could not make use of it unless there was
also an active faculty, either in me or in something else, which produced
or brought about these ideas. But this faculty cannot be in me, since
clearly it presupposes no intellectual act on my part,[8] and the ideas in
question are produced without my cooperation and often even against
my will. So the only alternative is that it is in another substance distinct

79

[4] The Latin term *corpus* as used here by Descartes is ambiguous as between 'body' (i.e. corporeal matter in general) and 'the body' (i.e. this particular body of mine). The French version preserves the ambiguity.
[5] '... that is, my soul, by which I am what I am' (added in French version).
[6] '... certain modes of thinking which are quite special and distinct from me' (French version).
[7] '... between the shapes, movements and other modes or accidents of a body and the body which supports them' (French version).
[8] '... cannot be in me in so far as I am merely a thinking thing, since it does not presuppose any thought on my part' (French version).

62

from me – a substance which contains either formally or eminently all the reality which exists objectively[9] in the ideas produced by this faculty (as I have just noted). This substance is either a body, that is, a corporeal nature, in which case it will contain formally <and in fact> everything which is to be found objectively <or representatively> in the ideas; or else it is God, or some creature more noble than a body, in which case it will contain eminently whatever is to be found in the ideas. But since God is not a deceiver, it is quite clear that he does not transmit the ideas to me either directly from himself, or indirectly, via some creature which contains the objective reality of the ideas not formally but only eminently. For God has given me no faculty at all for recognizing any such source for these ideas; on the contrary, he has given me a great propensity to believe that they are produced by corporeal things. So I do not see 80 how God could be understood to be anything but a deceiver if the ideas were transmitted from a source other than corporeal things. It follows that corporeal things exist. They may not all exist in a way that exactly corresponds with my sensory grasp of them, for in many cases the grasp of the senses is very obscure and confused. But at least they possess all the properties which I clearly and distinctly understand, that is, all those which, viewed in general terms, are comprised within the subject-matter of pure mathematics.

What of the other aspects of corporeal things which are either particular (for example that the sun is of such and such a size or shape), or less clearly understood, such as light or sound or pain, and so on? Despite the high degree of doubt and uncertainty involved here, the very fact that God is not a deceiver, and the consequent impossibility of there being any falsity in my opinions which cannot be corrected by some other faculty supplied by God, offers me a sure hope that I can attain the truth even in these matters. Indeed, there is no doubt that everything that I am taught by nature contains some truth. For if nature is considered in its general aspect, then I understand by the term nothing other than God himself, or the ordered system of created things established by God. And by my own nature in particular I understand nothing other than the totality of things bestowed on me by God.

---

[9] For the terms 'formally', 'eminently' and 'objectively', see notes, pp. 32 and 33 above.

There is nothing that my own nature teaches me more vividly than that I have a body, and that when I feel pain there is something wrong with the body, and that when I am hungry or thirsty the body needs food and drink, and so on. So I should not doubt that there is some truth in this.

81 Nature also teaches me, by these sensations of pain, hunger, thirst and so on, that I am not merely present in my body as a sailor is present in a ship,[10] but that I am very closely joined and, as it were, intermingled with it, so that I and the body form a unit. If this were not so, I, who am nothing but a thinking thing, would not feel pain when the body was hurt, but would perceive the damage purely by the intellect, just as a sailor perceives by sight if anything in his ship is broken. Similarly, when the body needed food or drink, I should have an explicit understanding of the fact, instead of having confused sensations of hunger and thirst. For these sensations of hunger, thirst, pain and so on are nothing but confused modes of thinking which arise from the union and, as it were, intermingling of the mind with the body.

I am also taught by nature that various other bodies exist in the vicinity of my body, and that some of these are to be sought out and others avoided. And from the fact that I perceive by my senses a great variety of colours, sounds, smells and tastes, as well as differences in heat, hardness and the like, I am correct in inferring that the bodies which are the source of these various sensory perceptions possess differences corresponding to them, though perhaps not resembling them. Also, the fact that some of the perceptions are agreeable to me while others are disagreeable makes it quite certain that my body, or rather my whole self, in so far as I am a combination of body and mind, can be affected by the various beneficial or harmful bodies which surround it.

82 There are, however, many other things which I may appear to have been taught by nature, but which in reality I acquired not from nature but from a habit of making ill-considered judgements; and it is therefore quite possible that these are false. Cases in point are the belief that any space in which nothing is occurring to stimulate my senses must be empty; or that the heat in a body is something exactly resembling the idea of heat which is in me; or that when a body is white or green,

---

[10] '. . . as a pilot in his ship' (French version).

the selfsame whiteness or greenness which I perceive through my senses is present in the body; or that in a body which is bitter or sweet there is the selfsame taste which I experience, and so on; or, finally, that stars and towers and other distant bodies have the same size and shape which they present to my senses, and other examples of this kind. But to make sure that my perceptions in this matter are sufficiently distinct, I must more accurately define exactly what I mean when I say that I am taught something by nature. In this context I am taking nature to be something more limited than the totality of things bestowed on me by God. For this includes many things that belong to the mind alone – for example my perception that what is done cannot be undone, and all other things that are known by the natural light;[11] but at this stage I am not speaking of these matters. It also includes much that relates to the body alone, like the tendency to move in a downward direction, and so on; but I am not speaking of these matters either. My sole concern here is with what God has bestowed on me as a combination of mind and body. My nature, then, in this limited sense, does indeed teach me to avoid what induces a feeling of pain and to seek out what induces feelings of pleasure, and so on. But it does not appear to teach us to draw any conclusions from these sensory perceptions about things located outside us without waiting until the intellect has examined[12] the matter. For knowledge of the truth about such things seems to belong to the mind alone, not to the combination of mind and body. Hence, although a star has no greater 83 effect on my eye than the flame of a small light, that does not mean that there is any real or positive inclination in me to believe that the star is no bigger than the light; I have simply made this judgement from childhood onwards without any rational basis. Similarly, although I feel heat when I go near a fire and feel pain when I go too near, there is no convincing argument for supposing that there is something in the fire which resembles the heat, any more than for supposing that there is something which resembles the pain. There is simply reason to suppose that there is something in the fire, whatever it may eventually turn out to be, which produces in us the feelings of heat or pain. And likewise, even though there is nothing in any given space that stimulates the senses, it does not follow that there is no body there. In these cases and many others I see

[11] '. . . without any help from the body' (added in French version).
[12] '. . . carefully and maturely examined' (French version).

that I have been in the habit of misusing the order of nature. For the proper purpose of the sensory perceptions given me by nature is simply to inform the mind of what is beneficial or harmful for the composite of which the mind is a part; and to this extent they are sufficiently clear and distinct. But I misuse them by treating them as reliable touchstones for immediate judgements about the essential nature of the bodies located outside us; yet this is an area where they provide only very obscure information.

I have already looked in sufficient detail at how, notwithstanding the goodness of God, it may happen that my judgements are false. But a further problem now comes to mind regarding those very things which nature presents to me as objects which I should seek out or avoid, and also regarding the internal sensations, where I seem to have detected errors[13] – e.g. when someone is tricked by the pleasant taste of some food into eating the poison concealed inside it. Yet in this case, what the man's nature urges him to go for is simply what is responsible for the pleasant taste, and not the poison, which his nature knows nothing about. The only inference that can be drawn from this is that his nature is not omniscient. And this is not surprising, since man is a limited thing, and so it is only fitting that his perfection should be limited.

And yet it is not unusual for us to go wrong even in cases where nature does urge us towards something. Those who are ill, for example, may desire food or drink that will shortly afterwards turn out to be bad for them. Perhaps it may be said that they go wrong because their nature is disordered, but this does not remove the difficulty. A sick man is no less one of God's creatures than a healthy one, and it seems no less a contradiction to suppose that he has received from God a nature which deceives him. Yet a clock constructed with wheels and weights observes all the laws of its nature just as closely when it is badly made and tells the wrong time as when it completely fulfils the wishes of the clockmaker. In the same way, I might consider the body of a man as a kind of machine equipped with and made up of bones, nerves, muscles, veins, blood and skin in such a way that, even if there were no mind in it, it would still perform all the same movements as it now does in those cases where movement is not under the control of the will or, consequently, of the

84

---

[13] '. . . and thus seem to have been directly deceived by my nature' (added in French version).

mind.[14] I can easily see that if such a body suffers from dropsy, for example, and is affected by the dryness of the throat which normally produces in the mind the sensation of thirst, the resulting condition of the nerves and other parts will dispose the body to take a drink, with the result that the disease will be aggravated. Yet this is just as natural as the body's being stimulated by a similar dryness of the throat to take a drink when there is no such illness and the drink is beneficial. Admittedly, when I consider the purpose of the clock, I may say that it is departing from its nature when it does not tell the right time; and similarly when I consider the mechanism of the human body, I may think that, in relation to the movements which normally occur in it, it too is deviating from its nature if the throat is dry at a time when drinking is not beneficial to its continued health. But I am well aware that 'nature' as I have just used it has a very different significance from 'nature' in the other sense. As I have just used it, 'nature' is simply a label which depends on my thought; it is quite extraneous to the things to which it is applied, and depends simply on my comparison between the idea of a sick man and a badly-made clock, and the idea of a healthy man and a well-made clock. But by 'nature' in the other sense I understand something which is really to be found in the things themselves; in this sense, therefore, the term contains something of the truth.

When we say, then, with respect to the body suffering from dropsy, that it has a disordered nature because it has a dry throat and yet does not need drink, the term 'nature' is here used merely as an extraneous label. However, with respect to the composite, that is, the mind united with this body, what is involved is not a mere label, but a true error of nature, namely that it is thirsty at a time when drink is going to cause it harm. It thus remains to inquire how it is that the goodness of God does not prevent nature, in this sense, from deceiving us.

The first observation I make at this point is that there is a great difference between the mind and the body, inasmuch as the body is by its very nature always divisible, while the mind is utterly indivisible. For when I consider the mind, or myself in so far as I am merely a thinking thing, I am unable to distinguish any parts within myself; I understand myself to be something quite single and complete. Although the whole

85

86

---

[14] '. . . but occurs merely as a result of the disposition of the organs' (French version).

mind seems to be united to the whole body, I recognize that if a foot or arm or any other part of the body is cut off, nothing has thereby been taken away from the mind. As for the faculties of willing, of understanding, of sensory perception and so on, these cannot be termed parts of the mind, since it is one and the same mind that wills, and understands and has sensory perceptions. By contrast, there is no corporeal or extended thing that I can think of which in my thought I cannot easily divide into parts; and this very fact makes me understand that it is divisible. This one argument would be enough to show me that the mind is completely different from the body, even if I did not already know as much from other considerations.

My next observation is that the mind is not immediately affected by all parts of the body, but only by the brain, or perhaps just by one small part of the brain, namely the part which is said to contain the 'common' sense.[15] Every time this part of the brain is in a given state, it presents the same signals to the mind, even though the other parts of the body may be in a different condition at the time. This is established by countless observations, which there is no need to review here.

I observe, in addition, that the nature of the body is such that whenever any part of it is moved by another part which is some distance away, it can always be moved in the same fashion by any of the parts which lie in between, even if the more distant part does nothing. For example, in a cord ABCD, if one end D is pulled so that the other end A moves, the exact same movement could have been brought about if one of the intermediate points B or C had been pulled, and D had not moved at all. In similar fashion, when I feel a pain in my foot, physiology tells me that this happens by means of nerves distributed throughout the foot, and that these nerves are like cords which go from the foot right up to the brain. When the nerves are pulled in the foot, they in turn pull on inner parts of the brain to which they are attached, and produce a certain motion in them; and nature has laid it down that this motion should produce in the mind a sensation of pain, as occurring in the foot. But since these nerves, in passing from the foot to the brain, must pass

87

---

[15] The supposed faculty which integrates the data from the five specialized senses (the notion goes back ultimately to Aristotle). 'The seat of the common sense must be very mobile, to receive all the impressions which come from the senses; but it must also be of such a kind as to be movable only by the spirits which transmit these impressions. Only the *conation* [pineal gland] fits this description' (letter to Mersenne, 21 April 1641: AT III 362; CSMK 180).

through the calf, the thigh, the lumbar region, the back and the neck, it can happen that, even if it is not the part in the foot but one of the intermediate parts which is being pulled, the same motion will occur in the brain as occurs when the foot is hurt, and so it will necessarily come about that the mind feels the same sensation of pain. And we must suppose the same thing happens with regard to any other sensation.

My final observation is that any given movement occurring in the part of the brain that immediately affects the mind produces just one corresponding sensation; and hence the best system that could be devised is that it should produce the one sensation which, of all possible sensations, is most especially and most frequently conducive to the preservation of the healthy man. And experience shows that the sensations which nature has given us are all of this kind; and so there is absolutely nothing to be found in them that does not bear witness to the power and goodness of God. For example, when the nerves in the foot are set in motion in a 88 violent and unusual manner, this motion, by way of the spinal cord, reaches the inner parts of the brain, and there gives the mind its signal for having a certain sensation, namely the sensation of a pain as occurring in the foot. This stimulates the mind to do its best to get rid of the cause of the pain, which it takes to be harmful to the foot. It is true that God could have made the nature of man such that this particular motion in the brain indicated something else to the mind; it might, for example, have made the mind aware of the actual motion occurring in the brain, or in the foot, or in any of the intermediate regions; or it might have indicated something else entirely. But there is nothing else which would have been so conducive to the continued well-being of the body. In the same way, when we need drink, there arises a certain dryness in the throat; this sets in motion the nerves of the throat, which in turn move the inner parts of the brain. This motion produces in the mind a sensation of thirst, because the most useful thing for us to know about the whole business is that we need drink in order to stay healthy. And so it is in the other cases.

It is quite clear from all this that, notwithstanding the immense goodness of God, the nature of man as a combination of mind and body is such that it is bound to mislead him from time to time. For there may be some occurrence, not in the foot but in one of the other areas through which the nerves travel in their route from the foot to the brain, or even in the brain itself; and if this cause produces the same motion which is generally produced by injury to the foot, then pain will be felt as if it were in the foot. This deception of the senses is natural, because a given motion in the brain must always produce the same sensation in the mind; and the origin of the motion in question is much more often going to be something which is hurting the foot, rather than something existing elsewhere. So it is reasonable that this motion should always indicate to the mind a pain in the foot rather than in any other part of the body. Again, dryness of the throat may sometimes arise not, as it normally does, from the fact that a drink is necessary to the health of the body, but from some quite opposite cause, as happens in the case of the man with dropsy. Yet it is much better that it should mislead on this occasion than that it should always mislead when the body is in good health. And the same goes for the other cases.

This consideration is the greatest help to me, not only for noticing all the errors to which my nature is liable, but also for enabling me to correct or avoid them without difficulty. For I know that in matters regarding the well-being of the body, all my senses report the truth much more frequently than not. Also, I can almost always make use of more than one sense to investigate the same thing; and in addition, I can use both my memory, which connects present experiences with preceding ones, and my intellect, which has by now examined all the causes of error. Accordingly, I should not have any further fears about the falsity of what my senses tell me every day; on the contrary, the exaggerated doubts of the last few days should be dismissed as laughable. This applies especially to the principal reason for doubt, namely my inability to distinguish between being asleep and being awake. For I now notice that there is a vast difference between the two, in that dreams are never linked by memory with all the other actions of life as waking experiences are. If, while I am awake, anyone were suddenly to appear to me and then disappear immediately, as happens in sleep, so that I could not see where he had come from or where he had gone to, it would not be unreasonable for me to judge that he was a ghost, or a vision created in my brain,[16] rather than a real man. But when I distinctly see where things come from and where and when they come to me, and when I can connect my perceptions of them with the whole of the rest of my life without a break,

---

[16] '... like those that are formed in the brain when I sleep' (added in French version).

then I am quite certain that when I encounter these things I am not asleep but awake. And I ought not to have even the slightest doubt of their reality if, after calling upon all the senses as well as my memory and my intellect in order to check them, I receive no conflicting reports from any of these sources. For from the fact that God is not a deceiver it follows that in cases like these I am completely free from error. But since the pressure of things to be done does not always allow us to stop and make such a meticulous check, it must be admitted that in this human life we are often liable to make mistakes about particular things, and we must acknowledge the weakness of our nature.

The Objections of Various Learned Men
to the foregoing Meditations
with the Replies of the Author
[Selections]

[On the First Meditation]

[The rejection of previous beliefs]

[It is objected that] I am asking for something impossible in wanting us AT IXA (203) to give up every kind of preconceived opinion ... But [my critic] has not realized that the term 'preconceived opinion' applies not to all the notions which are in our mind (which I admit it is impossible for us to get rid of) but only to all the opinions which we have continued to accept as a result of the previous judgements that we have made. And since making or not making a judgement is an act of will (as I have explained in the appropriate place)[1] it is evident that it is something in our power. For, after all, in order to get rid of every kind of preconceived opinion, all we need to do is resolve not to affirm or deny anything that we have previously affirmed or denied until we have examined it afresh. But this does not entail that we cease to retain all the same notions in our memory. Nevertheless, I did say that there was some difficulty expelling from our belief everything we have previously accepted. One reason for this is that before we can decide to doubt, we need some reason for doubting; and that is why in my First Meditation I put forward the principal reasons for doubt. Another reason is that no matter how much we resolved not to assert or deny anything, we easily forget our resolution afterwards if we have not strongly impressed it on

---

[1] Med. IV, p. 44ff, above.

75

our memory; and this is why I suggested that we should think about it very carefully. [*Appendix to Fifth Objections and Replies*: CSM II 270][2]

* * *

AT VII 481

Here I shall employ an everyday example to explain to my critic the rationale for my procedure, so as to prevent him misunderstanding it, or having the gall to pretend he does not understand it, in future. Suppose he had a basket full of apples and, being worried that some of the apples were rotten, wanted to take out the rotten ones to prevent the rot spreading. How would he proceed? Would he not begin by tipping the whole lot out of the basket? And would not the next step be to cast his eye over each apple in turn, and pick up and put back in the basket only those he saw to be sound, leaving the others? In just the same way, those who have never philosophized correctly have various opinions in their minds which they have begun to store up since childhood, and which they therefore have reason to believe may in many cases be false. They then attempt to separate the false beliefs from the others, so as to prevent their contaminating the rest and making the whole lot uncertain. Now the best way they can accomplish this is to reject all their beliefs together in one go, as if they were all uncertain and false. They can then go over each belief in turn and re-adopt only those which they recognize to be true and indubitable. Thus I was right to begin by rejecting all my beliefs ... [*Seventh Replies*: CSM II 324]

[The reliability of the senses]

When I said that the entire testimony of the senses should be regarded as uncertain and even as false, I was quite serious; indeed this point is so necessary for an understanding of my *Meditations* that if anyone is unwilling or unable to accept it, he will be incapable of producing any objection that deserves a reply. However we must note the distinction which I have insisted on in several passages between the actions of life and

---

[2] This extract is from Descartes's extended 'Letter to Clerselier', which was included in the first French translation of the *Meditations, Objections and Replies*, translated by Claude Clerselier, published in 1647. It responds to some additional criticisms made by Pierre Gassendi, author of the Fifth Set of Objections, which Gassendi had published in 1644. See 'Note on the Text and the Translation', p. lii, above, and see further CSM II 268, note 1.

the investigation of the truth.[3] For when it is a question of organizing our   351
life, it would, of course be foolish not to trust the senses, and the sceptics
who neglected human affairs to the point where friends had to stop them
falling off precipices deserved to be laughed at. Hence I pointed out in one
passage that no sane person ever seriously doubts such things.[4] But when
our inquiry concerns what can be known with complete certainty by the
human intellect, it is quite unreasonable to refuse to reject these things in
all seriousness as doubtful and even as false; the purpose here is to come to
recognize that certain other things which cannot be rejected in this way are
thereby more certain and in reality better known to us. [*Fifth Replies*:
CSM II 243]

* * *

Although there is deception or falsity, it is not to be found in the
senses; for the senses are quite passive and report only appearances,
which must appear in the way they do owing to their causes. The error
or falsity is in the judgement or the mind, which is not circumspect
enough and does not notice that things at a distance will for one reason
or another appear smaller and more blurred than when they are nearby,
and so on. Nevertheless, when deception occurs, we must not deny that
it exists; the only difficulty is whether it occurs all the time, thus
making it impossible for us ever to be sure of the truth of anything
which we perceive by the senses.

It is quite unnecessary to look for obvious examples here. With regard   333
to the cases you mention, or rather put forward as presenting a problem,
I will simply say that it seems to be quite uncontroversial that when we
look at a tower from nearby, and touch it, we are sure that it is square,
even though when we were further off we had occasion to judge it to be
round, or at any rate to doubt whether it was square or round or some
other shape.

Similarly the feeling of pain which still appears to occur in the foot or
hand after these limbs have been amputated[5] may sometimes give rise to
deception, because the spirits responsible for sensation have been accustomed to pass into the limbs and produce a sensation in them. But such
deception occurs, of course, in people who have suffered amputation;

---

[3] See pp. 12 and 66, above.   [4] Cf. Synopsis, p. 13, above.   [5] See Med. VI, pp. 60–1, above.

those whose bodies are intact are so certain that they feel pain in the foot or hand when they see it is pricked, that they cannot be in doubt.

Again, since during our lives we are alternately awake or dreaming, a dream may give rise to deception because things may appear to be present when they are not in fact present. But we do not dream all the time, and for as long as we are really awake we cannot doubt whether we are awake or dreaming. [*Fifth Objections*: CSM II 230–1]

Here you show quite clearly that you are relying entirely on a preconceived opinion which you have never got rid of. You maintain that we never suspect any falsity in situations where we have never detected it, and hence that when we look at a tower from nearby and touch it we are sure that it is square, if it appears square. You also 386 maintain that when we are really awake, we cannot doubt whether we are awake or asleep, and so on. But you have no reason to think that you have previously noticed all the circumstances in which error can occur; moreover, it is easy to prove that you are from time to time mistaken in matters which you accept as certain. [*Fifth Replies*: CSM II 264]

(418) Our *ninth* and most worrying difficulty is your assertion that we ought to mistrust the operations of the senses and that the reliability of the intellect is much greater than that of the senses.[6] But how can the intellect enjoy any certainty unless it has previously derived it from the senses when they are working as they should? How can it correct a mistake made by one of the senses unless some other sense first corrects the mistake? Owing to refraction, a stick which is in fact straight appears bent in water. What corrects the error? The intellect? Not at all; it is the sense of touch. And the same sort of thing must be taken to occur in other cases. Hence if you have recourse to all your senses when they are in good working order, and they all give the same report, you will achieve the greatest certainty of which man is naturally capable. But you will often fail to achieve it if you trust the operations of the mind; for the mind often goes astray in just those areas where it had previously supposed doubt to be impossible. [*Sixth Objections*: CSM II 281–2]

When people say that a stick in water 'appears bent because of refraction', this is the same as saying that it appears to us in a way which

---

[6] See above, Med. I, p. 16; Med. II, p. 25; Med. VI, p. 65.

would lead a child to judge that it was bent – and which may even lead us to make the same judgement, following the preconceived opinions which we have become accustomed to accept from our earliest years. But I cannot grant my critics' further comment that this error is corrected 'not by the intellect but by the sense of touch'. As a result of touching it, we may judge that the stick is straight, and the kind of judgement involved may be the kind we have been accustomed to make since childhood, and which is therefore referred to as the 'sense' of touch. But the sense alone does not suffice to correct the visual error: in addition we need to have some degree of reason which tells us that in this case we should believe the judgement based on touch rather than that elicited by vision. And since we did not have this power of reasoning in our infancy, it must be attributed not to the senses but to the intellect. Thus even in the very example my critics produce, it is the intellect alone which corrects the error of the senses; and it is not possible to produce any case in which error results from our trusting the operation of the mind more than the senses. [*Sixth Replies*: CSM II 296] 439

[The dreaming argument]

From what is said in this Meditation it is clear enough that there is no criterion enabling us to distinguish our dreams from the waking state and from veridical sensations. And hence the images we have when we are awake and having sensations are not accidents that inhere in external objects, and are no proof that any such external object exists at all. So if we follow our senses, without exercising our reason in any way, we shall be justified in doubting whether anything exists. I acknowledge the correctness of this Meditation. But since Plato and other ancient philosophers discussed this uncertainty in the objects of the senses, and since the difficulty of distinguishing the waking state from dreams is commonly pointed out, I am sorry that the author, who is so outstanding in the field of original speculations, should be publishing this ancient material. [*Third Objections*: CSM II 121] (171)

The arguments for doubting, which the philosopher here accepts as valid, are ones that I was presenting as merely plausible. I was not trying to sell them as novelties, but had a threefold aim in mind when I used them. Partly I wanted to prepare my readers' minds for the study of the 172 things which are related to the intellect, and help them to distinguish these things from corporeal things; and such arguments seem to be wholly necessary for this purpose. Partly I introduced the arguments so that I could reply to them in the subsequent Meditations. And partly I wanted to show the firmness of the truths which I propound later on, in the light of the fact that they cannot be shaken by these metaphysical doubts. Thus I was not looking for praise when I set out these arguments; but I think I could not have left them out, any more than a medical writer can leave out the description of a disease when he wants to explain how it can be cured. [*Third Replies*: CSM II 121]

[Certainty in dreams]

Has it never happened to you, as it has to many people, that things seemed clear and certain to you while you were dreaming, but that afterwards you discovered that they were doubtful or false? It is indeed
457 'prudent never to trust completely those who have deceived you even once'.[7] 'But', you reply, 'matters of the utmost certainty are quite different. They are such that they cannot appear doubtful even to those who are dreaming or mad.' But are you really serious in what you say? Can you pretend that matters of the utmost certainty cannot appear doubtful even to dreamers or madmen? What are these utterly certain matters? If things which are ridiculous or absurd sometimes appear certain, even utterly certain, to people who are asleep or insane, then why should not things which are certain, even utterly certain, appear false and doubtful? I know a man who once, when falling asleep, heard the clock strike four, and counted the strokes as 'one, one, one, one'. It then seemed to him that there was something absurd about this, and he shouted out: 'That clock must be going mad; it has struck one o'clock four times!' Is there really anything so absurd or irrational that it could not come into the mind of someone who is asleep or raving? There are no limits to what a dreamer may not 'prove' or believe, and indeed congratulate himself on, as if he had managed to invent some splendid thought. [*Seventh Objections*: CSM II 306]

---

[7] Med. I, above, p. 16.

My critic could have concluded from my writings that everything that anyone clearly and distinctly perceives is true, although the person in question may from time to time doubt whether he is dreaming or awake, and may even, if you like, be dreaming or mad. For no matter who the perceiver is, nothing can be clearly and distinctly perceived without its being just as we perceive it to be, i.e. without being true. But because it requires some care to make a proper distinction between what is clearly and distinctly perceived and what merely seems or appears to be, I am not surprised that my worthy critic should here mistake the one for the other. [*Seventh Replies*: CSM II 310]

462

[The scope of doubt]

I said at the end of the First Meditation that we may doubt all those things which we have not yet perceived with sufficient clarity, since our doubt is based on 'powerful and well thought-out reasons'. But I said this because at that point I was dealing merely with the kind of extreme doubt which, as I frequently stressed, is metaphysical and exaggerated and in no way to be transferred to practical life.[8] It was doubt of this type to which I was referring when I said that everything that could give rise to the slightest suspicion should be regarded as a sound reason for doubt. But my friendly and ingenious critic ... puts forward as an example of the things that I said we could doubt 'for powerful reasons' the question of whether there is an earth, or whether I have a body, and so on; the effect is that the reader, if he knows nothing of my 'metaphysical' doubt and refers the doubt to practical life, may think that I am not of sound mind.

460

... So long as we attend to a truth which we perceive very clearly, we cannot doubt it. But when, as often happens, we are not attending to any truth in this way, then even though we remember that we have previously perceived many things very clearly, nevertheless there will be nothing which we may not justly doubt so long as we do not know that whatever we clearly perceive is true. But my ... critic here takes 'nothing' quite differently. From the fact that at one point I said that there was nothing that we might not doubt – namely in the First

[8] Med. I, p. 19; Med. III, p. 30; Med. VI, p. 70; Synopsis, p. 12.

Meditation, where I was supposing that I was not attending to anything that I clearly perceived – he draws the conclusion that I am unable to know anything certain, even in the following Meditations. This is to suggest that the reasons which may from time to time give us cause to doubt something are not legitimate or sound unless they prove that the same thing must be permanently in doubt. [*Seventh Replies*: CSM II 308–9]

[On the Second Meditation]

[Cogito ergo sum ('I am thinking, therefore I exist')]

I see that you conclude that this proposition, *I am, I exist*, is true whenever it is put forward by you or conceived in your mind.[1] But I do not see that 259 you needed all this apparatus, when on other grounds you were certain, and it was true, that you existed. You could have made the same inference from any one of your other actions, since it is known by the natural light that whatever acts exists. [*Fifth Objections*: CSM II 180]

When you say that I 'could have made the same inference from any one (352) of my other actions' you are far from the truth, since I am not wholly certain of any of my actions, with the sole exception of thought (in using the word 'certain' I am referring to metaphysical certainty, which is the sole issue at this point). I may not, for example, make the inference 'I am walking, therefore I exist', except in so far as the awareness of walking is a thought. The inference is certain only if applied to this awareness, and not to the movement of the body which sometimes – in the case of dreams – is not occurring at all, despite the fact that I seem to myself to be walking. Hence from the fact that I think I am walking I can very well infer the existence of a mind which has this thought, but not the existence of a body that walks. And the same applies in other cases. [*Fifth Replies*: CSM II 244]

* * *

---

[1] Above, p. 21.

83

When someone says 'I am thinking, therefore I am, or I exist', he does not deduce existence from thought by means of a syllogism, but recognizes it as something self-evident by a simple intuition of the mind. This is clear from the fact that if he were deducing it by means of a syllogism, he would have to have had previous knowledge of the major premiss 'Everything which thinks is, or exists'; yet in fact he learns it from experiencing in his own case that it is impossible that he should think without existing. It is in the nature of our mind to construct general propositions on the basis of our knowledge of particular ones. [*Second Replies*: CSM II 100]

141

* * *

413 From the fact that we are thinking it does not seem to be entirely certain that we exist. For in order to be certain that you are thinking you must know what thought or thinking is, and what your existence is; but since you do not yet know what these things are, how can you know that you are thinking or that you exist? Thus neither when you say 'I am thinking' nor when you add 'therefore, I exist' do you really know what you are saying. Indeed, you do not even know that you are saying or thinking anything, since this seems to require that you should know that you know what you are saying; and this in turn requires that you be aware of knowing that you know what you are saying, and so on *ad infinitum*. Hence it is clear that you cannot know whether you exist or even whether you are thinking. [*Sixth Objections*: CSM II 278]

(422) It is true that no one can be certain that he is thinking or that he exists unless he knows what thought is and what existence is. But this does not require reflective knowledge, or the kind of knowledge that is acquired by means of demonstrations; still less does it require knowledge of reflective knowledge, i.e. knowing that we know, and knowing that we know that we know, and so on *ad infinitum*. This kind of knowledge cannot possibly be obtained about anything. It is quite sufficient that we should know it by that internal awareness which always precedes reflective knowledge. This inner awareness of one's thought and existence is so innate in all men that, although we may pretend that we do not have it if we are over whelmed by preconceived opinions and pay more attention to words than to their meanings, we cannot in fact fail to have it. Thus when anyone notices that he is thinking and that it follows from this that

84

he exists, even though he may never before have asked what thought is or what existence is, he still cannot fail to have sufficient knowledge of them both to satisfy himself in this regard. [*Sixth Replies*: CSM II 285]

[Sum res cogitans ('I am a thinking thing')]

I am a thinking thing: correct. For from the fact that I think, or have an image (whether I am awake or dreaming), it can be inferred that I am thinking; for 'I think' and 'I am thinking' mean the same thing. And from the fact that I am thinking it follows that I exist, since that which thinks is not nothing. But when the author adds 'that is, I am a mind, or intelligence, or intellect or reason',[2] a doubt arises. It does not seem to be a valid argument to say 'I am thinking, therefore I am thought' or 'I am using my intellect, hence I am an intellect.' I might just as well say 'I am walking, therefore I am a walk.' M. Descartes is identifying the thing which understands with intellection, which is an act of that which understands. Or at least he is identifying the thing which understands with the intellect, which is a power of that which understands. Yet all philosophers make a distinction between a subject and its faculties and acts, i.e. between a subject and its properties and its essences: an entity is one thing, its essence is another. Hence it may be that the thing that thinks is the subject to which mind, reason or intellect belong; and this subject may thus be something corporeal. The contrary is assumed, not proved. Yet this inference is the basis of the conclusion which M. Descartes seems to want to establish. [*Third Objections*: CSM II 122]   173

When I said 'that is, I am a mind, or intelligence, or intellect or reason',   (174)
what I meant by these terms was not mere faculties, but things endowed with the faculty of thought. This is what the first two terms are commonly taken to mean by everyone; and the second two are often understood in this sense. I stated this point so explicitly, and in so many places, that it seems to me there was no room for doubt.

There is no comparison here between 'a walk' and 'thought'. 'A walk' is usually taken to refer simply to the act of walking, whereas 'thought' is sometimes taken to refer to the act, sometimes to the faculty, and sometimes to the thing which possesses the faculty.

---

[2] Above, pp. 22–3.

I do not say that the thing which understands is the same as intellection. Nor, indeed, do I identify the thing which understands with the intellect, if 'the intellect' is taken to refer to a faculty; they are identical only if 'the intellect' is taken to refer to the thing which understands. Now I freely admit that I used the most abstract terms I could in order to refer to the thing or substance in question, because I wanted to strip away from it everything that did not belong to it. This philosopher, by contrast, uses absolutely concrete words, namely 'subject', 'matter' and 'body', to refer to this thinking thing, because he wants to prevent its being separated from the body. [*Third Replies*: CSM II 123]

* * *

What you promised in the title of this Meditation, namely that it would establish that the human mind is better known than the body, has not, so far as I can see, been achieved. Your aim was not to prove that the human mind exists, or that its existence is better known than the existence of the body, since its existence, at all events, is something which no one questions. Your intention was surely to establish that its nature is better known than the nature of the body, and this you have not managed to do. As regards the nature of the body, you have, O Mind, listed all the things we know: extension, shape, occupation of space, and so on. But what, after all your efforts, have you told us about yourself? You are not a bodily structure, you are not air, not a wind, not a thing which walks or senses, you are not this and not that. Even if we grant these results (though some of them you did in fact reject), they are not what we are waiting for. They are simply negative results; but the question is not what you are not, but what you are. And so you refer us to your principal result, that you are a thing that thinks – i.e. a thing that doubts, affirms etc. But to say first of all that you are a 'thing' is not to give any information. This is a general, imprecise and vague word which applies no more to you than it does to anything in the entire world that is not simply a nothing. You are a 'thing'; that is, you are not nothing, or, what comes to the same thing, you are something. But a stone is something and not nothing, and so is a fly, and so is everything else. When you go on to say that you are a *thinking* thing, then we know what you are saying; but we knew it already, and it was not what we were asking you to tell us. Who doubts that you are thinking? What we are

276

unclear about, what we are looking for, is that inner substance of yours whose property is to think. Your conclusion should be related to this inquiry, and should tell us not that you are a thinking thing, but what sort of thing this 'you' who thinks really is. If we are asking about wine, and looking for the kind of knowledge which is superior to common knowledge, it will hardly be enough for you to say 'wine is a liquid thing, which is compressed from grapes, white or red, sweet, intoxicating' and so on. You will have to attempt to investigate and somehow explain its internal substance, showing how it can be seen to be manufactured from spirits, tartar, the distillate, and other ingredients mixed together in such and such quantities and proportions. Similarly, given that you are looking for knowledge of yourself which is superior to common knowledge (that is, the kind of knowledge we have had up till now), you must see that it is certainly not enough for you to announce that you are a 277 thing that thinks and doubts and understands, etc. You should carefully scrutinize yourself and conduct, as it were, a kind of chemical investigation of yourself, if you are to succeed in uncovering and explaining to us your internal substance. If you provide such an explanation, we shall ourselves doubtless be able to investigate whether or not you are better known than the body whose nature we know so much about through anatomy, chemistry, so many other sciences, so many senses and so many experiments. [*Fifth Objections*: CSM II 192–3]

I am surprised that you should say here that all my considerations about the wax demonstrate that I distinctly know that I exist, but not that I know what I am or what my nature is; for one thing cannot be demonstrated without the other. Nor do I see what more you expect here, unless it is to be told what colour or smell or taste the human mind has, or the proportions of salt, sulphur and mercury from which it is compounded. You want us, you say, to conduct 'a kind of chemical investigation' of the mind, as we would of wine. This is indeed worthy of you, O Flesh, and of all those who have only a very confused conception 360 of everything, and so do not know the proper questions to ask about each thing. But as for me, I have never thought that anything more is required to reveal a substance than its various attributes; thus the more attributes of a given substance we know, the more perfectly we understand its nature. Now we can distinguish many different attributes in the wax: one, that it is white; two, that it is hard; three, that it can be melted; and so on. And there are correspondingly many attributes in the mind: one, that it has the power of knowing the whiteness of the wax; two, that it has the power of knowing its hardness; three, that it has the power of knowing that it can lose its hardness (i.e. melt), and so on. (Someone can have knowledge of the hardness without thereby having knowledge of the whiteness, e.g. a man born blind; and so on in other cases.) The clear inference from this is that we know more attributes in the case of our mind than we do in the case of anything else. For no matter how many attributes we recognize in any given thing, we can always list a corresponding number of attributes in the mind which it has in virtue of knowing the attributes of the thing; and hence the nature of the mind is the one we know best of all. [*Fifth Replies*: CSM II 248–9]

* * *

(413) When you say you are thinking and that you exist, someone might maintain that you are mistaken, and are not thinking but are merely in motion, and that you are nothing else but corporeal motion. For no one has yet been able to grasp that demonstration of yours by which you think you have proved that what you call thought cannot be a kind of corporeal motion. Have you used your method of analysis to separate off all the motions of that rarefied matter of yours? Is this what makes you so certain? And can you therefore show us (for we will give our closest attention and our powers of perception are, we think, reasonably keen) that it is self-contradictory that our thoughts should be reducible to these corporeal motions? [*Sixth Objections*: CSM II 278]

When someone notices that he is thinking, then, given that he understands what motion is, it is quite impossible that he should believe that he is mistaken and is 'not thinking but merely in motion'. Since the idea or notion which he has of thought is quite different from his idea of

(423) corporeal motion, he must necessarily understand the one as different from the other. Because, however, he is accustomed to attribute many different properties to one and the same subject without being aware of any connection between them, he may possibly be inclined to doubt, or may even affirm, that he is one and the same being who thinks and who moves from place to place. Notice that if we have different ideas of two things, there are two ways in which they can be taken to be one and the same thing: either in virtue of the unity or identity of their nature, or else

merely in respect of unity of composition. For example, the ideas which we have of shape and of motion are not the same, nor are our ideas of understanding and volition, nor are those of bones and flesh, nor are those of thought and of an extended thing. But nevertheless we clearly perceive that the same substance which is such that it is capable of taking on a shape is also such that it is capable of being moved, and hence that that which has shape and that which is mobile are one and the same in virtue of a unity of nature. Similarly, the thing that understands and the thing that wills are one and the same in virtue of a unity of nature. But our perception is different in the case of the thing that we consider under the form of bone and that which we consider under the form of flesh; and hence we cannot take them as one and the same thing in virtue of a unity of nature but can regard them as the same only in respect of unity of composition – i.e. in so far as it is one and the same animal which has bones and flesh. But now the question is whether we perceive that a thinking thing and an extended thing are one and the same by a unity of nature. That is to say, do we find between thought and extension the same kind of affinity or connection that we find between shape and motion, or understanding and volition? Alternatively, when they are said to be 'one and the same' is this not rather 424 in respect of unity of composition, in so far as they are found in the same man, just as bones and flesh are found in the same animal? The latter view is the one I maintain, since I observe a distinction or difference in every respect between the nature of an extended thing and that of a thinking thing, which is no less than that to be found between bones and flesh . . .

My critics ask whether I have used my method of analysis to separate off all the motions of that rarefied matter of mine. Is this (they ask) what makes me certain? And can I therefore show my critics, who are most attentive and (they think) reasonably perceptive men, that it is self-contradictory that our thoughts should be reduced to corporeal motions? By 'reduced' I take it that they mean that our thoughts and corporeal motions are one and the same. My reply is that I am very certain of this point, but I cannot guarantee that others can be convinced of it, however attentive they may be, and however keen, in their own judgement, their powers of perception may be. I cannot guarantee that they will be persuaded, at least so long as they focus their attention not on things which are objects of pure understanding but only on things which can be imagined. This mistake has obviously been made by those who have

425

imagined that the distinction between thought and motion is to be understood by making divisions within some kind of rarefied matter. The only way of understanding the distinction is to realize that the notions of a thinking thing and an extended or mobile thing are completely different, and independent of each other; and it is self-contradictory to suppose that things that we clearly understand as different and independent could not be separated, at least by God. Thus, however often we find them in one and the same subject – e.g. when we find thought and corporeal motion in the same man – we should not therefore think that they are one and the same in virtue of a unity of nature, but should regard them as the same only in respect of unity of composition. [*Sixth Replies*: CSM II 285–7]

[The nature of thought]

(214). The author lays it down as certain that there can be nothing in him, in so far as he is a thinking thing, of which he is not aware,[3] but it seems to me that this is false. For by 'himself, in so far as he is a thinking thing', he means simply his mind, in so far as it is distinct from the body. But all of us can surely see that there may be many things in our mind of which the mind is not aware. The mind of an infant in its mother's womb has the power of thought, but is not aware of it. And there are countless similar examples, which I will pass over. [*Fourth Objections*: CSM II 150]

As to the fact that there can be nothing in the mind, in so far as it is a thinking thing, of which it is not aware, this seems to me to be self-evident. For there is nothing that we can understand to be in the mind, regarded in this way, that is not a thought or dependent on a thought. If it were not a thought or dependent on a thought it would not belong to the mind *qua* thinking thing; and we cannot have any thought of which we are not aware at the very moment when it is in us. In view of this I do not doubt that the mind begins to think as soon as it is implanted in the body of an infant, and that it is immediately aware of its thoughts, even though it does not remember this afterwards because the impressions of these thoughts do not remain in the memory.

---

[3] Cf. Med. III, p 39.

But it must be noted that, although we are always actually aware of the acts or operations of our minds, we are not always aware of the mind's faculties or powers, except potentially. By this I mean that when we concentrate on employing one of our faculties, then immediately, if the faculty in question resides in our mind, we become actually aware of it, and hence we may deny that it is in the mind if we are not capable of becoming aware of it. [*Fourth Replies*: CSM II 171–2] 247

***

By 'thinking' you may mean that you understand and will and imagine and have sensations, and that you think in such a way that you can contemplate and consider your thought by a reflexive act. This would mean that when you think, you know and consider that you are thinking (and this is really what it is to be conscious and to have conscious awareness of some activity). Such consciousness, you claim, is a property 534 of a faculty or thing that is superior to matter and is wholly spiritual, and it is in this sense that you are a mind or a spirit. This claim is one you have not made before, but which should have been made, and which I was waiting for you to make; indeed, I often wanted to suggest it when I saw your method struggling ineffectively to bring it forth. But the claim, although *sound*, is nothing *new*, since we all heard it from our teachers long ago, and they heard it from their teachers, and so on, I would think, right back to Adam. [*Seventh Objections*: CSM II 364]

My critic says that to enable a substance to be superior to matter and wholly spiritual (and he insists on using the term 'mind' only in this restricted sense), it is not sufficient for it to think: it is further required that it should think that it is thinking, by means of a reflexive act, or that it should have awareness of its own thought. This is as deluded as our bricklayer's saying that a person who is skilled in architecture must employ a reflexive act to ponder on the fact that he has this skill before he can be an architect. It may in fact be that all architects frequently reflect on the fact that they have this skill, or at least are capable of so reflecting. But it is obvious that an architect does not need to perform this reflexive act in order to be an architect. And equally, this kind of pondering or reflecting is not required in order for a thinking substance to be superior to matter. The initial thought by means of which we become aware of something does not differ from the second thought by

91

means of which we become aware that we were aware of it, any more than this second thought differs from the third thought by means of which we become aware that we were aware that we were aware. And if it is conceded that a corporeal thing has the first kind of thought, then there is not the slightest reason to deny that it can have the second. Accordingly, it must be stressed that my critic commits a much more dangerous error in this respect than does the poor bricklayer. He removes the true and most clearly intelligible feature which differentiates corporeal things from incorporeal ones, *viz.* that the latter think, but not the former; and in its place he substitutes a feature which cannot in any way be regarded as essential, namely that incorporeal things reflect on their thinking, but corporeal ones do not. Hence he does everything he 560 can to hinder our understanding of the real distinction between the human mind and the body. [*Seventh Replies*: CSM II 382]

[The piece of wax]

Next you introduce the example of the wax, and you spend some time explaining that the so-called accidents of the wax are one thing, and the wax itself, or substance of the wax, is another. You say that in order to have a distinct perception of the wax itself or its substance we need only the mind or intellect, and not sensation or imagination.[4] But the first point is just what everyone commonly asserts, *viz.* that the concept of the wax or its substance can be abstracted from the concepts of its accidents. But does this really imply that the substance or nature of the wax is itself distinctly conceived? Besides the colour, the shape, the fact that it can melt, etc. we conceive that there is something which is the subject of the accidents and changes we observe; but what this subject is, or what its nature is, we do not know. This always eludes us; and it is only a kind of conjecture that leads us to think that there must be something underneath the accidents. So I am amazed at how you can 272 say that once the forms have been stripped off like clothes, you perceive more perfectly and evidently what the wax is. Admittedly, you perceive that the wax or its substance must be something over and above such forms; but what this something is you do not perceive, unless you are

---

[4] Cf. above, pp. 25–6.

misleading us. For this 'something' is not revealed to you in the way in which a man can be revealed when, after first of all seeing just his hat and garments, we then remove the clothes so as to find out who and what he is. Moreover, when you think you somehow perceive this underlying 'something', how, may I ask, do you do so? Do you not perceive it as something spread out and extended? For you do not conceive of it as a point, although it is the kind of thing whose extension expands and contracts. And since this kind of extension is not infinite but has limits, do you not conceive of the thing as having some kind of shape? And when you seem as it were to see it, do you not attach to it some sort of colour, albeit not a distinct one? You certainly take it to be something more solid, and so more visible, than a mere void. Hence even your 'understanding' turns out to be some sort of imagination. If you say you conceive of the wax apart from any extension, shape or colour, then you must in all honesty tell us what sort of conception you do have of it.

What you have to say about 'men whom we see, or perceive with the mind, when we make out only their hats or cloaks' does not show that it is the mind rather than the imagination that makes judgements. A dog, which you will not allow to possess a mind like yours, certainly makes a similar kind of judgement when it sees not its master but simply his hat or clothes. Indeed, even if the master is standing or sitting or lying down or reclining or crouching down or stretched out, the dog still always recognizes the master who can exist under all these forms, even though like the wax, he does not keep the same proportions or always appear under one form rather than another. And when a dog chases a hare that ²⁷³ is running away, and sees it first intact, then dead, and afterwards skinned and chopped up, do you suppose that he does not think it is the same hare? When you go on to say that the perception of colour and hardness and so on is 'not vision or touch but is purely mental scrutiny', I accept this, provided the mind is not taken to be really distinct from the imaginative faculty. You add that this scrutiny 'can be imperfect and confused or perfect and distinct depending on how carefully we concentrate on what the wax consists in'. But this does not show that the scrutiny made by the mind, when it examines this mysterious something that exists over and above all the forms, constitutes clear and distinct knowledge of the wax; it shows, rather, that such knowledge is constituted by the scrutiny made by the senses of all the possible accidents and changes which the wax is capable of taking on. From these we shall certainly be able to arrive at a conception and explanation of what we mean by the term 'wax'; but the alleged naked, or rather hidden, substance is something that we can neither ourselves conceive nor explain to others. [*Fifth Objections*: CSM II 189–91]

(359)   Here, as frequently elsewhere, you merely show that you do not have an adequate understanding of what you are trying to criticize. I did not abstract the concept of the wax from the concept of its accidents. Rather, I wanted to show how the substance of the wax is revealed by means of its accidents, and how a reflective and distinct perception of it (the sort of perception which you, O Flesh, seem never to have had) differs from the ordinary confused perception. I do not see what argument you are relying on when you lay it down as certain that a dog makes discriminating judgements in the same way as we do. Seeing that a dog is made of flesh you perhaps think that everything which is in you also exists in the dog. But I observe no mind at all in the dog, and hence believe there is nothing to be found in a dog that resembles the things I recognize in a mind. [*Fifth Replies*: CSM II 248]

[Definitions of 'thought', 'idea', 'substance' etc.][5]

Thought. I use this term to include everything that is in us in such a way that we are immediately aware of it. Thus all the operations of the will, the intellect, the imagination and the senses are thoughts. I say 'immediately' so as to exclude the consequences of thoughts; a voluntary movement, for example, originates in a thought but is not itself a thought.

Idea. I understand this term to mean the form of any given thought, immediate perception of which makes me aware of the thought. Hence whenever I express something in words and understand what I am saying, this very fact makes it certain that there is within me an idea of what is signified by the words in question. Thus it is not only the images depicted in the corporeal imagination which I call 'ideas'. Indeed, in so far

---

[5] These definitions are taken from Descartes's formal or 'geometrical' presentation of his proofs of the existence of God and the distinction between the soul and the body, which he included as a kind of appendix to the Second Set of Replies. The definitions are included here, since some are useful for understanding the Second Meditation, but others relate to the arguments of the Third and subsequent Meditations.

as these images are in the corporeal imagination, that is, are depicted in   161
some part of the brain, I do not call them 'ideas' at all; I call them 'ideas'
only in so far as they give form to the mind itself, when it is directed
towards part of the brain.

Objective reality of an idea. By this I mean the being of the thing which
is represented by an idea, in so far as this exists in the idea. In the same
way, we can talk of 'objective perfection', 'objective intricacy' and so on.
For whatever we perceive as being in the objects of our ideas exists
objectively in the ideas themselves.

Substance. This term applies to every thing in which whatever we
perceive immediate resides, as in a subject, or to every thing by means of
which whatever we perceive exists. By 'whatever we perceive' is meant
any property, quality or attribute of which we have a real idea. The only
idea we have of a substance itself, in the strict sense, is that it is the thing
in which whatever we perceive (or whatever has objective reality in one
of our ideas) exists, either formally or eminently. For we know by the
natural light that a real attribute cannot belong to nothing.

The substance in which thought immediately resides is called *mind*.
I use the term 'mind' rather than 'soul', since the word soul is ambiguous
and is often applied to something corporeal.[6]

The substance which is the immediate subject of local extension and
of the accidents which presuppose extension, such as shape, position,
local motion and so on, is called *body*. Whether what we call mind and
body are one and the same substance, or two different substances, is a
question which will have to be dealt with later on.   162

The substance which we understand to be supremely perfect, and in
which we conceive absolutely nothing that implies any defect or limitation in that perfection, is called *God*. ...

There are various *degrees of reality* or being: a substance has more reality
than an accident or a mode; and an infinite substance has more reality than
a finite substance. Hence there is more objective reality in the idea of a
substance than in the idea of an accident, and there is more objective
reality in the idea of an infinite substance than in the idea of a finite   166
substance. [*Second Replies:* CSM II 113–4, 116]

---

[6] E.g. a tenuous wind permeating the body. Cf. Med. II, p. 22, above.

[On the Third Meditation]

[Innate ideas]

When M. Descartes says that the ideas of God and of our souls are innate in us, I should like to know if the souls of people who are in a deep, dreamless sleep are thinking. If they are not, they do not have any ideas at the time. If follows that no idea is innate; for what is innate is always present. [*Third Objections*: CSM II 132]

When we say that an idea is innate in us, we do not mean that it is always there before us. This would mean that no idea is innate. We simply mean that we have within ourselves the faculty of summoning up the idea. [*Third Replies*: CSM II 132]

* * *

You next distinguish ideas (by which you mean thoughts in so far as they are like images) into three classes: innate, adventitious and made up. In the first class you put 'your understanding of what a thing is, what truth is and what thought is'. In the second class you put 'your hearing a noise, seeing the sun and feeling a fire'. And in the third class you put 'your invented idea of sirens and hippogriffs'. You add that all your ideas may perhaps be adventitious or they may all be innate or all made up, since you have not as yet clearly perceived their origin.[1] But in case some fallacy should creep in before you have managed to perceive the origin of your ideas, I should like to go further and note that all ideas seem to be

---

[1] Above, p. 31.

adventitious – to proceed from things which exist outside the mind and 280
come under one of our senses. The mind has the faculty (or rather is
itself the faculty) of perceiving adventitious ideas – those which it
receives through the senses and which are transmitted by things; these
ideas, I say, are quite unadorned and distinct, and are received just
exactly as they are. But in addition to this, the mind has the faculty of
putting these ideas together and separating them in various ways, of
enlarging them and diminishing them, of comparing them, and so on.

Hence the third class of ideas, at any rate, is not distinct from the
second. For the idea of a chimera is simply the idea of the head of a lion,
the body of a goat and the tail of a serpent, out of which the mind puts
together one idea, although the individual elements are adventitious.
Similarly the idea of a giant, or a man supposed to be as big as a
mountain or the whole world, is merely adventitious. It is the idea of a
man of ordinary size which the mind enlarges at will, although the more
the idea is enlarged the more confused the conception becomes. Again
the idea of a pyramid, or of a town, or of something else which we have
not so far seen, is simply the adventitious idea of a pyramid or town or
something else which we have seen, with the form somewhat modified so
that the idea is repeated and rearranged in a fairly confused way.

As for the forms which you say are innate, there do not seem to be
any: whatever ideas are said to belong to this category also appear to
have an external origin ... [Y]ou should also have raised and answered, (283)
amongst other things, the question of why a man born blind has no idea
of colour, or a man born deaf has no idea of sound. Surely this is
because external objects have not been able to transmit any images of
themselves to the minds of such unfortunates, because the doors have
been closed since birth, and there have always been barriers in place
which have prevented these images from entering. [*Fifth Objections*:
CSM II 195, 197]

I am amazed at the line of argument by which you try to prove that all (362)
our ideas are adventitious and that none of them are constructed by us.
You say that the mind has the faculty not just of perceiving adventitious
ideas but also 'of putting them together and separating them in various
ways, of enlarging them and diminishing them, of comparing them and
so on'. Hence you conclude that the ideas of chimeras, which the mind
makes up by the process of putting together and separating etc., are not

constructed by the mind but are adventitious. By this argument you could prove that Praxiteles never made any statues on the grounds that he did not get from within himself the marble from which he sculpted them; or you could prove that you did not produce these objections on the grounds that you composed them out of words which you acquired from others rather than inventing them yourself. But in fact the form of a chimera does not consist in the parts of the goat or lion, nor does the form of your objections consist in the individual words you have used; they both consist simply in the fact that the elements are put together in a certain way. . .

(363)   In addition to the arguments which I put forward against myself and refuted, you suggest the following: why is there no idea of colour in a man born blind, and no idea of sound in a man born deaf? Here you show plainly that you have no telling arguments to produce. How do you know that there is no idea of colour in a man born blind? From time to time we find in our own case that even though we close our eyes, sensations of light and colour are nevertheless aroused. And even if we grant what you say, those who deny the existence of material things may just as well attribute the absence of ideas of colour in the man born blind to the fact that his mind lacks the faculty for forming them; this is just as reasonable as your claim that he does not have the ideas because he is deprived of sight. [*Fifth Replies*: CSM II 250–1]

[The idea of God]

When I think of a man, I am aware of an idea or image made up of a certain shape and colour; and I can doubt whether this image is the likeness of a man or not. And the same applies when I think of the sky. When I think of a chimera, I am aware of an idea or an image; and I can be in doubt as to whether it is the likeness of a non-existent animal which is capable of existing, or one which may or may not have existed at some previous time.

But when I think of an angel, what comes to mind is an image, now of a flame, now of a beautiful child with wings; I feel sure that this image has no likeness to an angel, and hence that it is not the idea of an angel. But 180 I believe that there are invisible and immaterial creatures who serve God; and we give the name 'angel' to this thing which we believe in, or suppose to exist. But the idea by means of which I imagine an angel is composed of the ideas of visible things.

In the same way we have no idea or image corresponding to the sacred name of God. And this is why we are forbidden to worship God in the form of an image; for otherwise we might think that we were conceiving of him who is incapable of being conceived.

It seems, then, that there is no idea of God in us. A man born blind, who has often approached fire and felt hot, recognizes that there is something which makes him hot; and when he hears that this is called 'fire' he concludes that fire exists. But he does not know what shape or colour fire has, and has absolutely no idea or image of fire that comes before his mind. The same applies to a man who recognizes that there must be some cause of his images or ideas, and that this cause must have a prior cause, and so on; he is finally led to the supposition of an eternal cause which never began to exist and hence cannot have a cause prior to itself, and he concludes that something eternal must necessarily exist. But he has no idea which he can say is the idea of that eternal being; he merely gives the name or label 'God' to the thing that he believes in, or acknowledges to exist.

Now from the premiss that we have an idea of God in our soul, M. Descartes proceeds to prove the theorem that God (that is, the supremely wise and powerful creator of the world) exists. But he ought to have given a better explanation of this 'idea' of God, and he should have gone on to deduce not only the existence of God but also the creation of the world. [*Third Objections*: CSM II 126–7]

Here my critic wants the term 'idea' to be taken to refer simply to the images of material things which are depicted in the corporeal imagination; and if this is granted, it is easy for him to prove that there can be no proper idea of an angel or of God. But I make it quite clear in several places throughout the book, and in this passage in particular, that I am taking the word 'idea' to refer to whatever is immediately perceived by the mind. For example, when I want something, or am afraid of something, I simultaneously perceive that I want, or am afraid; and this is why I count volition and fear among my ideas. I used the word 'idea' because it was the standard philosophical term used to refer to the forms of perception belonging to the divine mind, even though we recognize that God does not possess any corporeal imagination. And besides, there was not any more appropriate term at my disposal. I think I did give a full enough explanation to the idea of God to satisfy those who are

181

prepared to attend to my meaning; I cannot possibly satisfy those who prefer to attribute a different sense to my words than the one I intended. As for the comment at the end regarding the creation of the world, this is quite irrelevant. [*Third Replies*: CSM II 127–8]

* * *

(286) You claim that there is in the idea of an infinite God more objective reality than in the idea of a finite thing.[2] But first of all, the human intellect is not capable of conceiving of infinity, and hence it neither has nor can contemplate any idea representing an infinite thing. Hence if someone calls something 'infinite' he attributes to a thing which he does not grasp a label which he does not understand. For just as the thing extends beyond any grasp of it he can have, so the negation of a limit which he attributes to its extension is not understood by him, since his intelligence is always confined within some limit. [*Fifth Objections*: CSM II 200]

365 You say: 'If someone calls something "infinite", he attributes to a thing which he does not grasp a label which he does not understand.' Here you fail to distinguish between, on the one hand, an understanding which is suited to the scale of our intellect (and each of us knows by his own experience quite well that he has this sort of understanding of the infinite) and, on the other hand, a fully adequate conception of things (and no one has this sort of conception either of the infinite or of anything else, however small it may be). Moreover, it is false that the infinite is understood through the negation of a boundary or limit; on the contrary, all limitation implies a negation of the infinite. [*Fifth Replies*: CSM II 252]

* * *

(96) [You make the inference] 'I am clearly and distinctly aware of an infinite being; hence this is a true entity and something real'. Yet will not someone ask '*Are* you clearly and distinctly aware of an infinite being? What, in that case, is the meaning of that well-worn maxim which is common knowledge: *the infinite qua infinite is unknown?*' When I think of a chiliagon, and

---

[2] pp. 32–3, above.

construct for myself a confused representation of some figure, I do not distinctly imagine the chiliagon itself, since I do not distinctly see the thousand sides. And if this is so, then the question obviously arises as to how the infinite can be thought of in a distinct as opposed to a confused manner, given that the infinite perceptions that make it up cannot be seen clearly 'before the eyes', as it were. [*First Objections*: CSM II 69–70]

My opponent ... shrewdly asks whether I am 'clearly and distinctly aware of the infinite'. I did try to anticipate this objection, but it is one that occurs so spontaneously to everyone that it is worthwhile replying to it at some length. So let me say first of all that the infinite, *qua* infinite, can in no way be grasped. But it can still be understood,[3] in so far as we can clearly and distinctly understand that something is such that no limitations can be found in it, and this amounts to understanding clearly that it is infinite.

Now I make a distinction here between the *indefinite* and the *infinite*. 113
I apply the term 'infinite', in the strict sense, only to that in which no limits of any kind can be found; and in this sense God alone is infinite. But in cases like the extension of imaginary space, or the set of numbers, or the divisibility of the parts of a quantity, there is merely some respect in which I do not recognize a limit; so here I use the term 'indefinite' rather than 'infinite', because these items are not limitless in every respect ...

When we look at the sea, our vision does not encompass its entirely, nor do we measure out its enormous vastness; but we are still said to 'see' it. In fact, if we look from a distance, so that our vision almost covers the entire sea at one time, we see it only in a confused manner, just as we have a confused picture of a chiliagon when we take in all its sides at once. But if we fix our gaze on some part of the sea at close quarters, then our view can be clear and distinct, just as our picture of a chiliagon can be, if it is confined to one or two of the sides. In the same way, God cannot be taken in by the human mind , and I admit this, along with all 114
theologians. Moreover, God cannot be distinctly known by those who look from a distance as it were, and try to make their minds encompass

---

[3] For the distinction between grasping (Latin *comprehendere*) and understanding (*intelligere*), see footnote 18, p. 37, above.

his entirety all at once. This is the sense in which St Thomas says ...
that the knowledge of God is within us 'in a somewhat confused
manner'.[4] But those who try to attend to God's individual perfections,
and try not so much to take hold of them as to be taken hold of by them,
using all the strength of their intellect to contemplate them, will certainly
find that God provides much more ample and straightforward subject-
matter for clear and distinct knowledge than any created thing. [*First
Replies*: CSM II 81–2]

* * *

From the idea of a supreme being, which you maintain is quite incapable
of originating from you, you venture to infer that there must necessarily
exist a supreme being who alone can be the origin of this idea which
appears in your mind.[5] However, we can find simply within ourselves a
sufficient basis for our ability to form the said idea, even supposing that
the supreme being did not exist, or that we did not know that he exists
and never thought about his existing. For surely I can see that, in so far
as I think, I have some degree of perfection, and hence that others
besides myself have a similar degree of perfection. And this gives me
the basis for thinking of an indefinite number of degrees and thus
positing higher and higher degrees of perfection up to infinity. Even if
there were just one degree of heat or light, I could always imagine
further degrees and continue the process of addition up to infinity. In
the same way, I can surely take a given degree of being, which I perceive
within myself, and add on a further degree, and thus construct the idea
of a perfect being from all the degrees which are capable of being added
on. You say, however, that an effect cannot possess any degree of reality
or perfection that was not previously present in the cause. But we see
that flies and other animals, and also plants, are produced from sun and
rain and earth, which lack life. Now life is something nobler than any
merely corporeal grade of being; and hence it does happen that an effect
may derive from its cause some reality which is nevertheless not present
in the cause. But leaving this aside, the idea of a perfect being is nothing
more than an entity of reason, which has no more nobility than your own
mind which is thinking. Moreover, if you had not grown up among

124

---

[4] Aquinas, *Summa theologiae*, Part I, Qu. 2, art. 2.   [5] Cf. Med. III, p. 36, above.

educated people, but had spent your entire life alone in some deserted spot, how do you know that the idea would have come to you? You derived this idea from earlier preconceptions, or from books or from discussion with friends and so on, and not simply from your mind or from an existing supreme being. So a clearer proof needs to be provided that this idea could not be present within you if a supreme being did not exist, and when you have provided it, we shall all surrender. However, the fact that the natives of Canada, the Hurons and other primitive peoples, have no awareness of any idea of this sort seems to establish that the idea does come from previously held notions. It is even possible for you to form the idea from a previous examination of corporeal things, so that your idea would refer to nothing but this corporeal world, which includes every kind of perfection that can be thought of by you. In that case you could not infer the existence of anything beyond an utterly perfect corporeal being, unless you were to add something further which lifts us up to an incorporeal or spiritual plane. We may add that you can form the idea of an angel just as you can form the idea of a supremely perfect being; but this idea is not produced in you by an angel, although the angel is more perfect than you. But in fact you do not have the idea of God, just as you do not have the idea of an infinite number or an infinite line (even if you may have the idea, the number is still impossible). Moreover, the idea of the unity and simplicity of one perfection that includes all others arises merely from an operation of the reasoning intellect, in the same way as those universal unities which do not exist in reality but merely in the intellect (as can be seen in the case of generic unity, transcendental unity, and so on). [*Second Objections*: CSM II 88–9]

When you say that we can find simply within ourselves a sufficient basis for forming the idea of God, your claim in no way differs from my own view. I expressly said at the end of the Third Meditation that 'this idea is innate in me'[6] – in other words, that it comes to me from no other source than myself. I concede also that 'we could form this idea even supposing that we did not know that the supreme being exists'; but I do not agree that we could form the idea 'even supposing that the supreme being did not exist'. On the contrary, I pointed out that the whole force of the

---

[6] p. 41, above.

argument lies in the fact that it would be impossible for me to have the power of forming this idea unless I were created by God.

Your remarks about flies, plants etc., do not go to show that there can be a degree of perfection in the effect which was not previously present in the cause. For, since animals lack reason, it is certain that they have no perfection which is not also present in inanimate bodies; or, if they do have any such perfections, it is certain that they derive them from some other source, and that the sun, the rain and the earth are not adequate causes of animals. Suppose someone does not discern any cause cooperating in the production of a fly which possesses all the degrees of perfection possessed by the fly; suppose further that he is not sure whether there is any additional cause beyond those which he does discern: it would be quite irrational for him to take this as a basis for doubting something which, as I shall shortly explain at length, is manifest by the very light of nature.

I would add that the claim regarding flies is based on a consideration of material things, and so it could not occur to those who follow my Meditations and direct their thought away from the things which are perceivable by the senses with the aim of philosophizing in an orderly manner.

As for your calling the idea of God which is in us an 'entity of reason', this is not a compelling objection. If by 'entity of reason' is meant something which does not exist, it is not true that the idea of God is an entity of reason in this sense. It is true only in the sense in which every operation of the intellect is an entity of reason, that is, an entity which has its origin in rational thought; and indeed this entire universe can be said to be an entity originating in God's reason, that is, an entity created by a single act of the divine mind. Moreover I have already insisted in various places that I am dealing merely with the objective perfection or reality of an idea; and this, no less than the objective intricacy in the idea of a machine of very ingenious design, requires a cause which contains in reality whatever is contained merely objectively in the idea.

I do not see what I can add to make it any clearer that the idea in question could not be present to my mind unless a supreme being existed. I can only say that it depends on the reader: if he attends carefully to what I have written he should be able to free himself from the preconceived opinions which may be eclipsing his natural light, and to accustom himself

134

135

to believing in the primary notions, which are as evident and true as anything can be, in preference to opinions which are obscure and false, albeit fixed in the mind by long habit.

The fact that 'there is nothing in the effect which was not previously present in the cause, either in a similar or in a higher form' is a primary notion which is as clear as any that we have; it is just the same as the common notion 'Nothing comes from nothing.' For if we admit that there is something in the effect that was not previously present in the cause, we shall also have to admit that this something was produced by nothing. And the reason why nothing cannot be the cause of a thing is simply that such a cause would not contain the same features as are found in the effect.

It is also a primary notion that 'all the reality or perfection which is present in an idea merely objectively must be present in its cause either formally or eminently'.[7] This is the sole basis for all the beliefs we have ever had about the existence of things located outside our mind. For what could ever have led us to suspect that such things exist if not the simple fact that ideas of these things reach our mind by means of the senses?

Those who give the matter their careful attention and spend time meditating with me will clearly see that there is within us an idea of a supremely powerful and perfect being, and also that the objective reality of this idea cannot be found in us, either formally or eminently. I cannot force this truth on my readers if they are lazy, 136 since it depends solely on their exercising their own powers of thought. [*Second Replies*: CSM II 96–7]

[Objective reality]

What is 'objective being in the intellect'? According to what I was taught, this is simply the determination of an act of the intellect by means of an object. And this is merely an extraneous label which adds nothing to the thing itself. Just as 'being seen' is nothing other than an act of vision attributable to myself, so 'being thought of', or having objective being in the intellect, is simply a thought of the mind which stops and terminates in

---

[7] Cf. Med. III, above pp. 33ff., and footnote 9, p. 33.

the mind. And this can occur without any movement or change in the thing itself, and indeed without the thing in question existing at all. So why should I look for a cause of something which is not actual, and which is simply an empty label, a non-entity?

'Nevertheless', says our ingenious author, 'in order for a given idea to contain such and such objective reality it must surely derive it from some cause.'[8] On the contrary, this requires no cause; for objective reality is a pure label, not anything actual. A cause imparts some real and actual influence; but what does not actually exist cannot take on anything, and so does not receive or require any actual causal influence. Hence, though I have ideas, there is no cause for these ideas, let alone some cause which is greater than I am, or which is infinite . . .

93

The author goes on to say, 'And yet the mode of being by which a thing exists objectively in the intellect by way of an idea, imperfect though it may be, is certainly not nothing, and so it cannot come from nothing'.[9] There is an equivocation here. If *nothing* is the same as an entity which does not actually exist, then this, since it is not actual, is nothing at all, and hence comes from nothing, that is, does not come from any cause . But if 'nothing' means something imaginary, or what they commonly call a 'conceptual entity',[10] then this is not 'nothing' but something real which is distinctly conceived. Nevertheless, since it is merely conceived and is not actual, although it can be conceived, it cannot in any way be caused. [*First Objections*: CSM II 66–7]

94

Now I wrote that an idea is the thing which is thought of in so far as it has objective being in the intellect. But to give me an opportunity of explaining these words more clearly the objector pretends to understand them in quite a different way from that in which I used them. 'Objective being in the intellect', he says, 'is simply the determination of an act of the intellect by means of an object, and this is merely an extraneous label which adds nothing to the thing itself.' Notice here that he is referring to the thing itself as if it were located outside the intellect, and in this sense 'objective being in the intellect' is certainly an extraneous label; but I was speaking of the idea, which is never outside the intellect, and in this sense 'objective being' simply means being in the intellect in the way in

[8] Med. III, above, p. 33.   [9] Med. III, above, p. 33.
[10] Lat. *ens rationis*, literally 'entity of reason'.

which objects are normally there. For example, if anyone asks what happens to the sun through its being objectively in my intellect, the best answer is that nothing happens to it beyond the application of an extraneous label which does indeed 'determine an act of the intellect by means of an object'. But if the question is about what the *idea* of the sun is, and we answer that it is the thing which is thought of, in so far as it has objective being in the intellect, no one will take this to be the sun itself with this extraneous label applied to it. 'Objective being in the intellect' will not here mean 'the determination of an act of the intellect by means of an object', but will signify the object's being in the intellect in the way in which its objects are normally there. By this I mean that the idea of the sun is the sun itself existing in the intellect – not of course formally existing, as it does in the heavens, but objectively existing, i.e. in the way in which objects normally are in the intellect. Now this mode 103 of being is of course much less perfect than that possessed by things which exist outside the intellect; but, as I did explain, it is not therefore simply nothing.[11]

When the learned theologian says there is an equivocation in what I say here, he apparently means to remind me of the point I have just made, in case I should forget it. He says, first of all, that when a thing exists in the intellect by means of an idea, it is not an actual entity, that is, it is not a being located outside the intellect; and this is quite true. Next he goes on to say that 'it is not something fictitious or a conceptual entity but something real which is distinctly conceived', and here he concedes everything which I have assumed. But he then adds 'since it is merely conceived and is not actual' – i.e. since it is merely an idea, and not a thing located outside the intellect – 'although it can be conceived it cannot in any way be caused'. This is to say that it does not require a cause enabling it to exist outside the intellect. This I accept; but it surely needs a cause enabling it to be conceived, which is the sole point at issue. Thus if someone has in his intellect the idea of a machine of a highly intricate design, it is perfectly fair to ask what is the cause of this idea. And it will not be an adequate reply to say that the idea is not anything outside the intellect and hence that it cannot be caused but can merely be conceived. Not will it suffice to say that the intellect itself is the cause of

[11] Med. III, above, p. 33.

104 the idea, in so far as it is the cause of its own operations; for what is at issue is not this, but the cause of the objective intricacy which is in the idea. For in order for the idea of the machine to contain such and such objective intricacy, it must derive it from some cause; and what applies to the objective intricacy belonging to this idea also applies to the objective reality belonging to the idea of God. Now admittedly there could be various causes of the intricacy contained in the idea of the machine. Perhaps the cause was a real machine of this design which was seen on some previous occasion, thus producing an idea resembling the original. Or the cause might be an extensive knowledge of mechanics in the intellect of the person concerned, or perhaps a very subtle intelligence which enabled him to invent the idea without any previous knowledge. But notice that all the intricacy which is to be found merely objectively in the idea must necessarily be found, either formally or eminently,[12] in its cause, whatever this turns out to be. And the same must apply to the objective reality in the idea of God. [*First Replies*: CSM II 74–5]

[God, author of my existence]

He goes on: 'I should like to go further and inquire whether I myself who have this idea could exist if no such being existed' (that is, as he says just before this, if there did not exist a being from whom my idea of a being more perfect than myself proceeds). He goes on: 'From whom, in that case, would I derive my existence? From myself, presumably, or from my parents or from others etc. Yet if I derived my existence from myself, then I should neither doubt nor want, nor lack anything at all; for I should have given myself all the perfections of which I have any idea, and thus I should myself be God.'[13] But if I derive my existence from some other, then if I trace the series back I will eventually come to a being which derives its existence from itself; and so the argument here becomes the same as the argument based on the supposition that I derive my existence from myself.[14] This is exactly the same approach as that taken by St Thomas: he called this way 'the way based on the causality of the efficient cause'.[15] He took the argument from Aristotle, although

---

[12] See above, p. 33, note 9.   [13] Med. III, above, p. 38.   [14] Cf. Med. III, above, p. 39–40.
[15] This is the second of Aquinas' 'Five Ways': *Summa Theologiae*, Part One, Qu. 2, art. 3. Cf. Aristotle, *Physics* VIII, 265 1ff; *Metaphysics* A, 1072ff.

neither he nor Aristotle was bothered about the causes of ideas. And perhaps they had no need to be; for can I not take a much shorter and more direct line of argument? 'I am thinking, therefore I exist; indeed, I am thought itself, I am a mind. But this mind and thought derives its existence either from itself, or from another. If the latter, then we continue to repeat the question – where does this other being derive its existence from? And if the former, if it derives its existence from itself, it is God. For what derives existence from itself will without difficulty have endowed itself with all things.'

I beg and beseech our author not to hide his meaning from a reader 95 who, though perhaps less intelligent, is eager to follow. The phrase 'from itself' has two senses. In the first, positive, sense, it means 'from itself as from a cause'. What derives existence from itself in this sense bestows its own existence on itself; so if by an act of premeditated choice it were to give itself what it desired, it would undoubtedly give itself all things, and so would be God. But in the second, negative sense, 'from itself' simply means 'not from another'; and this, as far as I remember, is the way in which everyone takes the phrase.

But now, if something derives its existence from itself in the sense of 'not from another', how can we prove that this being embraces all things and is infinite? This time I shall not listen if you say 'If it derives its existence from itself it could easily have given itself all things.' For it does not derive existence from itself as a cause, nor did it exist prior to itself so that it could choose in advance what it should subsequently be. [*First Objections*: CSM II 68–9]

At this point my critic has, through his excessive desire to be kind to me, put me in an unfortunate position. For in comparing my argument with one taken from St Thomas and Aristotle, he seems to be demanding an explanation for the fact that, after starting on the same road as they do, I have not kept to it in all respects. However, I hope he will allow me to avoid commenting on what others have said, and simply give an account of what I have written myself.

Firstly, then, I did not base my argument on the fact that I observed there to be an order or succession of efficient causes among the objects perceived by the senses. For one thing, I regarded the existence of God as much more evident than the existence of anything that can be perceived by the senses; and for another thing, I did not think that such a succession of causes could lead me anywhere except to a recognition of the imperfection of my intellect, since an infinite chain of such successive causes from eternity without any first cause is beyond my grasp. And my inability to grasp it certainly does not entail that there must be a first cause, any more than my inability to grasp the infinite number of divisions in a finite quantity entails that there is an ultimate division beyond which any further division is impossible. All that follows is that my intellect, which is finite, does not encompass the infinite. Hence I preferred to use my own existence as the basis of my argument, since it does not depend on any chain of causes and is better known to me than anything else could possibly be. And the question I asked concerning myself was not what was the cause that originally produced me, but what is the cause that preserves me at present. In this way I aimed to escape the whole issue of the succession of causes.

Next, in inquiring about what caused me, I was asking about myself, not in so far as I consist of mind and body, but only and precisely in so far as I am a thinking thing. This point is, I think, of considerable relevance. For such a procedure made it much easier for me to free myself from my preconceived opinions, to attend to the light of nature, to ask myself questions, and to affirm with certainty that there can be nothing within me of which I am not in some way aware. This is plainly a quite different approach from observing that my father begot me, inferring that my grandfather begot my father, and in view of the impossibility of going on *ad infinitum* in the search for parents of parents, bringing the inquiry to a close by deciding that there is a first cause.

Moreover, in inquiring about what caused me I was not simply asking about myself as a thinking thing; principally and most importantly I was asking about myself in so far as I observe, amongst my other thoughts, that there is within me the idea of a supremely perfect being. The whole force of my proof depends on this one fact. For, firstly, this idea contains the essence of God, at least in so far as I am capable of understanding it; and according to the laws of true logic, we must never ask about the existence of anything until we first understand its essence.[16] Secondly, it is this idea which provides me with the opportunity of inquiring whether I derive my existence from myself, or from another, and of recognizing

---

[16] Literally: 'we must never ask *if* it is (*an est*) until we first understand *what* it is (*quid est*)'.

my defects. And, lastly, it is this same idea which shows me not just that I have a cause, but that this cause contains every perfection, and hence that it is God ...

There are some who attend only to the literal and strict meaning of the (109) phrase 'efficient cause' and thus think it is impossible for anything to be the cause of itself. They do not see that there is any place for another kind of cause analogous to an efficient cause, and hence when they say that something derives its existence 'from itself' they normally mean simply that it has no cause. But if they would look at the facts rather than the words, they would readily observe that the negative sense of the phrase 'from itself' comes merely from the imperfection of the human 110 intellect and has no basis in reality. But there is a positive sense of the phrase which is derived from the true nature of things, and it is this sense alone which is employed in my argument. For example, if we think that a given body derives its existence from itself, we may simply mean that it has no cause; but our claim here is not based on any positive reason, but merely arises in a negative way from our ignorance of any cause. Yet this is a kind of imperfection in us, as we will easily see if we consider the following. The separate divisions of time do not depend on each other; hence the fact that the body in question is supposed to have existed up till now 'from itself', that is, without a cause, is not sufficient to make it continue to exist in future, unless there is some power in it that as it were recreates it continuously. But when we see that no such power is to be found in the idea of a body, and immediately conclude that the body does not derive its existence from itself, we shall then be taking the phrase 'from itself' in the positive sense. Similarly, when we say that God derives his existence 'from himself', we can understand the phrase in the negative sense, in which case the meaning will simply be that he has no cause. But if we have previously inquired into the cause of God's existing or continuing to exist, and we attend to the immense and incomprehensible power that is contained within the idea of God, then we will have recognized that this power is so exceedingly great that it is plainly the cause of his continuing existence, and nothing but this can be the cause. And if we say as a result that God derives his existence from himself, we will not be using the phrase in its negative sense but in an absolutely positive sense. There is no need to say that God is the efficient cause of himself, for this might give rise to a verbal dispute. But the fact 111 that God derives his existence from himself, or has no cause apart from himself, depends not on nothing but on the real immensity of his power; hence, when we perceive this, we are quite entitled to think that in a sense he stands in the same relation to himself as an efficient cause does to its effect, and hence that he derives his existence from himself in the positive sense. And each one of us may ask himself whether he derives his existence from himself in this same sense. Since he will find no power within himself which suffices to preserve him even for one moment of time, he will be right to conclude that he derives his existence from another being, and indeed that this other being derives its existence from itself (there is no possibility of an infinite regress here, since the question concerns the present, not the past or the future). Indeed, I will now add something which I have not put down in writing before, namely that the cause we arrive at cannot merely be a secondary cause; for a cause which possesses such great power that it can preserve something situated outside itself must, *a fortiori*, preserve itself by its own power, and hence derive its existence from itself. [*First Replies*: CSM II 77–8, 79–80]

[On The Fourth Meditation]

[The cause of error]

You say that although you have no power to avoid error through having a clear perception of things, you can still avoid it by firmly resolving to adhere to the rule of not assenting to anything which you do not clearly perceive.[1] But although you can always keep this rule carefully in mind, is it not still an imperfection not to perceive clearly matters which you need to decide upon, and hence to be perpetually liable to the risk of error?

You say that error resides in the mental operation itself in so far as it proceeds from you and is a kind of privation, but not in the faculty God gave you, nor in its operation in so far as it depends on him.[2] But although the error does not immediately reside in the faculty God gave you, it does indirectly attach to it, since it was created with the kind of imperfection which makes error possible. Admittedly, as you say, you have no cause for complaint against God who, despite owing you nothing, bestowed on you the good gifts which you should thank him for. But there is still cause to wonder why he did not bestow more perfect gifts on you, given that he had the knowledge and the power and was not malevolent.

You go on to say that you have no cause to complain that God's concurrence is involved in your acts when you go wrong. For in so far as these acts depend on God, they are all true and good; and your ability to perform them means that there is, in a sense, more perfection in you

[1] Cf. above, p. 49. [2] Cf. above, p. 47.

113

than would be the case if you lacked this ability. You continue: 'As for the privation involved – which is all that the essential definition of falsity and wrong consists in – this does not in any way require the concurrence of God, since it is not a thing and should not be referred to him.'[3] But although this is a subtle distinction it is not quite enough to resolve the problem. For even if God does not concur in the privation in which the falsity and error of the act consists, he nonetheless concurs in the act itself; and if he did not concur in it, there would be no privation. In any case, he is the author of that power in you which is subject to deception and error; and hence he is the author of a power which is, so to speak, ineffective. Thus the defect in the act should not, it seems, be referred so much to the power which is ineffective as to the author who made it ineffective and did not choose to make it effective, or more effective, though he was able to do so. It is certainly no fault in a workman if he does not trouble to make an enormous key to open a tiny box; but it is a fault if, in making the key small, he gives it a shape which makes it difficult or impossible to open the box. Similarly, God is admittedly not to be blamed for giving puny man a faculty of judging that is too small to cope with everything, or even with most things or the most important things; but this still leaves room to wonder why he gave man a faculty which is uncertain, confused and inadequate even for the few matters which he did want us to decide upon.

You next ask what is the cause of error or falsity in you.[4] First of all, I do not question your basis for saying the intellect is simply the faculty of being aware of ideas, or of apprehending things simply and without any affirmation or negation; nor do I dispute your calling the will or freedom of choice a faculty of judging whose function is to affirm or deny, to give or withhold assent. My only question concerns why, on your account, our will or freedom of choice is not restricted by any limits, whereas the intellect is restricted. In fact it seems that these two faculties have an equally broad scope; certainly the scope of the intellect is at the very least no narrower than that of the will, since the will never aims at anything which the intellect has not already perceived.

I said that the scope of the intellect was 'at the very least no narrower'; in fact its scope seems to be even wider than that of the will. For the will

---

[3] Above, p. 48.   [4] Above, pp. 44f.

or choice or judgement, and hence our selection or pursuit or avoidance of something, never occurs unless we have previously apprehended that thing, or unless the idea of that thing has been previously perceived and set before us by the intellect. What is more, there are many things which we understand only obscurely, so that no judgement or pursuit or avoidance occurs in respect of them. Also, the faculty of judgement is 315 often undecided, and if there are reasons of equal weight on either side, or no reasons at all, no judgement follows; but the intellect still continues to apprehend the matters on which no judgement has been passed.

You say that you can always understand the possibility of your understanding more and more, including the intellectual faculty itself, of which you can form an infinite idea. But this itself shows that the intellect is not any more limited than the will, since it can extend itself even to an infinite object. You say that you recognize your will to be equal to that of God – not, indeed, in respect of its extent, but essentially. But surely the same could be said of the intellect too, since you have defined the essential notion of the intellect in just the same way as you have defined that of the will. In short, will you please tell us if the will can extend to anything that escapes the intellect? [*Fifth Objections*: CSM II 217–19]

You here ask me to say briefly whether the will can extend to anything that escapes the intellect. The answer is that this occurs whenever we happen to go wrong. Thus when you judge that the mind is a kind of rarefied body, you can understand that the mind is itself, i.e. a thinking thing, and that a rarefied body is an extended thing; but the proposition 377 that it is one and the same thing that thinks and is extended is one which you certainly do not understand. You simply want to believe it, because you have believed it before and do not want to change your view. It is the same when you judge that an apple, which may in fact be poisoned, is nutritious: you understand that its smell, colour and so on, are pleasant, but this does not mean that you understand that this particular apple will be beneficial to eat; you judge that it will because you want to believe it. So, while I do admit that when we direct our will towards something, we always have some sort of understanding of some aspect of it, I deny that our understanding and our will are of equal scope. In the case of any given object, there may be many things about it that we desire but very few things of which we have knowledge. And when we make a bad judgement, it is not that we exercise our will in a bad fashion, but that the object of our will happens to be bad. Again, we never understand anything in a bad fashion; when we are said to 'understand in a bad fashion', all that happens is that we judge that our understanding is more extensive than it in fact is. [*Fifth Replies*: CSM II 259]

[The indifference of the will]

[T]he difficulty arises in connection with the indifference that belongs to our judgement, or liberty. This indifference, you claim, does not belong to the perfection of the will but has to do merely with its imperfection; thus, according to you, indifference is removed whenever the mind clearly perceives what it should believe or do or refrain from doing.[5] But do you not see that by adopting this position you are

417 destroying God's freedom, since you are removing from his will the indifference as to whether he shall create this world rather than another world or no world at all? Yet it is an article of faith that God was from eternity indifferent as to whether he should create one world, or innumerable worlds, or none at all. But who doubts that God has always perceived with the clearest vision what he should do or refrain from doing? Thus, a very clear vision and perception of things does not remove indifference of choice; and if indifference cannot be a proper part of human freedom, neither will it find a place in divine freedom, since the essences of things are, like numbers, indivisible and immutable. Therefore indifference is involved in God's freedom of choice no less than it is in the case of human freedom of choice. [*Sixth Objections*: CSM II 280–1]

As for the freedom of the will, the way in which it exists in God is quite different from the way in which it exists in us. It is self-contradictory to

432 suppose that the will of God was not indifferent from eternity with respect to everything which has happened or will ever happen; for it is impossible to imagine that anything is thought of in the divine intellect as good or true, or worthy of belief or action or omission, prior to the decision of the divine will to make it so. I am not speaking here of temporal priority: I mean that there is not even any priority of order, or

---

[5] Med. IV, above, p. 46.

nature, or of 'rationally determined reason' as they call it, such that God's idea of the good impelled him to choose one thing rather than another. For example, God did not will the creation of the world in time because he saw that it would be better this way than if he had created it from eternity; nor did he will that the three angles of a triangle should be equal to two right angles because he recognized that it could not be otherwise, and so on. On the contrary, it is because he willed to create the world in time that it is better this way than if he had created it from eternity; and it is because he willed that the three angles of a triangle should necessarily equal two right angles that this is true and cannot be otherwise; and so on in other cases. There is no problem in the fact that the merit of the saints may be said to be the cause of their obtaining eternal life; for it is not the cause of this reward in the sense that it determines God to will anything, but is merely the cause of an effect of which God willed from eternity that it should be the cause. Thus the supreme indifference to be found in God is the supreme indication of his omnipotence. But as for man, since he finds that the nature of all goodness and truth is already determined by God, and his will cannot tend towards anything else, it is evident that he will embrace what is good and true all the more willingly, and hence more freely, in proportion as he sees it more clearly. He is never indifferent except when he does not know which of the two alternatives is the better or truer, or at least when he does not see this clearly enough to rule out any possibility of doubt. Hence the indifference which belongs to human freedom is very different from that which belongs to divine freedom. The fact that the essences of things are said to be indivisible is not relevant here. For, firstly, no essence can belong univocally to both God and his creatures; and, secondly, indifference does not belong to the essence of human freedom, since not only are we free when ignorance of what is right makes us indifferent, but we are also free – indeed at our freest – when a clear perception impels us to pursue some object. [*Sixth Replies*: CSM II 291–2]

433

[Faith, reason and the natural light]

If the will exposes itself to danger by following a conception of the intellect (126) which is wholly lacking in clarity and distinctness, then note what follows from this. A Turk, or any other unbeliever, not only does not sin in refusing to embrace the Christian religion, but what is more, he sins if he does embrace it, since he does not possess clear and distinct knowledge of its truth. Indeed, if this rule of yours is true, then there is almost nothing that the will is going to be allowed to embrace, since there is almost nothing that we know with the clarity and distinctness which you require for that kind of certainty which is beyond any doubt. [*Second Objections*: CSM II 90]

When I judge that obscurity must be removed from our conceptions to enable us to assent to them without any danger of going wrong ... it should be noted that the clarity or transparency which can induce our will to give its assent is of two kinds: the first comes from the natural light, while the second comes from divine grace. Now although it is commonly said that faith concerns matters which are obscure, this refers solely to the thing or subject matter to which our faith relates: it does not imply that the formal reason which leads us to assent to matters of faith is obscure. On the contrary, this formal reason consists in a certain inner light which comes from God, and when we are supernaturally illumined by it we are confident that what is put forward for us to believe has been revealed by God himself. And it is quite impossible for him to lie; this is more certain than any natural light, and is often even more evident because of the light of grace.

The sin that Turks and other infidels commit by refusing to embrace the Christian religion does not arise from their unwillingness to assent to obscure matters (for obscure they indeed are), but from their resistance to the impulses of divine grace within them, or from the fact that they make themselves unworthy of grace by their other sins. ... Furthermore, those who read my books will not be able to suppose that I did not recognize this supernatural light, since I expressly stated in the Fourth Meditation, where I was looking into the cause of falsity, that it produces in our inmost thought a disposition of the will, without lessening our freedom.[6]

However, I should like you to remember here that, in matters which may be embraced by the will, I made a very careful distinction between the conduct of life and the contemplation of the truth. As far as the conduct of life is concerned, I am very far from thinking that we should assent only to

---

[6] Cf. above, p. 46.

what is clearly and distinctly perceived. On the contrary, I do not think that we should always wait even for probable truths; from time to time we will have to choose one of many alternatives about which we have no knowledge, and once we have made our choice, so long as no reasons against it can be produced, we must stick to it as firmly as if it had been chosen for transparently clear reasons. I explained this in ... the *Discourse on the Method*.[7] But when we are dealing solely with the contemplation of the truth, surely no one has ever denied that we should refrain from giving assent to matters which we do not perceive with sufficient distinctness. Now in my *Meditations* I was dealing solely with the contemplation of the truth; the whole enterprise shows this to be the case, as well as my express declaration at the end of the First Meditation where I said that I could not possibly go too far in my distrustful attitude, since the task in hand involved not action but merely the acquisition of knowledge.[8] [*Second Replies*: CSM II 105–6]

[The rejection of final causes]

Your rejection of the employment of final causes in physics[9] might have been correct in a different context, but since you are dealing with God, there is obviously a danger that you may be abandoning the principal argument for establishing by the natural light the wisdom, providence and power of God, and indeed his existence. Leaving aside the entire world, the heavens and its other main parts, how or where will you be able to get any better evidence for the existence of such a God than from the function of the various parts in plants, animals, man and yourself (or your body), seeing that you bear the likeness of God? We know that certain great thinkers have been led by a study of anatomy not just to achieve a knowledge of God but also to sing thankful hymns to him for having organized all the parts and harmonized their functions in such a way as to deserve the highest praise for his care and providence. [*Fourth Objections*: CSM II 215]

The points you make to defend the notion of a final cause should be applied to efficient causation. The function of the various parts of plants and animals etc. makes it appropriate to admire God as their

309

---

[7] See *Discourse*, Part Three (AT VII; CSM I 123).   [8] Above, p. 19.   [9] See above, p. 44.

375 efficient cause – to recognize and glorify the craftsman though examining his works; but we cannot guess from this what purposes God has in creating any given thing. In ethics, then, where we may often legitimately employ conjectures, it may admittedly be pious on occasion to try to guess what purpose God may have had in mind in his direction of the universe; but in physics, where everything must be backed up by the strongest arguments, such conjectures are futile. We cannot pretend that some of God's purposes are more out in the open that others; all are equally hidden in the inscrutable abyss of his wisdom. [*Fourth Replies*: CSM II 258]

[On the Fifth Meditation]

[Whether God's essence implies his existence]

You next attempt to demonstrate the existence of God, and the thrust of your argument is contained in the following passage:

When I concentrate, it is quite evident that existence can no more be separated from the essence of God than the fact that its three angles equal two right angles can be separated from the essence of a triangle, or than the idea of a mountain can be separated from the idea of a valley. Hence it is just as much of a contradiction to think of God (that is, a supremely perfect being) lacking existence (that is, lacking a perfection) as it is to think of a mountain without a valley.[1]

But we must note here that the kind of comparison you make is not wholly fair.

It is quite all right for you to compare essence with essence, but instead of going on to compare existence with existence or a property with a property, you compare existence with a property. It seems that you should have said that omnipotence, for example, can no more be separated from the essence of God than the fact that its angles equal two right angles can be separated from the essence of a triangle. Or, at any rate, you should have said that the existence of God can no more be separated from his essence than the existence of a triangle can be separated from its essence. If you had done this, both your comparisons would have been satisfactory, and I would have granted you not only the first one but the second one as well. But you would not for all that have

323

---

[1] Above, p. 52.

established that God necessarily exists, since a triangle does not necessarily exist either, even though its essence and existence cannot in actual fact be separated. Real separation is impossible no matter how much the mind may separate them or think of them apart from each other – as indeed it can even in the case of God's essence and existence.

Next we must note that you place existence among the divine perfections, but do not place it among the perfections of a triangle or mountain, though it could be said that in its own way it is just as much a perfection of each of these things. In fact, however, existence is not a perfection either in God or in anything else; it is that without which no perfections can be present.

For surely, what does not exist has no perfections or imperfections, and what does exist and has several perfections does not have existence as one of its individual perfections; rather, its existence is that in virtue of which both the thing itself and its perfections are existent, and that without which we cannot say that the thing possesses the perfections or that the perfections are possessed by it. Hence we do not say that existence 'exists in a thing' in the way perfections do; and if a thing lacks existence, we do not say it is imperfect, or deprived of a perfection, but say instead that it is nothing at all.

Thus, just as when you listed the perfections of the triangle you did not include existence or conclude that the triangle existed, so when you listed the perfections of God you should not have included existence among them so as to reach the conclusion that God exists, unless you wanted to beg the question . . .

(324) You say that you are not free to think of God without existence (that is, a supremely perfect being without a supreme perfection) as you are free to imagine a horse with or without wings. The only comment to be added to this is as follows. You are free to think of a horse not having wings without thinking of the existence which would, according to you, be a perfection in the horse if it were present; but, in the same way, you are free to think of God as having knowledge and power and other

325 perfections without thinking of him as having the existence which would complete his perfection, if he had it. Just as the horse which is thought of as having the perfection of wings is not therefore deemed to have the existence which is, according to you, a principal perfection, so the fact that God is thought of as having knowledge and other perfections does not therefore imply that he has existence. This remains to be proved.

And although you say that both existence and all the other perfections are included in the idea of a supremely perfect being, here you simply assert what should be proved, and assume the conclusion as a premiss. Otherwise I could say that the idea of a perfect Pegasus contains not just the perfection of his having wings but also the perfection of existence. For just as God is thought of as perfect in every kind of perfection, so Pegasus is thought of as perfect in his own kind. It seems that there is no point that you can raise in this connection which, if we preserve the analogy, will not apply to Pegasus if it applies to God, and *vice versa*. [*Fifth Objections*: CSM II 224–6]

Here I do not see what sort of thing you want existence to be, nor why it cannot be said to be a property just like omnipotence – provided, of course, that we take the word 'property' to stand for any attribute, or for whatever can be predicated of a thing; and this is exactly how it should be taken in this context. Moreover, in the case of God necessary existence is in fact a property in the strictest sense of the term, since it applies to him alone and forms a part of his essence as it does of no other thing. Hence the existence of a triangle should not be compared with the existence of God, since the relation between existence and essence is manifestly quite different in the case of God from what it is in the case of the triangle.

To list existence among the properties which belong to the nature of God is no more 'begging the question' than listing among the properties of a triangle the fact that its angles are equal to two right angles.

Again, it is not true to say that in the case of God, just as in the case of a triangle, existence and essence can be thought of apart from one another; for God is his own existence, but this is not true of the triangle. I do not, however, deny that possible existence is a perfection in the idea of a triangle, just as necessary existence is a perfection in the idea of God; for this fact makes the idea of a triangle superior to the ideas of chimeras, which cannot possibly be supposed to have existence. Thus at no point have you weakened the force of my argument in the slightest ... [*Fifth Replies*: CSM II 262–3]

Let us then concede that someone does possess a clear and distinct idea of a supreme and utterly perfect being. What is the next step you will take from here? You will say that this infinite being exists, and that his existence is so certain that 'I ought to regard the existence of God as having at least the same level of certainty as I have hitherto attributed to the truths of mathematics. Hence it is just as much of a contradiction to think of God (that is, a supremely perfect being) lacking existence (that is, lacking a perfection), as it is to think of a mountain without a valley.'[2] This is the lynchpin of the whole structure; to give in on this point is to be obliged to admit defeat. But since I am taking on an opponent whose strength is greater than my own, I should like to have a preliminary skirmish with him, so that, although I am sure to be beaten in the end, I may at least put off the inevitable for a while.

98

I know we are basing our argument on the reason alone and not on appeals to authority. But to avoid giving the impression that I am wilfully taking issue with such an outstanding thinker as M. Descartes, let me nevertheless begin by asking you to listen to what St Thomas says. He raises the following objection to his own position:

> As soon as we understand the meaning of the word 'God', we immediately grasp that God exists. For the word 'God' means 'that than which nothing greater can be conceived'. Now that which exists in reality as well as in the intellect is greater than that which exists in the intellect alone. Hence, since God immediately exists in the intellect as soon as we have understood the word 'God', it follows that he also exists in reality.[3]

This argument may be set out formally as follows. 'God is that than which nothing greater can be conceived. But that than which nothing greater can be conceived includes existence. Hence God, in virtue of the very word or concept of "God", contains existence; and hence he cannot lack, or be conceived of as lacking, existence.' But now please tell me if this is not the selfsame argument as that produced by M. Descartes? St Thomas defines God as 'that than which nothing greater can be conceived'. M. Descartes calls him 'a supremely perfect being'; but of course nothing greater than this can be conceived. St Thomas's next step is to say 'that than which nothing greater can be conceived includes existence', for otherwise something greater could be conceived, namely a being conceived of as also including existence. Yet surely M. Descartes' next step is identical to this. God, he says, is a supremely perfect being;

---

[2] Med. V, above, p. 52f.
[3] *Summa Theologiae*, Part One, Qu. 2, art 1. Aquinas is in fact criticizing St Anselm's version of the ontological argument.

and a supremely perfect being includes existence, for otherwise it would not be a supremely perfect being. St. Thomas's conclusion is that 'since God immediately exists in the intellect as soon as we have understood the word "God", it follows that he also exists in reality'. In other words, since the very concept or essence of 'a being than which nothing greater can be conceived' implies existence, it follows that this very being exists. M. Descartes' conclusion is the same: 'From the very fact that I cannot think of God except as existing, it follows that existence is inseparable from God and hence that he really exists.'[4] But now let St Thomas reply both to himself and to M. Descartes. 'Let it be granted', he says,

> that we all understand that the word 'God' means what it is claimed to mean, namely 'that than which nothing greater can be thought of'. However, it does not follow that we all understand that what is signified by this word exists in the real world. All that follows is that it exists in the apprehension of the intellect. Nor can it be shown that this being really exists unless it is conceded that there really is something such that nothing greater can be thought of; and this premiss is denied by those who maintain that God does not exist.

My own answer to M. Descartes, which is based on this passage, is briefly this. Even if it is granted that a supremely perfect being carries the implication of existence in virtue of its very title, it still does not follow that the existence in question is anything actual in the real world; all that follows is that the concept of existence is inseparably linked to the concept of a supreme being. So you cannot infer that the existence of God is anything actual unless you suppose that the supreme being actually exists; for then it will actually contain all perfections, including the perfection of real existence.

Pardon me, gentlemen: I am now rather tired and propose to have a little fun. The complex 'existing lion' includes both 'lion' and 'existence', and it includes them essentially, for if you take away either element it will not be the same complex. But now, has not God had clear and distinct knowledge of this composite from all eternity? And does not the idea of this composite, as a composite, involve both elements essentially? In other words, does not existence belong to the essence of the composite 'existing lion'? Nevertheless the distinct knowledge of God, the distinct knowledge he has from eternity, does not compel either element in the composite to exist, unless we assume that the composite itself exists (in which case it will contain all its essential perfections including actual existence). Similarly even if I have distinct knowledge of a supreme being, and even if the supremely perfect being includes existence as an essential part of the concept, it still does not follow that the existence in question is anything actual, unless we suppose that the supreme being exists (for in that case it will include actual existence along with all its other perfections). Accordingly we must look elsewhere for a proof that the supremely perfect being exists. [*First Objections*: CSM II 70–2]

The author of the objections here again compares one of my arguments with one of St Thomas's, thus as it were forcing me to explain how one argument can have any greater force than the other. I think I can do this without too much unpleasantness. For, first, St Thomas did not put forward the argument as his own; second, he did not arrive at the same conclusion as I do; and lastly, on this issue I do not differ from the Angelic Doctor in any respect. St Thomas asks whether the existence of God is self-evident as far as we are concerned, that is, whether it is obvious to everyone; and he answers, correctly, that it is not. The argument which he then puts forward as an objection to his own position can be stated as follows. 'Once we have understood the meaning of the word "God", we understand it to mean 'that than which nothing greater can be conceived". But to exist in reality as well as in the intellect is greater than to exist in the intellect alone. Therefore, once we have understood the meaning of the word "God" we understand that God exists in reality as well as in the understanding.' In this form the argument is manifestly invalid, for the only conclusion that should have been drawn is: 'Therefore, once we have understood the meaning of the word "God" we understand that what is conveyed is that God exists in reality as well as in the understanding.' Yet because a word conveys something, that thing is not therefore shown to be true. My argument however was as follows: 'That which we clearly and distinctly understand to belong to the true and immutable nature, or essence, or form of something, can truly be asserted of that thing. But once we have made a sufficiently careful investigation of what God is, we clearly and distinctly understand that existence belongs to his true and immutable nature.

116

Hence we can now truly assert of God that he does exist.' Here at least the conclusion does follow from the premises. But, what is more, the major premiss cannot be denied, because it has already been conceded that whatever we clearly and distinctly understand is true. Hence only the minor premiss remains, and here I confess that there is considerable difficulty. In the first place we are so accustomed to distinguishing existence from essence in the case of all other things that we fail to notice how closely existence belongs to essence in the case of God as compared with that of other things. Next, we do not distinguish what belongs to the true and immutable essence of a thing from what is attributed to it merely by a fiction of the intellect. So, even if we observe clearly enough that existence belongs to the essence of God, we do not draw the conclusion that God exists, because we do not know whether his essence is immutable and true, or merely invented by us.

But to remove the first part of the difficulty we must distinguish between possible and necessary existence. It must be noted that possible existence is contained in the concept or idea of everything that we clearly and distinctly understand; but in no case is necessary existence so contained, except in the case of the idea of God. Those who carefully attend to this difference between the idea of God and every other idea will undoubtedly perceive that even though our understanding of other things always involves understanding them as if they were existing things, it does not follow that they do exist, but merely that they are capable of existing. For our understanding does not show us that it is necessary for actual existence to be conjoined with their other properties. But, from the fact that we understand that actual existence is necessarily and always conjoined with the other attributes of God, it certainly does follow that God exists.

To remove the second part of the difficulty, we must notice a point about ideas which do not contain true and immutable natures but merely ones which are invented and put together by the intellect. Such ideas can always be split up by the same intellect, not simply by an abstraction but by a clear and distinct intellectual operation, so that any ideas which the intellect cannot split up in this way were clearly not put together by the intellect. When, for example, I think of a winged horse or an actually existing lion, or a triangle inscribed in a square, I readily understand that I am also able to think of a horse without wings, or a lion which does not exist, or a triangle apart from a square, and so on; hence these things do

117

127

not have true and immutable natures. But if I think of a triangle or a square (I will not now include the lion or the horse, since their natures are not transparently clear to us), then whatever I apprehend as being contained in the idea of a triangle – for example that its three angles are equal to two right angles – I can with truth assert of the triangle. And the same applies to the square with respect to whatever I apprehend as being contained in the idea of a square. For even if I can understand what a triangle is if I abstract the fact that its three angles are equal to two right angles, I cannot deny that this property applies to the triangle by a clear and distinct intellectual operation – that is, while at the same time understanding what I mean by my denial. Moreover, if I consider a triangle inscribed in a square, with a view not to attributing to the square properties that belong only to the triangle, or attributing to the triangle properties that belong to the square, but with a view to examining only the properties which arise out of the conjunction of the two, then the nature of this composite will be just as true and immutable as the nature of the triangle alone or the square alone. And hence it will be quite in order to maintain that the square is not less than double the area of the triangle inscribed within it, and to affirm other similar properties that belong to the nature of this composite figure.

But if I were to think that the idea of a supremely perfect body contained existence, on the grounds that it is a greater perfection to exist both in reality and in the intellect than it is to exist in the intellect alone, I could not infer from this that the supremely perfect body exists, but only that it is capable of existing. For I can see quite well that this idea has been put together by my own intellect which has linked together all bodily perfections; and existence does not arise out of the other bodily perfections because it can equally well be affirmed or denied of them. Indeed, when I examine the idea of a body, I perceive that a body has no power to create itself or maintain itself in existence; and I rightly conclude that necessary existence – and it is only necessary existence that is at issue here – no more belongs to the nature of a body, however perfect, than it belongs to the nature of a mountain to be without a valley, or to the nature of a triangle to have angles whose sum is greater than two right angles. But instead of a body, let us now take a thing – whatever this thing turns out to be – which possesses all the perfections which can exist together. If we ask whether existence should be included among these perfections, we will admittedly be in some doubt at first. For our mind, which is finite, normally thinks of these perfections only separately, and hence may not immediately notice the necessity of their being joined together. Yet if we attentively examine whether existence belongs to a supremely powerful being, and what sort of existence it is, we shall be able to perceive clearly and distinctly the following facts. First, possible existence, at the very least, belongs to such a being, just as it belongs to all the other things of which we have a distinct idea, even to those which are put together through a fiction of the intellect. Next, when we attend to the immense power of this being, we shall be unable to think of its existence as possible without also recognizing that it can exist by its own power; and we shall infer from this that this being does really exist and has existed from eternity, since it is quite evident by the natural light that what can exist by its own power always exists. So we shall come to understand that necessary existence is contained in the idea of a supremely powerful being, not by any fiction of the intellect, but because it belongs to the true and immutable nature of such a being that it exists. And we shall also easily perceive that this supremely powerful being cannot but possess within it all the other perfections that are contained in the idea of God; and hence these perfections exist in God and are joined together not by any fiction of the intellect but by their very nature. [*First Replies*: CSM II 82–5]

[Eternal truths and God]

How can the truths of geometry or metaphysics, such as those you refer to, be immutable and eternal and yet not be independent of God? What sort of causal dependence on God do they have? Could he have brought 418 it about that there has never been any such thing as the nature of a triangle? And how, may we ask, could he have made it untrue from eternity that twice four makes eight, or that a triangle has three angles? Either these truths depend solely on the intellect, while it is thinking of them, or on existing things, or else they are independent, since it seems that God could not have brought it about that any of these essences or truths did not obtain from all eternity. [*Sixth Objections*: CSM II 281]

If anyone attends to the immeasurable greatness of God he will find it manifestly clear that there can be nothing whatsoever which does not depend on him. This applies not just to everything that subsists, but to all order, every law, and every reason for anything's being true or good.

If this were not so, then ... God would not be completely indifferent with respect to the creation of what he did in fact create. If some reason for something's being good had existed prior to his preordination, this would have determined God to prefer those things which it was best to do. But, on the contrary, just because he resolved to prefer those things which are now to be done, for this very reason, in the words of Genesis, 436 'they are very good';[5] in other words, the reason for their goodness depends on the fact that he exercised his will to make them so. There is no need to ask what category of causality is applicable to the dependence of this goodness upon God, or to the dependence on him of other truths, both mathematical and metaphysical. For since the various kinds of cause were enumerated by thinkers who did not, perhaps, attend to this type of causality, it is hardly surprising that they gave no name to it. But in fact they did give it a name, for it can be called efficient causality, in the sense that a king may be called the efficient cause of a law, although the law itself is not a thing which has physical existence, but is merely what they call a 'moral entity'. Again, there is no need to ask how God could have brought it about from eternity that it was not true that twice four makes eight, and so on; for I admit this is unintelligible to us. Yet on the other hand I do understand, quite correctly, that there can be nothing in any category of being that does not depend on God; I also understand that it would have been easy for God to ordain certain things such that we human beings cannot understand the possibility of their being otherwise than they are. And therefore it would be irrational for us to doubt what we do understand correctly just because there is something which we do not understand and which, so far as we can see, there is no reason why we should understand. Hence we should not suppose that eternal truths 'depend on the human intellect or on other existing things'; they depend on God alone, who, as the supreme legislator, has ordained them for eternity. [*Sixth Replies*: CSM II 293–4]

[Clear and distinct perception and the 'Cartesian Circle']

125 You are not yet certain of the existence of God, and you say that you are not certain of anything, and cannot know anything clearly and distinctly

---

[5] Genesis 1:31.

until you have achieved clear and certain knowledge of the existence of God.[6] It follows from this that you do not yet clearly and distinctly know that you are a thinking thing, since, on your own admission, that knowledge depends on the clear knowledge of an existing God; and this you have not yet proved in the passage where you draw the conclusion that you clearly know what you are.

Moreover, an atheist is clearly and distinctly aware that the three angles of a triangle are equal to two right angles; but so far is he from supposing the existence of God that he completely denies it. According to the atheist, if God existed there would be a supreme being and a supreme good; that is to say, the infinite would exist. But the infinite in every category of perfection excludes everything else whatsoever – every kind of being and goodness, as well as every kind of non-being and evil. Yet in fact there are many kinds of being and goodness, and many kinds of non-being and evil. We think you should deal with this objection, so that the impious have no arguments left to put forward. [*Second Objections*: CSM II 89]

When I said that we can know nothing for certain until we are aware that God exists, I expressly declared that I was speaking only of knowledge of those conclusions which can be recalled when we are no longer attending to the arguments by means of which we deduced them.[7] Now awareness of first principles is not normally called 'knowledge' by dialectitians . . . (140)

The fact that an atheist can be 'clearly aware that the three angles of a triangle are equal to two right angles' is something I do not dispute. But I maintain that this awareness of his is not true knowledge, since no act of awareness that can be rendered doubtful seems fit to be called knowledge.[8] Now since we are supposing that this individual is an atheist, he cannot be certain that he is not being deceived on matters which seem to him to be very evident (as I fully explained). And although this doubt may not occur to him, it can still crop up if someone (141)

---

[6] Cf. Med. III, above, p. 30; Med. V, above, p. 54. [7] Cf. Med. V, above, p. 54.

[8] Descartes seems to distinguish here between an isolated cognition or act of awareness (*cognitio*) and systematic, properly grounded knowledge (*scientia*). Compare the remarks in *The Search for Truth* about the need to acquire 'a body of knowledge firm and certain enough to deserve the name "science"': AT X 513; CSM II 408.

else raises the point or if he looks into the matter himself. So he will never be free of this doubt until he acknowledges that God exists.

It does not matter that the atheist may think he has demonstrations to prove that there is no God. For, since these proofs are quite unsound, it will always be possible to point out their flaws to him, and when this happens he will have to abandon his view. [*Second Replies*: CSM II 100–1]

(126) It is not, however, necessary to suppose that God is a deceiver in order to explain your being deceived about matters which you think you clearly and distinctly know. The cause of this deception could lie in you, though you are wholly unaware of it. Why should it not be in your nature to be subject to constant – or at least very frequent – deception? How can you establish with certainty that you are not deceived, or capable of being deceived, in matters which you think you know clearly and distinctly? Have we not often seen people turn out to have been deceived in matters where they thought their knowledge was as clear as the sunlight? Your principle of clear and distinct knowledge thus requires a clear and distinct explanation, in such a way as to rule out the possibility that anyone of sound mind may be deceived on matters which he thinks he knows clearly and distinctly. Failing this, we do not see that any degree of certainty can possibly be within your reach or that of mankind in general. [*Second Objections*: CSM II 90]

From time to time it does appear that we are really deceived by the natural instinct which God gave us, as in the case of the thirst felt by those who suffer from dropsy. These patients have a positive impulse to drink which derives from the nature that God has bestowed on the body in order to preserve it; yet this nature does deceive them because on this occasion the drink will have a harmful effect. Nevertheless, this is not inconsistent with the goodness or veracity of God, and I have explained why in the Sixth Meditation.[9]

In the case of our clearest and most careful judgements, however, this
144 kind of explanation would not be possible, since if such judgements were false they could not be corrected by any clearer judgements or by means of any other natural faculty. In such cases I simply assert that it is

[9] Above, p. 69.

impossible for us to be deceived. Since God is the supreme being, he must also be supremely good and true, and it would therefore be a contradiction that anything should be created by him which positively tends towards falsehood. Now everything real which is in us must have been bestowed on us by God (this was proved when his existence was proved); moreover, we have a real faculty for recognizing the truth and distinguishing it from falsehood, as is clear merely from the fact that we have within us ideas of truth and falsehood. Hence this faculty must tend towards the truth, at least when we use it correctly (that is, by assenting only to what we clearly and distinctly perceive, for no other correct method of employing this faculty can be imagined). For if it did not so tend then, since God gave it to us, he would rightly have to be regarded as a deceiver.

Hence you see that once we have become aware that God exists it is necessary for us to imagine that he is a deceiver if we wish to cast doubt on what we clearly and distinctly perceive. And since it is impossible to imagine that he is a deceiver, whatever we clearly and distinctly perceive must be completely accepted as true and certain.

But since I see that you are still stuck fast in the doubts which I put forward in the First Meditation, and which I thought I had very carefully removed in the succeeding Meditations, I shall now expound for a second time the basis on which it seems to me that all human certainty can be founded.

First of all, as soon as we think that we correctly perceive something, we are spontaneously convinced that it is true. Now if this conviction is so firm that it is impossible for us ever to have any reason for doubting what we are convinced of, then there are no further questions for us to ask: we have everything that we could reasonably want. What is it to us that someone may make out that the perception whose truth we are so firmly convinced of may appear false to God or an angel, so that it is, absolutely speaking, false? Why should this 'absolute falsity' bother us, since we neither believe in it nor have even the smallest suspicion of it? For the supposition which we are making here is of a conviction so firm that it is quite incapable of being destroyed; and such a conviction is clearly the same as the most perfect certainty.

But it may be doubted whether any such certainty, or firm and immutable conviction, is in fact to be had.

145

It is clear that we do not have this kind of certainty in cases where our perception is even the slightest bit obscure or confused, for such obscurity, whatever its degree, is quite sufficient to make us have doubts in such cases. Again, we do not have the required kind of certainty with regard to matters which we perceive solely by means of the senses, however clear such perception may be. For we have often noted that error can be detected in the senses, as when someone with dropsy feels thirsty or when someone with jaundice sees snow as yellow; for when he sees it as yellow he sees it just as clearly and distinctly as we do when we see it as white. Accordingly, if there is any certainty to be had, the only remaining alternative is that it occurs in matters that are clearly perceived by the intellect and nowhere else.

Now some of these are so transparently clear and at the same time so simple that we cannot ever think of them without believing them to be true. The fact that I exist so long as I am thinking, or that what is done cannot be undone, are examples of truths in respect of which we manifestly possess this kind of certainty. For we cannot doubt them unless we think of them; but we cannot think of them without at the same time believing they are true, as was supposed. Hence we cannot doubt them without at the same time believing they are true; that is, we can never doubt them.

It is no objection to this to say that we have often seen people 'turn out to have been deceived in matters where they thought their knowledge was as clear as the sunlight'. For we have never seen, indeed no one could possibly see, this happening to those who have relied solely on the intellect in their quest for clarity in their perceptions; we have seen it happen only to those who tried to derive such clarity from the senses or from some false preconceived opinion.

It is also no objection for someone to make out that such items might appear false to God or to an angel. For the evident clarity of our perceptions does not allow us to listen to anyone who makes up this kind of story.

There are other matters which are perceived very clearly by our intellect so long as we attend to the arguments on which our knowledge of them depends; and we are therefore incapable of doubting them during this time. But we may forget the arguments in question and later remember simply the conclusions which were deduced from them. The question will now arise as to whether we possess the same firm and immutable conviction concerning these conclusions, when we simply recollect that they were previously deduced from quite evident principles (our ability to call them 'conclusions' presupposes such a recollection). My reply is that the required certainty is indeed possessed by those whose knowledge of God enables them to understand that the intellectual faculty which he gave them cannot but tend towards the truth; but the required certainty is not possessed by others. This point was explained so clearly at the end of the Fifth Meditation[10] that it does not seem necessary to add anything further here. [*Second Replies*: CSM II 102–5]

I have one further worry, namely how the author avoids reasoning in a (214) circle when he says that we are sure that what we clearly and distinctly perceive is true only because God exists.[11]

But we can be sure that God exists only because we clearly and distinctly perceive this. Hence, before we can be sure that God exists, we ought to be able to be sure that whatever we perceive clearly and evidently is true. [*Fourth Objections*: CSM II 150]

Lastly, as to the fact that I was not guilty of circularity when I said that the only reason we have for being sure that what we clearly and distinctly perceive is true is the fact that God exists, but that we are sure that God 246 exists only because we perceive this clearly: I have already given an adequate explanation of this point in my reply to the Second Objections, where I made a distinction between what we in fact perceive clearly and what we remember having perceived clearly on a previous occasion.[12] To begin with, we are sure that God exists because we attend to the arguments which prove this; but subsequently it is enough for us to remember that we perceived something clearly in order for us to be certain that it is true. This would not be sufficient if we did not know that God exists and is not a deceiver. [*Fourth Replies*: CSM II 171]

---

[10] Above, pp. 54f.   [11] Cf. Med. V, above, p. 55.   [12] See above, pp. 131 and 134.

[On the Sixth Meditation]

[The real distinction between mind and body]

It is clear that the question he promised to answer still remains outstanding: how does it follow, from the fact that he is aware of nothing else belonging to his essence, that nothing else does in fact belong to it?[1] I must confess that I am somewhat slow, but I have been unable to find anywhere in the Second Meditation an answer to this question. As far as I can gather, however, the author does attempt a proof of this claim in the Sixth Meditation, since he takes it to depend on his having clear knowledge of God, which he had not yet arrived at in the Second Meditation. This is how the proof goes:

> I know ... that everything which I clearly and distinctly understand is capable of being created by God so as to correspond exactly with my understanding of it. Hence the fact that I can clearly and distinctly understand one thing apart from another is enough to make me certain that the two things are distinct, since they are capable of being separated, at least by God. The question of what kind of power is required to bring about such a separation does not affect the judgement that the two things are distinct... Now on the one hand I have a clear and distinct idea of myself, in so far as I am simply a thinking, non-extended thing; and on the other hand I have a distinct idea of body, in so far as this is simply an extended, non-thinking thing. And accordingly, it is certain that I am really distinct from my body, and can exist without it.[2]

200

---

[1] See Preface, above, p. 8.   [2] Above, pp. 61–2.

We must pause a little here, for it seems to me that in these few words lies the crux of the whole difficulty.

First of all, if the major premiss of this syllogism is to be true, it must be taken to apply not to any kind of knowledge of a thing, nor even to clear and distinct knowledge; it must apply solely to knowledge which is adequate. For our distinguished author admits in his reply to the theologian, that if one thing can be conceived distinctly and separately from another 'by an abstraction of the intellect which conceives the thing inadequately', then this is sufficient for there to be a formal distinction between the two, but it does not require that there be a real distinction. And in the same passage he draws the following conclusion:

> By contrast, I have a complete understanding of what a body is when I think that it is merely something having extension, shape and motion, and I deny that it has anything which belongs to the nature of a mind. Conversely, I understand the mind to be a complete thing, which doubts, understands, wills, and so on, even though I deny that it has any of the attributes which are contained in the idea of a body. Hence there is a real distinction between the body and the mind.[3]

But someone may call this minor premiss into doubt and maintain that the conception you have of yourself when you conceive of yourself as a thinking, non-extended thing is an inadequate one; and the same may be true of your conception of yourself[4] as an extended, non-thinking thing. Hence we must look at how this is proved in the earlier part of the argument. For I do not think that this matter is so clear that it should be assumed without proof as a first principle that is not susceptible of demonstration.

As to the first part of your claim, namely that you have a complete understanding of what a body is when you think that it is merely 201 something having extension, shape, motion etc., and you deny that it has anything which belongs to the nature of a mind, this proves little. For those who maintain that our mind is corporeal do not on that account suppose that every body is a mind. On their view, body would be related to mind as a genus is related to a species. Now a genus can be understood apart from a species, even if we deny of the genus what is

---

[3] *First Replies*: AT VII 121; CSM II 86.   [4] '. . . i.e. your body' (supplied in French version).

proper and peculiar to the species – hence the common maxim of logicians, 'The negation of the species does not negate the genus.' Thus I can understand the genus 'figure' apart from my understanding of any of the properties which are peculiar to a circle. It therefore remains to be proved that the mind can be completely and adequately understood apart from the body.

I cannot see anywhere in the entire work an argument which could serve to prove this claim, apart from what is suggested at the beginning: 'I can deny that any body exists, or that there is any extended thing at all, yet it remains certain to me that I exist, so long as I am making this denial or thinking it. Hence I am a thinking thing, not a body, and the body does not belong to the knowledge I have of myself.'[5]

But so far as I can see, the only result that follows from this is that I can obtain some knowledge of myself without knowledge of the body. But it is not yet transparently clear to me that this knowledge is complete and adequate, so as to enable me to be certain that I am not mistaken in excluding body from my essence. I shall explain the point by means of an example.

Suppose someone knows for certain that the angle in a semi-circle is a right angle, and hence that the triangle formed by this angle and the diameter of the circle is right-angled. In spite of this, he may doubt, or not yet have grasped for certain, that the square on the hypotenuse is equal to the squares on the other two sides; indeed he may even deny this if he is misled by some fallacy. But now, if he uses the same argument as that proposed by our illustrious author, he may appear to have confirmation of his false belief, as follows: 'I clearly and distinctly perceive', he may say, 'that the triangle is right-angled; but I doubt that the square on the hypotenuse is equal to the squares on the other two sides; therefore it does not belong to the essence of the triangle that the square on its hypotenuse is equal to the squares on the other sides.'

Again, even if I deny that the square on the hypotenuse is equal to the square on the other two sides, I still remain sure that the triangle is right-angled, and my mind retains the clear and distinct knowledge that one of its angles is a right angle. And given that this is so, not even God could bring it about that the triangle is not right-angled.

202

---

[5] Not an exact quotation. Cf. Med. II, above, pp. 22–3.

I might argue from this that the property which I doubt, or which can be removed while leaving my idea intact, does not belong to the essence of the triangle.

Moreover, 'I know', says M. Descartes, 'that everything which I clearly and distinctly understand is capable of being created by God as to correspond exactly with my understanding of it. And hence the fact that I can clearly and distinctly understand one thing apart from another is enough to make me certain that the two things are distinct, since they are capable of being separated by God.'[6] Yet I clearly and distinctly understand that this triangle is right-angled, without understanding that the square on the hypotenuse is equal to the squares on the other sides. It follows on this reasoning that God, at least, could create a right-angled triangle with the square on its hypotenuse not equal to the squares on the other sides.

I do not see any possible reply here, except that the person in this example does not clearly and distinctly perceive that the triangle is right-angled. But how is my perception of the nature of my mind any clearer than his perception of the nature of the triangle? He is just as certain that the triangle in the semi-circle has one right angle (which is the criterion of a right-angled triangle) as I am certain that I exist because I am thinking.

Now although the man in the example clearly and distinctly knows that the triangle is right-angled, he is wrong in thinking that the aforesaid relationship between the squares on the sides does not belong to the nature of the triangle. Similarly, although I clearly and distinctly know my nature to be something that thinks, may I, too, not perhaps be wrong in thinking that nothing else belongs to my nature apart from the fact that I am a thinking thing? Perhaps the fact that I am an extended thing may also belong to my nature.

Someone may also make the point that since I infer my existence from the fact that I am thinking, it is certainly no surprise if the idea that I form by thinking of myself in this way represents to my mind nothing other than myself as a thinking thing. For the idea was derived entirely from my thought. Hence it seems that this idea cannot provide any evidence that nothing belongs to my essence beyond what is contained in the idea.

[6] Med. VI, above, p. 61.

It seems, moreover, that the argument proves too much, and takes us back to the Platonic view (which M. Descartes nonetheless rejects) that nothing corporeal belongs to our essence, so that man is merely a rational soul, and the body merely a vehicle for the soul – a view which gives rise to the definition of man as 'a soul which makes use of a body'.

If you reply that body is not straightforwardly excluded from my essence, but is ruled out only and precisely in so far as I am a thinking thing, it seems that there is a danger that someone will suspect that my knowledge of myself as a thinking thing does not qualify as knowledge of a being of which I have a complete and adequate conception; it seems instead that I conceive of it only inadequately, and by a certain intellectual abstraction ...

Geometers conceive of a line as a length without breadth, and they conceive of a surface as length and breadth without depth, despite the fact that no length exists without breadth, and no breadth without depth. In the same way, someone may perhaps suspect that every thinking thing is also an extended thing – an extended thing which, besides the attributes it has in common with other extended things, such as shape, motion etc., also possesses the peculiar power of thought. This would mean that although, simply in virtue of this power, it can by an intellectual abstraction be apprehended as a thinking thing, in reality bodily attributes may belong to this thinking thing. In the same way, although quantity can be conceived in terms of length alone, in reality breadth and depth belong to every quantity along with length.

(204)   The difficulty is increased by the fact that the power of thought appears to be attached to bodily organs, since it can be regarded as dormant in infants and extinguished in the case of madmen. And this is an objection strongly pressed by those impious people who try to do away with the soul altogether. [*Fourth Objections*: CSM II 140–3]

Now the mind can be perceived distinctly and completely (that is, sufficiently for it to be considered a complete thing) without any of the forms or attributes by which we recognize that body is a substance, as I think I showed quite adequately in the Second Meditation. And similarly a body can be understood distinctly and as a complete thing, without any of the attributes which belong to the mind.

But here my distinguished critic argues that although I can obtain some knowledge of myself without knowledge of the body, it does not

140

follow that this knowledge is complete and adequate, so as to enable me to be certain that I am not mistaken in excluding body from my essence. He explains the point by using the example of a triangle inscribed in a semi-circle, which we can clearly and distinctly understand to be right-angled although we do not know, or may even deny, that the square on the hypotenuse is equal to the squares on the other sides. But we cannot infer from this that there could be a right-angled triangle such that the square on the hypotenuse is not equal to the squares on the other sides. 224

But this example differs in many respects from the case under discussion.

First of all, though a triangle can perhaps be taken concretely as a substance having a triangular shape, it is certain that the property of having the square on the hypotenuse equal to the squares on the other sides is not a substance. So neither the triangle nor the property can be understood as a complete thing in the way in which mind and body can be so understood; nor can either item be called a 'thing' in the sense in which I said 'it is enough that I can understand one thing (that is, a complete thing) apart from another' etc.[7] This is clear from the passage which comes next: 'Besides I find in myself faculties' etc. I did not say that these faculties were *things*, but carefully distinguished them from things or substances.

Secondly, although we can clearly and distinctly understand that a triangle in a semi-circle is right-angled without being aware that the square on the hypotenuse is equal to the squares on the other two sides, we cannot have a clear understanding of a triangle having the square on its hypotenuse equal to the squares on the other sides without at the same time being aware that it is right-angled. And yet we can clearly and distinctly perceive the mind without the body and the body without the mind. 225

Thirdly, although it is possible to have a concept of a triangle inscribed in a semi-circle which does not include the fact that the square on the hypotenuse is equal to the squares on the other sides, it is not possible to have a concept of the triangle such that no ratio at all is understood to hold between the square on the hypotenuse and the squares on the other sides. Hence, though we may be unaware of what that ratio is, we cannot say that any given ratio does not hold unless we clearly understand that it does not belong to the triangle; and where the

[7] Med. VI, above, p. 61.

141

ratio is one of equality, this can never be understood. Yet the concept of body includes nothing at all which belongs to the mind, and the concept of mind includes nothing at all which belongs to the body.

So although I said 'it is enough that I can clearly and distinctly understand one thing apart from another' etc., one cannot go on to argue 'yet I clearly and distinctly understand that this triangle is right-angled without understanding that the square on the hypotenuse' etc. There are three reasons for this. First, the ratio between the square on the hypotenuse and the squares on the other sides is not a complete thing. Secondly, we do not clearly understand the ratio to be equal except in the case of a right-angled triangle. And thirdly, there is no way in which the triangle can be distinctly understood if the ratio which obtains between the square on the hypotenuse and the squares on the other sides is said not to hold.

But now I must explain how the mere fact that I can clearly and distinctly understand one substance apart from another is enough to make me certain that one excludes the other.[8]

The answer is that the notion of a *substance* is just this – that it can exist by itself, that is without the aid of any other substance. And there is no one who has ever perceived two substances by means of two different concepts without judging that they are really distinct.

Hence, had I not been looking for greater than ordinary certainty, I should have been content to have shown in the Second Meditation that the mind can be understood as a subsisting thing despite the fact that nothing belonging to the body is attributed to it, and that, conversely, the body can be understood as a subsisting thing despite the fact that nothing belonging to the mind is attributed to it. I should have added nothing more in order to demonstrate that there is a real distinction between the mind and the body, since we commonly judge that the order in which things are mutually related in our perception of them corresponds to the order in which they are related in actual reality. But one of the exaggerated doubts which I put forward in the First Meditation went so far as to make it impossible for me to be certain of this very point (namely whether things do in reality correspond to our perception of them), so long as I was supposing myself to be ignorant of the author of

226

---

[8] Cf. Med. VI, above, p. 61.

my being. And this is why everything I wrote on the subject of God and truth in the Third, Fourth and Fifth Meditations contributes to the conclusion that there is a real distinction between the mind and the body, which I finally established in the Sixth Meditation.

And yet, says M. Arnauld, 'I have a clear understanding of a triangle inscribed in a semi-circle without knowing that the square on the hypotenuse is equal to the squares on the other sides.' It is true that the triangle is intelligible even though we do not think of the ratio which obtains between the square on the hypotenuse and the squares on the other sides; but it is not intelligible that this ratio should be denied of the triangle. In the case of the mind, by contrast, not only do we understand it to exist without the body, but, what is more, all the attributes which belong to a body can be denied of it. For it is of the nature of substances that they should mutually exclude one another.

M. Arnauld goes on to say: 'Since I infer my existence from the fact that I am thinking, it is certainly no surprise if the idea that I form in this way represents me simply as a thinking thing.' But this is no objection to my argument. For it is equally true that when I examine the nature of the body, I find nothing at all in it which savours of thought. And we can have no better evidence for a distinction between two things than the fact that if we examine either of them, whatever we find in one is different from what we find in the other ...

I thought I was very careful to guard against anyone inferring from this that man was simply 'a soul which makes use of a body'. For in the Sixth Meditation, where I dealt with the distinction between the mind and the body, I also proved at the same time that the mind is substantially united with the body.[9] And the arguments which I used to prove this are as strong as any I can remember ever having read. ... [But] the substantial union does not prevent our having a clear and distinct concept of the mind on its own, as a complete thing. The concept is thus very different from that of a surface or a line, which cannot be understood as complete things unless we attribute to them not just length and breadth, but also depth.

Finally, the fact that 'the power of thought is dormant in infants and extinguished in madmen' (I should say not 'extinguished' but 'disturbed')

227

228

[9] See p. 64, above.

does not show that we should regard it as so attached to bodily organs that it cannot exist without them. The fact that thought is often impeded by bodily organs, as we know from our own frequent experience, does not at all entail that it is produced by those organs. This latter view is one for which not even the slightest proof can be adduced.

229   I must admit, however, that the fact that the mind is closely conjoined with the body, which we experience constantly through our senses, does result in our not being aware of the real distinction between mind and body unless we attentively meditate on the subject. But I think that those who repeatedly ponder on what I wrote in the Second Meditation will be easily convinced that the mind is distinct from the body, and distinct not just by a fiction or abstraction of the intellect: it can be known as a distinct thing because it is in reality distinct. [*Fourth Replies*: CSM II 157–60]

* * *

We ask you to provide in addition a reliable rule and some firm criteria which will make us utterly sure of the following point: when we understand something entirely apart from some other thing, in the way you describe, is it indeed certain that the one is so distinct from the other that they could subsist apart – at least through the power of God?[10] That is,

419   how can we know for sure, clearly and distinctly, that when our intellect makes this distinction, the distinction does not arise solely from the intellect but arises from the nature of the things themselves? For when we contemplate the immensity of God while not thinking of his justice, or when we contemplate his existence when not thinking of the Son or the Holy Spirit, do we not have a complete perception of that existence, or of God as existing, entirely apart from the other Persons of the Trinity? So could not an unbeliever deny that these Persons belong to God on the same reasoning that leads you to deny that the mind or thought belongs to the body? If anyone concludes that the Son and the Holy Spirit are essentially distinct from God the Father or that they can be separated from him, this will be an unsound inference; and in the same way, no one will grant you that thought, or the human mind, is distinct from the body, despite the fact that you conceive one apart from

[10] Cf. Med. VI, above, p. 61.

the other and deny the one of the other, and despite your belief that this does not come about simply through an abstraction of your mind. [*Sixth Objections*: CSM II 282]

When, on the basis of the arguments set out in these Meditations, I first 440 drew the conclusion that the human mind is really distinct from the body, better known than the body, and so on, I was compelled to accept these results because everything in the reasoning was coherent and was inferred from quite evident principles in accordance with the rules of logic. But I confess that for all that I was not entirely convinced; I was in the same plight as astronomers who have established by argument that the sun is several times larger than the earth, and yet still cannot prevent themselves judging that it is smaller, when they actually look at it. However, I went on from here, and proceeded to apply the same fundamental principles to the consideration of physical things. First I attended to the ideas or notions of each particular thing which I found within myself, and I carefully distinguished them one from the other so that all my judgements should match them. I observed as a result that nothing whatever belongs to the concept of body except the fact that it is something which has length, breadth and depth and is capable of various shapes and motions; moreover, these shapes and motions are merely modes which no power whatever can cause to exist apart from body. But colours, smells, tastes and so on, are, I observed, merely certain sensations which exist in my thought, and are as different from bodies as pain is different from the shape and motion of the weapon which produces it. And lastly, I observed that heaviness and hardness and the power to heat or to attract, or to purge, and all the other qualities which we experience in bodies, consist solely in the motion of bodies, or its absence, and the configuration and situation of their parts.

Since these opinions were completely different from those which I had 441 previously held regarding physical things, I next began to consider what had led me to take a different view before. The principal cause, I discovered, was this. From infancy I had made a variety of judgements about physical things in so far as they contributed to preserving the life which I was embarking on; and subsequently I retained the same opinions I had originally formed of these things. But at that age the mind employed the bodily organs less correctly than it now does, and was more firmly attached to them; hence it had no thoughts apart from them and perceived things only in a confused manner. Although it was aware of its own nature and had within itself an idea of thought as well as an idea of extension, it never exercised its intellect on anything without at the same time picturing something in the imagination. It therefore took thought and extension to be one and the same thing, and referred to the body all the notions which it had concerning things related to the intellect. Now I had never freed myself from these preconceived opinions in later life, and hence there was nothing that I knew with sufficient distinctness, and there was nothing I did not suppose to be corporeal; however, in the case of those very things that I supposed to be corporeal, the ideas or concepts which I formed were frequently such as to refer to minds rather than bodies.

For example, I conceived of gravity[11] as if it were some sort of real quality, which inhered in solid bodies; and although I called it a 'quality', thereby referring it to the bodies in which it inhered, by adding that it was 'real' I was in fact thinking that it was a substance. In the same way clothing, regarded in itself, is a substance, even though when referred to the man who wears it, it is a quality. Or again, the mind, even though it is in fact a substance, can nonetheless be said to be a quality of the body to which it is joined. And although I imagined gravity to be scattered throughout the whole body that is heavy, I still did not attribute to it the extension which constitutes the nature of a body. For the true extension of a body is such as to exclude any interpenetration of the parts, whereas I thought that there was the same amount of gravity in a ten foot piece of wood as in a one foot lump of gold or other metal – indeed I thought that the whole of the gravity could be contracted to a mathematical point. Moreover, I saw that the gravity, while remaining coextensive with the heavy body, could exercise all its force in any one part of the body; for if the body were hung from a rope attached to any part of it, it would still pull the rope down with all its force, just as if all the gravity existed in the part actually touching the rope instead of being scattered through the remaining parts. This is exactly the way in which I now understand the mind to be coextensive with the body – the whole mind in the whole body and the whole mind in any one of its parts. But what makes it especially clear that my idea of gravity was taken largely from the idea I had of the mind is the fact that I thought that gravity carried bodies towards the centre of the earth as if it had some knowledge of the centre within itself. For this surely

442

---

[11] Lat. *gravitas*, literally 'heaviness'.

could not happen without knowledge, and there can be no knowledge except in a mind. Nevertheless I continued to apply to gravity various other attributes which cannot be understood to apply to a mind in this way – for example its being divisible, measurable and so on.

But later on I made the observations which led me to make a careful 443 distinction between the idea of the mind and the ideas of body and corporeal motion; and I found that all those other ideas of 'real qualities' or 'substantial forms' which I had previously held were ones which I had put together or constructed from those basic ideas. And thus I very easily freed myself from all the doubts that my critics here put forward. First of all, I did not doubt that I 'had a clear idea of my mind', since I had a close inner awareness of it. Nor did I doubt that 'this idea was quite different from the ideas of other things', and that 'it contained nothing of a corporeal nature'. For I had also looked for true ideas of all these 'other things', and I appeared to have some general acquaintance with all of them; yet everything I found in them was completely different from my idea of the mind. Moreover, I found that the distinction between things such as mind and body, which appeared distinct even though I attentively thought about both of them, is much greater than the distinction between things which are such that when we think of both of them we do not see how one can exist apart from the other (even though we may be able to understand one without thinking of the other). For example, we can understand the immeasurable greatness of God even though we do not attend to his justice; but if we attend to both, it is quite self-contradictory to suppose that he is immeasurably great and yet not just. Again, it is possible to have true knowledge of the existence of God even though we lack knowledge of the Persons of the Holy Trinity, since the latter can be perceived only by a mind which faith has illuminated; yet when we do perceive them, I deny that it is intelligible to suppose that there is a real distinction between them, at least as far as the divine essence is concerned, although such a distinction may be admitted as far as their mutual 444 relationship is concerned. [*Sixth Replies*: CSM II 296–9]

* * *

However much we ponder on the question of whether the idea of our (420) mind (or a human mind), i.e. our knowledge and perception, contains anything corporeal, we cannot go so far as to assert that what we call thought cannot in any way belong to a body subject to some sort of motion. For since we see that there are some bodies that do not think and others, namely human bodies, and perhaps those of the brutes, which do think, will you not yourself convict us of sophistry and of making rash judgements if we infer from this that there are no bodies that think? ...

(421)   Lastly since we do not know what can be done by bodies and their motions, and since you confess that without a divine revelation no one can know everything which God has imparted or could impart to any object, how can you possibly have known that God has not implanted in certain bodies a power or property enabling them to doubt, think etc.? [*Sixth Objections*: CSM II 283, 284]

I was not afraid ... that I might have made the mistake suggested by my critics: seeing that there are 'certain bodies which do not think' (or, rather, clearly understanding that certain bodies can exist without thought), I preferred, they claim, to assert that thought does not belong to the nature of the body rather than to notice that there are certain bodies, namely human ones, which do think, and to infer that thought is a mode of the body. In fact I have never seen or perceived that human bodies think; all I have seen is that there are human beings, who possess both thought and a body. This happens as a result of a thinking thing's being combined with a corporeal thing: I perceived this from the fact that when I examined a thinking thing on its own, I discovered nothing in it which belonged to body, and similarly when I considered corporeal nature on its own I discovered no thought in it. On the contrary, when I examined all the modes of body and mind, I did not observe a single mode the concept of which did not depend on the concept of the thing of which it was a mode. Also, the fact that we often see two things joined together does not license the inference that they are one and the same; but the fact that we sometimes observe one of them apart from the other entirely justifies the inference that they are different. Nor should the power of God deter us from making this inference. For it is a conceptual contradiction to suppose that two things which we clearly perceive as different should become one and the same (that is intrinsically one and

445   the same, as opposed to by combination); this is no less a contradiction than to suppose that two things which are in no way distinct should be separated. Hence, if God has implanted the power of thought in certain

bodies (as he in fact has done in the case of human bodies), then he can remove this power from them, and hence it still remains really distinct from them. [*Sixth Replies*: CSM II 296–9]

[Interaction between soul and body]

There are two further questions they add: how can the soul move the body if it is in no way material, and how can it receive the forms of corporeal objects? . . . These questions presuppose amongst other things an explanation of the union between the soul and the body, which I have not yet dealt with at all. But I will say, for your benefit at least, that the whole problem contained in such questions arises simply from a supposition that is false and cannot in any way be proved, namely that, if the soul and the body are two substances whose nature is different, this prevents them from being able to act on each other. [*Appendix to Fifth Replies*: CSM II 275][12]

AT IXA (213)

[The immortality of the soul]

You say not one word about the immortality of the human mind. Yet this is something you should have taken special care to prove and demonstrate, to counter those people, themselves unworthy of immortality, who utterly deny and even perhaps despise it. What is more . . . it does not seem to follow from the fact that the mind is distinct from the body that it is incorruptible or immortal. What if its nature were limited by the duration of the life of the body, and God had endowed it with just so much strength and existence as to ensure that it came to an end with the death of the body? [*Second Objections*: CSM II 91]

AT VII 128

As to why I wrote nothing concerning the immortality of the soul, I did already explain this in the Synopsis of my *Meditations*. And . . . I did provide an adequate proof of the fact that the soul is distinct from every body. However, you go on to say that it does not follow from the fact that the soul is distinct from the body that it is immortal, since it could still be claimed that God gave it such a nature that its duration comes to an end simultaneously with the end of the body's life. Here I admit that I cannot

153

---

[12] For this 'Appendix', see above, p. 76, note 2.

refute what you say. For I do not take it upon myself to try to use the power of human reason to settle any of those matters which depend on the free will of God. Our natural knowledge tells us that the mind is distinct from the body, and that it is a substance. But in the case of the human body, the difference between it and other bodies consists merely in the arrangement of the limbs and other accidents of this sort; and the final death of the body depends solely on a division or change of shape. Now we have no convincing evidence or precedent to suggest that the death or annihilation of a substance like the mind must result from such a trivial cause as a change in shape, for this is simply a mode, and what is more not a mode of the mind, but a mode of the body which is really distinct from the mind. Indeed, we do not even have any convincing evidence or precedent to suggest that any substance can perish. And this entitles us to conclude that the mind, in so far as it can be known by

154 natural philosophy, is immortal. [*Second Replies*: CSM II 108–9]

[Mechanical bodily movement in humans and animals]

As far as the souls of the brutes are concerned, M. Descartes elsewhere
205 suggests clearly enough that they have none. All they have is a body which is constructed in a particular manner, made up of various organs in such a way that all the operations which we observe can be produced in it and by means of it.[13]

But I fear that this view will not succeed in finding acceptance in people's minds unless it is supported by very solid arguments. For at first sight it seems incredible that it can come about, without the assistance of any soul, that the light reflected from the body of a wolf onto the eyes of a sheep should move the minute fibres of the optic nerves, and that on reaching the brain this motion should spread the animal spirits[14] through the nerves in the manner necessary to precipitate the sheep's flight. [*Fourth Objections*: CSM II 144]

As far as the souls of the brutes are concerned, this is not the place to examine the subject, and, short of giving an account of the whole of physics, I cannot add to the explanatory remarks I made in Part Five of

---

[13] Cf. *Discourse on the Method*, Part Five, AT VI 55ff.; CSM I 139ff.
[14] The 'animal spirits' were a fine gas or vapour supposed in Descartes's time to flow along the neural pathways.

the *Discourse on the Method.* But to avoid passing over the topic in silence, I will say that I think the most important point is that, both in our bodies and those of the brutes, no movement can occur without the presence of all the organs or instruments which would enable the same movement to be produced in a machine. So even in our own case, the mind does not directly move the external limbs, but simply controls the animal spirits which flow from the heart via the brain into the muscles, and sets up certain motions in them; for the spirits are by their nature adapted with equal facility to a great variety of actions. Now a very large number of the motions occurring inside us do not depend in any way on the mind. These include heartbeat, digestion, nutrition, respiration when we are asleep, and also such waking actions as walking, singing, and the like, when these occur without the mind attending to them. When people take a fall, and stick out their hands so as to protect their head, it is not reason that instructs them to do this; it is simply that the sight of the impending fall reaches the brain and sends the animal spirits into the nerves in the manner necessary to produce this movement even without any mental volition, just as it would be produced in a machine. And since our own experience reliably informs us that this is so, why should we be so amazed that 'the light reflected from the body of a wolf onto the eyes of a sheep' should equally be capable of arousing the movement of flight in the sheep? [*Fourth Replies*: CSM II 161]

[The three grades of sensory response]

If we are to get a clear view of what sort of certainty attaches to the senses, we must distinguish three grades of sensory response. The first is limited to the immediate stimulation of the bodily organs by external objects; this can consist in nothing but the motion of the particles of the organs, and any change of shape and position resulting from this motion. The second grade comprises all the immediate effects produced in the mind as a result of its being united with a bodily organ which is affected in this way. Such effects include the perceptions of pain, pleasure, thirst, hunger, colours, sound, taste, smell, heat, cold and the like, which arise from the union and as it were intermingling of mind and body, as explained in the Sixth Meditation.[15] The third grade includes all the

15 Above, pp. 64ff.

judgements about things outside us which we have been accustomed to make from our earliest years – judgements which are occasioned by the movements of these bodily organs.

For example, when I see a stick, it should not be supposed that certain 'intentional forms' fly off the stick towards the eye,[16] but simply that rays of light are reflected off the stick and set up certain movements in the optic nerve and, via the optic nerve, in the brain, as I have explained at some length in the *Optics*.[17] This movement in the brain, which is common to us and the brutes, is the first grade of sensory response. This leads to the second grade, which extends to the mere perception of the colour and light reflected from the stick; it arises from the fact that the mind is so intimately conjoined with the body that it is affected by the movements which occur in it. Nothing more than this should be referred to the sensory faculty, if we wish to distinguish it carefully from the intellect. But suppose that as a result of being affected by this sensation of colour, I judge that a stick, located outside me, is coloured; and suppose that on the basis of the extension of the colour and its boundaries together with its position in relation to the parts of the brain, I make a rational calculation about the size, shape and distance of the stick; although such reasoning is commonly assigned to the senses (which is why I have
438 referred it to the third grade of sensory response), it is clear that it depends solely on the intellect. I demonstrated in the *Optics* how size, distance and shape can be perceived by reasoning alone, which works out any one feature from the other features. The only difference is that when we now make a judgement for the first time because of some new observation, then we attribute it to the intellect; but when from our earliest years we have made judgements, or even rational inferences, about the things which affect our senses, then, even though these judgements were made in exactly the same way as those we make now, we refer them to the senses. The reason for this is that we make the calculation and judgement at great speed because of habit, or rather we remember the judgements we have long made about similar objects; and so we do not distinguish these operations from simple sense-perception.

---

[16] According to the scholastic theory referred to here, what is directly perceived via the senses is not the object itself but a 'form' or 'semblance' (Lat. *species*) transmitted from object to observer.
[17] AT VI 133ff: CSM I 169ff.

It is clear from this that when we say 'The reliability of the intellect is much greater than that of the senses'[18] this means merely that when we are grown up the judgements which we make as result of various new observations are more reliable than those which we formed without any reflection in our early childhood; and this is undoubtedly true. It is clear that we are not here dealing with the first and second grades of sensory response, because no falsity can occur in them. [*Sixth Replies*: CSM II 294–5]

[Coherence and memory in waking life]

You say 'I now notice that there is a vast difference between [the waking state and dreams] in that dreams are never linked by memory with all the other actions of life'.[19] But consider someone who dreams that he is in doubt as to whether he is dreaming or not. My question is whether such a man could not dream that his dream fits in with his ideas of a long series of past events. If this is possible, then what appear to the dreamer to be actions belonging to his past life could be judged to be true occurrences, just as if he were awake. Moreover, as the author himself asserts, the certainty and truth of all knowledge depends solely on our knowledge of the true God. But in that case an atheist cannot infer that he is awake on the basis of memory of his past life. The alternative is that someone *can* know that he is awake without knowledge of the true God. [*Third Objections*: CSM II 137] 196

A dreamer cannot really connect his dreams with the ideas of past events, though he may dream that he does. For everyone admits that a man may be deceived in his sleep. But afterwards, when he wakes up, he will easily recognize his mistake.

An atheist can infer that he is awake on the basis of memory of his past life. But he cannot know that this criterion is sufficient to give him the certainty that he is not mistaken, if he does not know that he was created by a non-deceiving God. [*Third Replies*: CSM II 137].

---

[18] Cf. Med. I, p. 16; Med. II, p. 25; Med. VI, pp. 64–6.   [19] Above, p. 70.

Index

Cambridge Texts In The History of Philosophy

Titles published in the series thus far

Aquinas *Disputed Questions on the Virtues* (edited by E.M. Atkins and Thomas Williams)

Aquinas *Summa Theologiae, Questions on God* (edited by Brian Davies and Brian Leftow)

Aristotle *Eudemian Ethics* (edited by Brad Inwood and Raphael Woolf)

Aristotle *Nicomachean Ethics* Revised Edition (edited by Roger Crisp)

Arnauld and Nicole *Logic or the Art of Thinking* (edited by Jill Vance Buroker)

Augustine *On the Free Choice of the Will, On Grace and Free Choice, and Other Writings* (edited by Peter King)

Augustine *On the Trinity* (edited by Gareth Matthews)

Bacon *The New Organon* (edited by Lisa Jardine and Michael Silverthorne)

Berkeley *Philosophical Writings* (edited by Desmond M. Clarke)

Boyle *A Free Enquiry into the Vulgarly Received Notion of Nature* (edited by Edward B. Davis and Michael Hunter)

Bruno *Cause, Principle and Unity and Essays on Magic* (edited by Richard Blackwell and Robert de Lucca with an introduction by Alfonso Ingegno)

Cavendish *Observations upon Experimental Philosophy* (edited by Eileen O'Neill)

Cicero *On Moral Ends* (edited by Julia Annas, translated by Raphael Woolf)

Clarke *A Demonstration of the Being and Attributes of God and Other Writings* (edited by Ezio Vailati)

Classic and Romantic German Aesthetics (edited by J.M. Bernstein)

Condillac *Essay on the Origin of Human Knowledge* (edited by Hans Aarsleff)

Conway *The Principles of the Most Ancient and Modern Philosophy* (edited by Allison P. Coudert and Taylor Corse)

Cudworth *A Treatise Concerning Eternal and Immutable Morality with A Treatise of Freewill* (edited by Sarah Hutton)

Descartes *Meditations on First Philosophy, with selections from the Objections and Replies*, Second Edition (translated and edited by John Cottingham)

Descartes *The World and Other Writings* (edited by Stephen Gaukroger)

Fichte *Attempt at a Critique of All Revelation* (edited by Allen Wood, translated by Garrett Green)

Fichte *Foundations of Natural Right* (edited by Frederick Neuhouser, translated by Michael Baur)

Fichte *The System of Ethics* (edited by Daniel Breazeale and Günter Zöller)

Greek and Roman Aesthetics (edited by Oleg V. Bychkov and Anne Sheppard)

Hamann *Philosophical Writings* (edited by Kenneth Haynes)

Heine *On the History of Religion and Philosophy in Germany and Other Writings* (edited by Terry Pinkard, translated by Howard Pollack-Milgate)

Herder *Philosophical Writings* (edited by Michael Forster)

Hobbes and Bramhall on Liberty and Necessity (edited by Vere Chappell)

Humboldt *On Language* (edited by Michael Losonsky, translated by Peter Heath)

Hume *Dialogues Concerning Natural Religion and Other Writings* (edited by Dorothy Coleman)

Hume *An Enquiry concerning Human Understanding* (edited by Stephen Buckle)

Kant *Anthropology from a Pragmatic Point of View* (edited by Robert B. Louden with an introduction by Manfred Kuehn)

Kant *Critique of Practical Reason* Revised Edition (edited by Mary Gregor with an introduction by Andrews Reath)

Kant *Groundwork of the Metaphysics of Morals* Revised Edition (edited by Mary Gregor and Jens Timmermann, with an introduction by Christine M. Korsgaard)

Kant *Metaphysical Foundations of Natural Science* (edited by Michael Friedman)

Kant *The Metaphysics of Morals* (edited by Mary Gregor with an introduction by Roger Sullivan)

Kant *Observations on the Feeling of the Beautiful and Sublime and Other Writings* (edited by Patrick Frierson and Paul Guyer)

Kant *Prolegomena to any Future Metaphysics* Revised Edition (edited by Gary Hatfield)

Kant *Religion within the Boundaries of Mere Reason and Other Writings* (edited by Allen Wood and George di Giovanni with an introduction by Robert Merrihew Adams)

Kierkegaard *Concluding Unscientific Postscript* (edited by Alastair Hannay)

Kierkegaard *Fear and Trembling* (edited by C. Stephen Evans and Sylvia Walsh)

La Mettrie *Machine Man and Other Writings* (edited by Ann Thomson)

Leibniz *New Essays on Human Understanding* (edited by Peter Remnant and Jonathan Bennett)

Lessing *Philosophical and Theological Writings* (edited by H.B. Nisbet)

Locke on Toleration (edited by Richard Vernon)

Malebranche *Dialogues on Metaphysics and on Religion* (edited by Nicholas Jolley and David Scott)

Malebranche *The Search after Truth* (edited by Thomas M. Lennon and Paul J. Olscamp)

Medieval Islamic Philosophical Writings (edited by Muhammad Ali Khalidi)

Medieval Jewish Philosophical Writings (edited by Charles Manekin)

Melanchthon *Orations on Philosophy and Education* (edited by Sachiko Kusukawa, translated by Christine Salazar)

Mendelssohn *Philosophical Writings* (edited by Daniel O. Dahlstrom)

Newton *Philosophical Writings* Revised Edition (edited by Andrew Janiak)

Nietzsche *The Antichrist, Ecce Homo, Twilight of the Idols and Other Writings* (edited by Aaron Ridley and Judith Norman)

Nietzsche *Beyond Good and Evil* (edited by Rolf-Peter Horstmann and Judith Norman)

Nietzsche *The Birth of Tragedy and Other Writings* (edited by Raymond Geuss and Ronald Speirs)

Nietzsche *Daybreak* (edited by Maudemarie Clark and Brian Leiter, translated by R.J. Hollingdale)

Nietzsche *The Gay Science* (edited by Bernard Williams, translated by Josefine Nauckhoff)

Nietzsche *Human, All Too Human* (translated by R.J. Hollingdale with an introduction by Richard Schacht)

Nietzsche *Thus Spoke Zarathustra* (edited by Adrian Del Caro and Robert B. Pippin)

Nietzsche *Untimely Meditations* (edited by Daniel Breazeale, translated by R.J. Hollingdale)

Nietzsche *Writings from the Early Notebooks* (edited by Raymond Geuss and Alexander Nehamas, translated by Ladislaus Löb)

Nietzsche *Writings from the Late Notebooks* (edited by Rüdiger Bittner, translated by Kate Sturge)

Novalis *Fichte Studies* (edited by Jane Kneller)

Plato *Meno, Phaedo* (edited by David Sedley and Alex Long)

Plato *Theaetetus and the Sophist* (edited by Christopher Rowe)

Plato *The Symposium* (edited by M.C. Howatson and Frisbee C.C. Sheffield)

Reinhold *Letters on the Kantian Philosophy* (edited by Karl Ameriks, translated by James Hebbeler)

Schleiermacher *Hermeneutics and Criticism* (edited by Andrew Bowie)

Schleiermacher *Lectures on Philosophical Ethics* (edited by Robert Louden, translated by Louise Adey Huish)

Schleiermacher *On Religion: Speeches to its Cultured Despisers* (edited by Richard Crouter)

Schopenhauer *Prize Essay on the Freedom of the Will* (edited by Günter Zöller)

Sextus Empiricus *Against the Logicians* (edited by Richard Bett)

Sextus Empiricus *Outlines of Scepticism* (edited by Julia Annas and Jonathan Barnes)

Shaftesbury *Characteristics of Men, Manners, Opinions, Times* (edited by Lawrence Klein)

Adam Smith *The Theory of Moral Sentiments* (edited by Knud Haakonssen)

Spinoza *Theological-Political Treatise* (edited by Jonathan Israel, translated by Michael Silverthorne and Jonathan Israel)

Voltaire *Treatise on Tolerance and Other Writings* (edited by Simon Harvey)